Empanadas, Pupusas, and Greens on the Side

Empanadas, Pupusas, and Greens on the Side

Language and Latinidad in the Nation's Capital

Amelia Tseng

Georgetown University Press / Washington, DC

© 2025 Amelia Tseng. All rights reserved. No part of this book may be reproduced or utilized in any form or by any means, electronic or mechanical, including photocopying and recording, or by any information storage and retrieval system, without permission in writing from the publisher.

The publisher is not responsible for third-party websites or their content.
URL links were active at time of publication.

Library of Congress Cataloging-in-Publication Data

Names: Tseng, Amelia, 1979- author.
Title: Empanadas, pupusas, and greens on the side : language and Latinidad in the nation's capital / Amelia Tseng.
Description: Washington, DC : Georgetown University Press, 2025. | Includes bibliographical references and index.
Identifiers: LCCN 2024031120 (print) | LCCN 2024031121 (ebook) | ISBN 9781647125899 (hardcover) | ISBN 9781647125905 (paperback) | ISBN 9781647125912 (ebook)
Subjects: LCSH: Spanish language—Washington (D.C.) | Latin Americans—Washington (D.C.)—Language. | Latin Americans—Washington (D.C.)—Ethnic identity. | Latin Americans—Washington (D.C.)—Social life and customs.
Classification: LCC PC4829.W18 T84 2024 (print) | LCC PC4829.W18 (ebook) | DDC 305.7/610753--dc23/eng/20250129
LC record available at https://lccn.loc.gov/2024031120
LC ebook record available at https://lccn.loc.gov/2024031121

EU GPSR Authorized Representative
LOGOS EUROPE, 9 rue Nicolas Poussin, 17000, LA ROCHELLE, France
Email: Contact@logoseurope.eu

26 25   9 8 7 6 5 4 3 2   First printing

Cover design by TG Design Studio
Cover photo by Nancy Shia
Interior design by Paul Hotvedt

Contents

	List of Illustrations	*vii*
	Acknowledgments	*ix*
	Transcription Conventions	*xiii*
	Introduction	1
1	Languaging Identity in the Nation's Capital: Raciomultilingual Dynamics in Washington, DC	19
2	"Empanadas, pupusas, and greens on the side": DC Latinidad	43
3	"En la viña de Dios hay de todo": Spanish and Identity	71
4	"Blacks and Latinos sort of roll in the same circles": Sociolinguistic Socialization	108
5	"¿Qué pasó vos?": Voicing the Raciomultilingual Self and Other	129
6	"We're Washingtonians": Constructing Local Identity and Authenticity	160
	Conclusion: "We're so rich with different types of culture"	198
	Notes	*217*
	Bibliography	*245*
	Index	*279*
	About the Author	*289*

Illustrations

Figures

1.1.	Multiscalar model of interacting sociolinguistic ideologies and emerging new meanings in diaspora	27
2.1.	The four quadrants of Washington, DC	45
2.2.	Salsa legends Celia Cruz and Tito Puente with DC organizer Willy Vásquez at the Latino Festival, 1985. Photo by Nancy Shia, used with permission	54
2.3.	March for El Salvador going down Columbia Road NW, Washington, DC, 1982. Photo by Nancy Shia, used with permission	55
2.4.	Latinx multilingual repertoires	60

Tables

I.1	Latin American Origins	9
I.2	Immigrant Generation	9
I.3	Participant Ages	11
I.4	Language Choice	12
2.1	Race/Ethnicity in the DC Metropolitan Area, 2022	49
2.2	Local versus Nonlocal *Washington Post* Items by Latino/Hispanic versus Salvadoran, 1990–2012	61
2.3	El Salvador/Salvadoran versus Mexico/Mexican in *Washington Hispanic* and *El Tiempo Latino*, 2017–2019	61
3.1	Spanish Proficiency: Survey Self-Reporting	74
3.2	Spanish Spoken with Family of the Same Generation	74
3.3	Use of Spanish with Close Friends	74
3.4	Use of Spanish at Parties with Friends	74
3.5	Descriptions of DC Spanish	85
3.6	Salvadoran /s/ Realization by Generation	89
3.7	DC Dialect Attitudes Hierarchy	98

4.1	Survey Participants' English	109
4.2	Latinx English versus Learner English	113
4.3	Interviews: Latinx and African American English Features	116
4.4	Surveys: Latinx and African American English Features	117
4.5	African American English Morphology and Syntax	118
6.1	Characteristics of Washingtonians and Gentrifiers	166

Acknowledgments

This book has been a labor of love and community to bring to fruition.

From its seed when I first moved to DC for graduate school, through life's pathways and the world-halting COVID-19 pandemic, it's been a fulfilling journey and a very rewarding one, if at times longer than anticipated.

I am deeply appreciative of the support of those around me at different stages throughout this journey.

Early research was funded by the National Science Foundation. I received invaluable support for this book as a research associate at the Smithsonian Center for Folklife and Cultural Heritage, and the public-facing anthropology of my colleagues there was an inspiration. I also received much support at American University and Georgetown University.

I am indebted to my colleague, Noemí Enchautegui-de-Jesús, for her collaboration on the Bilingualism and Latin@s in Washington, DC project, which contributed data to this book, and the American University Center for Latin American and Latino Studies and American University Metropolitan Policy Center, which supported that project through a seed grant and research award.

I am profoundly grateful to Ana Celia Zentella, Carmen Fought, Andrew Lynch, and Olivia Cadaval for their feedback at a book workshop supported by a Book Incubator grant from the American University College of Arts and Sciences. The book grew a great deal from your insights. An ADVANCE AU career grant for faculty in STEM research provided further writing support and enabled me to work with Patti Bower and her editorial eagle eye.

Naomi Baron was a fount of encouragement. She generously read the entire manuscript early on and helped me to find my book voice. Lars Hinrichs gave invaluable feedback on drafts that contributed to this work at different stages, as did Betsy Sneller.

I have benefited tremendously from conversations with my colleagues along the way. Deep thanks to Jonathan Rosa and Nelson Flores for their insights and generosity as scholars; to Jen Nycz; to Ana Nylund for reading drafts at various stages of the process and for her support and friendship always; and to my dissertation committee—Natalie Schilling, Anna De Fina, and Otto Santa Ana—for helping me plant this book's seed. Thanks also to Brenda Werth for being an excellent colleague and friend; Nicole Holliday, Holman Tse, and the Pomodoros crew for many writing sessions and camaraderie; and way back in the day, my graduate school writing group—Jessi Grieser, Julie Lake, Kaitlyn Tagarelli, and Laura West.

My research also benefited from conference audiences, particularly New Ways of Analyzing Variation (NWAV) 41; the Ninth National Symposium on Spanish as a Heritage Language; the Ninety-Second Annual Meeting of the Linguistic Society of America; the 2017 LSA Linguistic Institute; the Third International Conference on the Sociolinguistics of Immigration; the American Anthropological Association; Sociolinguistics Symposium; Latino/a Studies Association; and the 2022 NSF Build and Broaden panel, "What Is the Social in Sociolinguistics?"

And of course thanks are due to the anonymous reviewers who read this manuscript and provided thoughtful feedback.

Deep thanks to Hope LeGro, editor extraordinaire, and the Georgetown University Press team for their amazing work, and to Carole Sargent and the Georgetown University Office of Scholarly Publications for support early in the process. I also thank the research assistants and interns that I worked with over the years at American University, Georgetown University, and the Smithsonian Institution, particularly Gennesis Sánchez and Brenda López.

My students always inspire me with their curiosity to understand language, identity, who they are in the world, and how to make it a better place.

I can't thank my DC family enough: Olivia Cadaval, an inspiration as a person, scholar, mentor, and activist; Quique Avilés and Hilary Binder, Hugo Nájera, María Sprehn, and the many community members I have been privileged to speak with over the years. Nancy

Shia lent her years of photography in the DC Latinx community to the images in the book and its cover. I value the conversations I had with Michelle Banks, Camila Bryce-LaPorte, José Centeno-Meléndez, Sabiyha Prince, Ana Patricia Rodríguez, Roland Roebuck, Pat Scallen, Ranald Woodaman, and many others.

Finally, I would like to dedicate this book to my family. My son, Luchito, mi corazón, was born halfway through the writing process. And my beautiful daughter Alicia was born just as this book was going into print. The best distractions anyone could have, mijito, mi niña linda, son la luz de mis ojos y mi felicidad, mi razón para seguir adelante. Trilingual parenthood has enriched the way I see language and identity and deepened the roots I've put down in the area. My parents' journey to the US made me who I am, and their experiences, and those of many other friends and family, inspire me and inform my perspective with love and humor. 衷心感謝. Muchas gracias.

My deepest thanks to everyone who has been part of the journey and helped me make this book a reality. If I have inadvertently left someone out, it is a reflection of my memory, not my gratitude.

Transcription Conventions for Excerpts

Spanish is noted by italics. Phonetic detail, where needed, is indicated through **bolding**. Intonation, pausing, volume, vowel or consonant lengthening, interruptions and overlap, and laughter are also indicated. Dialectal features, as set forth in the body of each chapter, are described below the relevant places in discourse. Translations are provided immediately after the relevant excerpts.

Italics	Spanish
?	Rising intonation followed by noticeable pause, as at the end of an interrogative sentence
.	Falling intonation followed by noticeable pause, as at the end of a declarative sentence
,	Continuing intonation; may be a slight rise or fall in contour; may not be followed by pause
(.)	Noticeable pause, untimed
TEXT	Louder than surrounding talk
-	Self-interruption
[text	Overlapping talk
[text	
=	Latching talk, when one turn follows another without pause
=	
[text]	Variable usage, that is, researcher-supplied missing information to make the quote make sense, such as a pronoun that is obligatory in English but not Spanish; other essential referent so the reader can follow the quote; and phonetic features
[phonetic description]	
:	Vowel or consonant lengthening

Transcription Conventions for Excerpts

↑	High intonation
. . .	Text has been omitted
(text)	Researcher notes and asides

Introduction

One fall day in 2019 my husband and I stood on the sidewalk in Mount Pleasant, a historic Washington, DC, neighborhood, watching a group of older men tearing up some bongos. The drum circle was singing, "*Los Nacionales campeones, los Nacionales campeones.*" The Washington Nationals had just won the World Series, the city was celebrating, and Latinxs returned to the barrio to celebrate the momentous occasion.

The event's location in the streets of the barrio was significant. Mount Pleasant is a deeply important place for the Latinx community of DC. One of the original barrios, it was the cradle of community life for decades. DC Latinidad in a real sense was forged in this neighborhood and in nearby Adams Morgan and Columbia Heights. The Latino Festival was born in its streets in the 1970s.[1] The Mount Pleasant disturbances against police brutality and other abuses took place here in 1991. These are variously referred to as an "uprising" or "riots," depending on whether one consults official sources or those who lived through it. Ethnographies have been written about Mount Pleasant's gentrification, and the street corner ("*La Esquina*") where men have gathered for decades to play checkers remains relevant—and controversial—in debates about the neighborhood and the changing city.[2]

Gentrification and rising prices have driven many Latinxs into satellite communities in the surrounding metropolitan area. Nevertheless, Mount Pleasant continues to be an important community site. Working-class Latinxs still live in the area, vendors sell snack bags of fruit in the streets, and venerable shops and restaurants cling on. Events such as Día de los Muertos and community theater are held here, and Latinxs—many who lived in Mount Pleasant when they first arrived and others who were raised there—come back to the city for them. Holding social events in public spaces provides continuity and visibility and echoes the communal Latin American spirit of the neighborhood in years past.[3]

The music we heard that day was also significant. Collective drumming is a tradition in much of Latin America and in DC. In neighboring Columbia Heights—another iconic Latinx neighborhood—a drum circle has met every Sunday for more than fifty years in Meridian Hill Park, which is also called Malcolm X Park. The tradition began in the Black community with a single drummer when Martin Luther King Jr. was assassinated; some say it traces back further, to emancipation.[4] Latinxs have been participating for decades, and the drum circle is a feature of multicultural DC life. As with many aspects of DC culture, new residents complained about the drum circle as the neighborhood gentrified, but it endures as a vibrant part of local culture. Spontaneous drumming in the streets of Mount Pleasant to celebrate the Nationals' win evokes this richly interwoven cultural history.

The musicians' chant—"*Los Nacionales campeones, los Nacionales campeones*" (The Nationals [are] champions)—celebrated the "all-American pastime" in Spanish, a form of ownership through language and of embracing the occasion. But what was really being celebrated went beyond baseball. The Nationals are a recently acquired team that, according to my conversations with old-time Washingtonians, does not enjoy the same long-term "hometown team" devotion as, say, the Washington Commanders football team. What was being celebrated was DC having a win, the exultation manifesting spontaneously through a particularly DC—and particularly Latinx—form of cultural expression.

Washington, DC, the nation's capital, is a vibrant city with its own culture. Indeed, locals often distinguish between "Washington" (the political city) and local "DC" life. However, Washington, DC—possibly the most powerful city in the world—occupies an unusual role in the United States imaginary: at once highly symbolic and somewhat overlooked. Its license plates say, "END TAXATION WITHOUT REPRESENTATION," reflecting its lack of statehood or representation in Congress. Its governance, which has to be approved by Congress, is often a political bargaining chip or an afterthought. The city gets no airtime in pop culture except for in politics-focused television shows like *The West Wing* and does not typically feature in the broader American consciousness except in dog-whistle rhetoric about "urban crime" or "draining the (political) swamp." When the Nationals won the pennant, Donald Trump had won his first presidency by playing to these fears, and he remained hostile to the city while in office.[5] In this context, the celebration of the Nationals' win was an assertion of local pride and identity in the face of silencing and disdain, a statement that "we are here!" with a much-needed win. The statement took place through the lens of a DC Latinx cultural institution with continuity and familiarity to those in the audience. In 1987, amid a wave of Central American migration to DC, the Smithsonian Folklife Festival featured the theme "Making a New Place Home." This book views through the lens of language how Latinx immigrants made—and continue to make—Washington, DC, their home.

A Sociolinguistics of Place and Identity

Language and identity are intimately connected. Through language, communities are forged and senses of self are sustained, reimagined, and contested in relation to others and the social environment. As Latinxs put down roots in the area, being Washingtonian—and how this is imagined to look, sound, and behave—became part of their identity. Washingtonian Latinidad reflects an ongoing process of reflection for individuals and within the community and reflects the social circumstances of the broader DC region.

DC Latinxs reflect the diversity of the nation's capital itself, which draws people from all over the world, from diplomats to refugees and undocumented workers. Historically home to a large African American population, the city's demographics changed dramatically at the end of the twentieth century as ongoing gentrification displaced former working- and middle-class residents of color. Intensive Central American migration since the 1980s makes the DC area the only place in the United States where this group holds the majority among Latinx, but DC Latinxs come from all over the

Spanish-speaking world. Nevertheless, little linguistic research has been conducted on Latinxs in the area.

I came to DC for graduate school with a long-standing interest in sociolinguistics and bilingualism. Over time, I realized that the models I studied could not by themselves account for the rich diversity of local language and identity that I encountered. DC, and the Latinxs who live here, were too complex for traditional models that assumed "one language, one culture, one identity" to be adequate to account for the language present and what it meant to people. Broad patterns of language use and attitudes held—such as Spanish bilingualism and its role as an important index of Latinx identity—but were intricately interwoven with local nuances particular to DC's social tapestry as well as different aspects of the immigrant experience. A new perspective was needed.

How does Spanish dialect diversity play into language and identity? Much research shows that Central Americans in the United States tend to accommodate to local Spanish norms, partly as a form of protective camouflage and partly because Central American Spanish is often stigmatized. However, as with much US Latinx research, this phenomenon has largely been studied in California and Texas, where Central Americans are in the minority. What happens when they are the majority group, as in DC? Do they keep their language? Do other Latinxs adopt Central American norms? What about Latinx English, again primarily studied elsewhere in the United States, and linguistic contact between Latinxs and African Americans? While Latino English is often documented as having African American English features, rigorous ethnographic investigation of different contact situations is necessary. Much of the research around language and identity in this area has been conducted in regions with substantial Caribbean populations, which tend to be of African descent, such as early work by William Labov and Walt Wolfram on New York Puerto Ricans, Ana Celia Zentella's research, or Benjamin Bailey's study of Dominican youth. In contrast, Salvadorans—the largest DC Latinx group—are not stereotypically associated with Black phenotypes and have their own history of erasure of Blackness. How do these dynamics play out in terms of language in a city that until recently had a proud Black majority and that has always elected Black mayors since "home rule"—the right to vote for this office—was enacted in 1973?

Toward a Raciomultilingual Perspective

What could explain the attitudes and ideologies that underlie the complex sociolinguistic dynamics of Washingtonian Latinx identity? This question brought me to a complex *raciomultilingual framework* in which I study the elements of the bilingual repertoire in interaction with each other and with the complex social environment in order to understand what language means as a whole to its speakers and their understandings of the Self and Other. This framework centers bilingualism itself within the influential raciolinguistic paradigm set forth by Jonathan Rosa and Nelson Flores,[6] among others, while underscoring how racialization affects bilingual repertoires and experiences. I consider the bilingual repertoire to be a dynamic and unitary whole, in line with scholars such as Ofelia García and Li Wei.[7] However, I still consider the structural elements of Spanish and English in depth and, like Daniel Erker, recognize the importance of these named languages to speakers themselves.[8] I consider how the idea of Spanish and English, and how they are spoken, factors into how speakers see themselves and others. At the same time, I engage with how notions of "language" and "identity" themselves are social constructs whose boundaries are more porous than is often imagined, by examining new practices that emerge in the local context and blur established lines between groups. Important for studying diasporic communities, I take multiple centers of reference—in the DC area, in the United States, and in Latin America—into account to examine how immigrants and their descendants make sense of the sociolinguistic world. The raciomultilingual model thus accounts for discourses that seem to contradict each other—such as stigma and pride—but that coexist by operating at different local, national, and transnational levels of awareness.

A new look at the questions outlined above goes directly to foundational concepts in sociolinguistics, such as markedness, stigma, and prestige; how they affect linguistic repertoires; and their relationship with identity and social context. It also provides insight into philosophical questions that underscore how we conduct research, such as the assignment of "authentic" language to a group,[9] and when they are considered to be "crossing" boundaries.[10] DC Latinidad presents an engrossing view on polyphonous identity and the relationship between language, ethnocultural identity, and the broader social imaginary.

These topics are of perennial importance in understanding and improving society, and particularly so under the increasingly diverse and mobile conditions of late modernity. Sociolinguistic insights, coupled with education and outreach, can help decrease the number and intensity of stereotypes that reduce groups to monoliths associated with one single or primary language and that devalue their linguistic identities as part of broader racial/ethnic discrimination. This raciolinguistic discrimination disproportionately affects minorities, depriving them of language rights, damaging their self-esteem, and limiting their opportunities. In sum, the Washington, DC, metropolitan area presents a fascinating context for the study of language and identity construction among Latinxs of diverse backgrounds in a distinct global-city environment and for the implications of this research for sociolinguistic research and understandings of language and society more broadly.

Conducting the Research

I take an interdisciplinary approach that combines sociolinguistic investigation with discourse analysis, ethnography, and archival research. Throughout my research, I spoke with a wide range of DC Latinxs, primarily regular people but also activists and community leaders. I chose this approach to give a broad perspective on language and identity among local Latinxs, although, as with any work of this kind, it cannot pretend to capture the full range of experiences. Language and identity are ever changing, and many stories remain to be told.

Data collection took several forms. Ethnography was an ongoing project. I have lived in DC and its *afueras* and been involved with the Latinx community for more than a decade. This gave me the opportunity for much participant observation, from community events such as the "*Nacionales campeones*" gathering that opens this chapter and the annual Día de Muertos (Day of the Dead) celebration in Mount Pleasant, to parties, volunteering, shopping, protests, arts and cultural events, and just hanging out. Through these and other interactions I was able to speak with many community members, gain insights into culture and local dynamics, and build connections.

Through Olivia Cadaval, my mentor at the Smithsonian Center for Folklife and Cultural Heritage, for example, I spoke with a woman who had participated as a child in one of the 1980s Smithsonian Folklife Festival recordings. This was invaluable firsthand insight into the social dynamics of Latinx/African American contact in the 1980s and beyond, as we talked about her school experiences, friends, and teachers and about where life has taken them. I remember another conversation with a young, DC-born Salvadoran man who carefully explained to me the proper way to eat *pupusas* with your fingers (never a fork!). Another time, a father worried that his daughter was falling in with bad company, while his daughter perceived this concern as racism, accusing him of not liking her friends because they are Black.

Additionally, I consulted with DC-area Afro-Latinxs and African American community members and scholars, and many other Washingtonians, for additional insights into social dynamics and gentrification. Local media by and about Latinxs, such as websites and newspaper articles, provided further insight. For example, controversy about the "*Esquineros*" project, which looks at gentrification in Mount Pleasant through the perspectives of the men who have for decades gathered to socialize on the street corner there ("*La Esquina*"), underscored that the debate about "who belongs" in a changing barrio remains as relevant today as when Galey Modan documented it in Mount Pleasant in 2008.

The Smithsonian archives provided a rich source of historical material to ground my contemporary data in a deeper understanding of DC Latinxs' sociolinguistic context. The archival material I analyzed includes recordings of Latinx language in the 1980s and many community artifacts. I also drew on macrodata such as the US Census for broad demographic information and patterns of bilingualism and Spanish's language vitality.

I conducted many interviews in order to understand language and identity among DC Latinxs. The people I interviewed with came from a diverse range of Latin American backgrounds: Mexico, El Salvador, Honduras, Guatemala, Panama, Puerto Rico, the Dominican Republic, Venezuela, Ecuador, Colombia, Peru, Bolivia, Paraguay, Chile, Argentina, and Uruguay (see table I.1). Salvadorans were the largest group by national origin (50 percent), and Central Americans the largest regional group overall (63 percent). South Americans made up 18 percent of participants, of which Peruvians were the largest group, at 6 percent of the total, followed by Colombians (4 percent). Mexicans were 6 percent of total participants—a difference with research in other areas of the United States, where they tend to be the largest population. Caribbeans, primarily Puerto Ricans, made up 5 percent of the total. And 7 percent of participants were of mixed origins. Of these, 5 percent had parents from different Spanish-speaking countries, and 2 percent had one non-Latinx parent. All but one of the mixed-background participants were born in the United States, reflecting the mixed marriages common in the DC area.

Fifty-three percent of participants were first-generation immigrants (born abroad). Those who were born abroad but arrived in the United States before adulthood (G1.5, or the "1.5 generation") and second-generation immigrants (born in the United States) were 27 percent and 20 percent, respectively. Second-generation participants were primarily of Salvadoran origin; mixed-heritage participants were also second-generation.

The term "1.5 generation" refers to immigrants who came as children or adolescents, but there is no consensus among scholars about the cutoff age of arrival.[11] As Farahnaz Faez notes, G1.5's inherent broadness means that the term encompasses a range of experiences and backgrounds.[12] However, the term's breadth should not be seen as a limitation but as a flexible means of accessing experiences that, while diverse, have in common their differences from the generations

Table I.1. Latin American Origins

Region	N	%
North America	6	6.1
Mexico	6	6.1
Central America	62	63.3
El Salvador	49	50.0
Guatemala	4	4.1
Honduras	6	6.1
Panama	3	3.1
South America	18	18.2
Argentina	1	1.0
Bolivia	2	2.0
Chile	1	1.0
Colombia	4	4.1
Ecuador	1	1.0
Paraguay	1	1.0
Peru	6	6.1
Uruguay	1	1.0
Venezuela	1	1.0
Caribbean	5	5.1
Dominican Republic	1	1.0
Puerto Rico	4	4.1
Mixed	7	7.1
Total	98	99.8

Table I.2. Immigrant Generation

Generation	N	%
G1	52	53.1
G1.5	26	26.5
G2	20	20.4
Total	98	100

that precede and follow them. G1.5's social and educational experiences, cultural orientation, and linguistic competencies differ from those of both G1 adult immigrants and the second generation born in the new country. Since this book is primarily concerned with DC Latinxs' language experiences and understandings, and since high school is a well-documented period of language and identity development and flux,[13] I take a broad approach to G1.5 as up to eighteen years of age, and I take individual ages of arrival into account for nuanced analysis.

Participant ages encompassed a wide range, from eighteen to seventy. Most were of school or working age, with the majority being in their twenties or thirties, followed by the eighteen-to-twenty- and forty-to-fifty-year-old cohorts (see table I.3). Overall, they were working or middle class, employed in occupations ranging from cleaning, hospitality, and construction to office work, government jobs, education, and real estate. There were also full-time students, stay-at-home mothers, and community elders.

The ninety-eight interviews analyzed in this book reflect ongoing research and are grouped into two batches collected between 2013 and 2018, a period of much change and debate in the city as intensive gentrification displaced local residents, and just after DC lost its historic Black majority in 2011.[14] A snapshot of this moment in time provides powerful insight into social and linguistic processes many years in the making, which continue in the present day. The interviews were semistructured and conversational, centered on questions about language, identity, and Latinx life in the DC area. For example, interviews elicited information about local Spanish and English, changes in the city, experiences with discrimination, language attitudes, and cultural pride. The interviews allowed me to observe participants' actual and reported language practices in a guided conversational context, their stylistic and discursive identity construction, and metalinguistic commentary. Interviews were typically an hour long; some were shorter, some longer. Participants were assured that they could use English, Spanish, or both as they were more comfortable. I then followed their language leads.

I collected the first batch of interviews as part of my dissertation project, supplemented with existing interviews from the Georgetown University Language and Communication in Washington, DC project, for a total of thirty-six interviews.[15] Two interview participants also agreed to self-record interactions with family and friends in their daily lives, which provided examples of how they spoke in different naturalistic social encounters.

Table I.3. Participant Ages

Ages	N	%
18–20	15	15.3
20s	31	31.6
30s	30	30.6
40s	15	15.3
50s	3	3.1
60s	4	4.1
Total	98	100

These interviews were sourced using the snowball sampling method and conducted in public spaces, such as coffee shops, and homes as participants preferred. I met these participants largely through mutual acquaintances. This method is one I prefer as it increases confidence and yields rich conversations and relationships. For example, I met "Marcos" through a friend at a social event and interviewed him at his home. The result was particularly rich data—partly because of his outgoing personality and strong opinions, partly because I was a "known quantity"—and I was able to conduct a follow-up interview. Similarly, I was able to speak with "Héctor" multiple times after the initial interview, yielding follow-up conversations and a self-recording, and we are still in touch. These personal relationships have enriched my life tremendously as well as my research. Over the years I have been to housewarmings, weddings, house parties, cookouts, and many community events. I've also been invited to collaborate on community projects and give talks at schools and in the community. I'm always happy to do so, since relationships are a two-way street. Rather than assuming an all-knowing stance, I believe that researchers should give back to the communities they interact with in line with the communities' own needs and desires.

The second batch of interviews included the same conversational topics but added a survey component with targeted questions about sociolinguistic attitudes, bilingualism across the lifespan, social networks, and language proficiency self-rating, among others. These interviews were collected through the Bilingualism and Latin@s in Washington, DC project, a project that examined Latinx

Table I.4. Language Choice

	Spanish % (n)	English % (n)	Total % (n)
G1	66.1 (41)	1.6 (1)	67.7 (42)
G1.5	6.5 (4)	9.7 (6)	16.1 (10)*
G2	3.2 (2)	12.9 (8)	16.1 (10)
Total	75.8 (47)	24.2 (15)	99.9 (62)

*Some rows do not sum because of rounding error.

bilingualism, identity, and access to resources and yielded sixty-two recordings. I conducted interviews with my colleague Noemí Enchautegui-de-Jesús and our research assistants, who were primarily second-generation Latinas of diverse backgrounds: Salvadoran, Colombian, Guatemalan, and more.[16] We recruited participants at community organizations and conducted them wherever space was provided: empty classrooms, libraries, nurseries, auditoriums, hallways.

While the first group spoke mainly English in their interviews, the second group of interviews showed a generational trend in language preferences. First-generation immigrants preferred to speak in Spanish and second-generation immigrants in English. The 1.5 generation was a mix but generally preferred English (see table I.4).

Using community centers as recruitment sites may have influenced overall participant demographics. Working-class, first-generation Salvadoran women were particularly well represented in this group, likely due to the nature of community organization services and clientele and to gendered social roles. Eighty percent of the first-generation immigrants in the interviews overall were interviewed at community centers. This makes sense, as community organizations tend to serve immigrants who need help accessing services and establishing themselves in the new country. Similarly, while the total ratio of men to women participants was approximately 1:4 (twenty-five men and seventy-three women), the gender ratio was more imbalanced (20 percent male) in the community center interviews than in the interviews recruited through snowball sampling. This pattern may reflect gendered differences in family roles, where women are more responsible for childcare and education, family health, and other family needs that are served by community organizations.

Analyzing the Data

The relationship between linguistic style, discourse, and identity construction is an important framework for interpreting my data.[17] Together with metalinguistic commentary, these approaches shed light on speakers' language beliefs as well as on how different elements of language contribute to identity construction.

One aspect of this is *stance* and *positioning*: examining how speakers discursively construct identity as they orient to different topics and create groups by aligning or disaligning themselves and others in terms of social qualities, feelings, and behaviors.[18] I pay close attention to *dialect variation* and to *translanguaging*—speakers drawing on the full range of resources in their linguistic repertoires, including bilingualism, to achieve communicative goals—as part of stances and in my discourse analysis more broadly.[19] I also examine *narratives* as an effective medium for understanding identity construction, as the stories people tell simultaneously present themselves and others as particular "kinds of people"; perform interactional work, such as providing epistemic support for points the speaker wishes to argue; and co-construct social reality.[20] Finally, I use discourse analysis to examine connections between DC Latinxs' sociolinguistic beliefs and the particularities of DC's history and cultural context as well as the reification of broader national and transnational discourses about language and aspects of identity such as race, ethnicity, and social class. This approach provides insight into how common beliefs about language and social identity are understood locally in relation to broader US and Latin American ideologies and how these broader systems of belief in turn are challenged, negotiated, and supported at the local level.[21]

The focus here is a holistic examination of the linguistic repertoire and indexicalities of language and identity, not documentation of linguistic variation in the classic paradigm. Nevertheless, English and Spanish linguistic features form part of my analysis. It bears mentioning that neither Spanish varieties nor Latinx and African American English are monoliths; all show regional and class variation. For my purposes, I concentrate on features that characterize the different varieties and are generally socially salient. These features are /s/ in Spanish and several features associated with Latinx English and African American English.

Full realization of /s/ and various aspects of weakening, such as elision and aspiration, are well documented in Central American Spanish and elsewhere. Nonstandard second-person morphosyntax known as *"voseo"* for use of the pronoun *"vos"* instead of or in combination with *"tú"* is also a feature of Central American Spanish.[22] Tokens were identified using impressionistic auditory coding and visually inspected using the phonetics analysis software Praat. Formant measurements were also taken for a subset of interview participants' /ae/ tokens.[23]

Latinx English is an ethnic dialect of American English that shows long-term effects of Spanish contact, such as light or apical /l/, as in the word "Latino";[24] low or backed prenasal /ae/, as in the words "bat" and "ban";[25] and r-trilling, as in the word "three," which has not previously been discussed in Latinx English but which I observe.[26] I also examine the well-established African American English features of r-lessness in certain phonetic contexts, as in "here"; weakening of the /aɪ/ diphthong ("my") toward a monophthongal realization; and /l/ vocalization ("feel"). I will explain this methodology further, as with my methodology in general, as necessary throughout the book.

Researcher Positionality

Interpersonally, I would classify myself as a peripheral community member based on how my relationship to the local Latinx community has been described by friends and participants. In fact, a friend and mentor who has been well respected in activism and cultural events for decades described my position as "peripheral insider" in terms of knowing people and being involved with, yet not central to, the community. I have been involved with the DC Latinx community for over a decade through research; outreach; engagement with social, cultural, political, and educational community events; and friendships. My positionality as a child of non-White[27] immigrant parents, who speaks fluent Spanish, with a Peruvian husband and extended family also informs my positionality and how I am perceived. These experiences have shaped my worldview and resonate with others of similar backgrounds. For example, conversations about immigrant family experiences, adjustment, and cultural maintenance frequently arise on social occasions and through arts and cultural events, providing a framework of commonality in my interviews, as does a shared awareness of being othered as not "real Americans." However, my Chinese American background and racialized appearance mean that I do not have the same lived and cultural experiences as US Latinxs. Further, as an Asian person, I am always racialized and seen as Other or potentially "foreign"—there is no "neutral setting" for me in Western social perception. That said, it is important to note that Latinx is an ethnic rather than racial identity, and Latinxs come from all racial backgrounds, although racial ideologies continue to be at work among them. The burgeoning conversation around Afro-Latinidad in Latin America and the United States speaks to this diversity, as does the work I have done on raciolinguistic representations of Latinxs of Asian descent.[28] Racialized imaginaries that seek to fit minoritized peoples into neatly delineated separate categories are based in Western colonial logics, but they continue to affect social thought and organization in the present day.

These nuances of participation in different communities can be seen from the way that community members introduce me to others in different contexts. On social occasions, it is often simply as a friend; in others, my research and allyship with DC Latinxs and diversity efforts are highlighted; in some, my professional credentials are mentioned. I recall that a friend and sometime interview participant once introduced me by saying, "She's cool, she hangs with Latinos." Since this statement was directed to a person I had never met before, I took it as a means of vouching for me on a personal level to explain my presence in the group and interest in Latinx language even though I am not Latinx. My Peruvian connection by marriage sometimes also helps Latinxs "place" me as someone with a personal connection to Latinidad. The Peruvian aspect specifically perhaps also makes me more legible as a Spanish-speaking Asian, since Peru has a large Asian-descent population.

Structure of the Book

Chapter 1 orients the reader to the book. I put forth foundational issues of language, identity, society, and migration within the context of Washington, DC, and I articulate a raciomultilingual perspective that can adequately address the extreme diversity and the divisions that remain within it, exemplified by the capital of the United States, its Latinx community, and global cities more broadly. Chapter 2 situates Latinx history and demographics within the unique environment of the Washington, DC, metropolitan area. This discussion sets the stage for my insights into DC-area Latinx linguistic identities that follow in chapters 3–6. My description sketches demographics and immigration in DC and the DC metropolitan area. It begins with key aspects of DC's history as a majority-Black but also segregated city, the debate around gentrification, and the region's evolution as a site of global contact and influence. I then present a brief history of Latinx settlement and relations among themselves and with others, drawing connections with other areas that have been better studied in terms of US Latinxs and noting the importance of both US and Latin American social relations in community dynamics.

In the chapters that follow I offer my theories concerning different aspects of Latinx linguistic repertoires and their relationship to identity and social context. I trace how multifaceted understandings of language and identity operate on multiple, simultaneous scales, such as the coexistence of discourses of commonality and difference among DC-area Latinxs. I address ways that local, national, and transnational ideologies of language and identity affect DC-area Latinxs across the range of their raciomultilingual repertoires and how they navigate internal Latinx hierarchies as well as socialization with other groups and the US social context more broadly. I am particularly interested in how new indexical meanings related to language and identity emerge, yet others stay the same. Relatedly, I show how sociolinguistic ideologies recenter or develop multiple centers of reference in global cities.[29]

Chapter 3 explores Spanish and its social meaning among DC Latinxs. Findings confirm that Spanish is seen as an important part of ethnocultural identity. However, dialect attitudes reveal ambivalent attitudes of stigma and pride toward the most-spoken dialect, Salvadoran Spanish, for reasons that have to do with the group's local positionality but also reference Latin American dynamics. I note that a discourse celebrating sociolinguistic diversity among Latinxs exists alongside this dynamic. Further, the association of Spanish with Latinx identity can cause shame for the US-born generation.

Chapter 4 focuses on how different kinds of English play into "sounding Latinx." Here I focus on DC-area Latinxs' attitudes toward the different Englishes they speak. In addition to Latinx English features and translanguaging, I pay attention to the history of contact that normalized African American English in local Latinxs' repertoires. However, language attitudes also stigmatize Black language due to hegemonic attitudes current in both the United States and Latin America.

Chapter 5 provides a deeper discursive analysis of the indexicalities adhering to speakers' multilingualism. I examine how intersectional ideologies of race and class come together across language boundaries in the imagination of a particular local Latinx identity. While the previous two chapters focused on Spanish and English separately for the sake of convenience, this chapter looks at the ways in which ideology crosses language and national boundaries.

Chapter 6 presents a case study of raciomultilingual identity construction in relationship to Latinx history in the area, DC's place identity as an African American city, and the perceived Whiteness of gentrifiers. I examine how "Marcos," a second-generation Washingtonian Latinx, draws on different aspects of his linguistic repertoire as he stylistically and discursively constructs a hybridized local Latinx identity. This identity construction—much of which takes place through narratives—is part of a broader argument in which he argues for the authenticity of "real" Washingtonians, and thus their rights to the city, against "outsiders."

The book concludes by returning to the broader picture of sociolinguistic and multilingual inquiry, and the contributions of a raciomultilingual framework to these areas of study. One key topic is the complex positioning of minority languages in intersection with discourses of race/ethnicity, class, diversity, and discrimination in global cities. Another is the proliferation and scalar organization of ideologies about languages and language proficiency that accompany multilingual repertoires, at the same time that traditional beliefs—often reductivist or essentializing—continue to hold sway. A third key theme is problematizing hegemonically imposed notions of homogeneous minoritized groups versus the actual diversity present within diasporic communities. This point also subverts paradigmatic assumptions that White mainstream America and mainstream American English are the primary reference for immigrants' assimilation, or lack thereof. Finally, I discuss the insights that this research can make for linguistics and related fields, and I conclude with future directions for investigation of social and linguistic diversity among Latinxs, in DC and more generally.

1

Languaging Identity in the Nation's Capital
Raciomultilingual Dynamics in Washington, DC

I spoke with many local residents during my research over the course of ten years, research that comprises almost 100 sociolinguistic surveys and interviews as well as archival recordings, ethnography, and other information. I'll begin here by introducing some of the key participants you will meet in these pages, and there are many more.

"Marcos" (all participant names have been changed) is a proud and vocal Washingtonian, born and raised, of mixed Mexican and Salvadoran parentage. He grew up in pre-gentrified DC in the 1970s and 1980s, when, as he describes it, the city was still very Latinx in the barrios and very Black in the other neighborhoods he grew up in. Marcos's mother once had to throw him out of a window into his father's waiting arms as they escaped an immigration raid. He describes Black neighbors babysitting him while his mother was at work: older men with "the breasted suit, the vests underneath, the feather in their caps, I mean those were the guys that I was hanging out with. . . . You know, they were taking care of me," and he learned to braid hair.[1] As he describes it, although DC struggled with drugs, poverty, and violence, there was a sense of community, and people helped each other. Prostitutes and drug dealers were common on the streets, but old people monitored goings-on from porches, and communities protected children. Now, as an adult with his own family, Marcos in his interview with me reflects on what it means to be Washingtonian, as he thinks about his own experience and that of his son in a city in which diversity, multiculturalism, and fluidity remain defining characteristics even as DC has changed around them.

And as he tells these stories, Marcos uses Washingtonian Latinx language to depict characters, enrich narratives of home, and construct a sense of Washingtonian identity that stands in contrast to that of gentrifiers.

"Emanuel," who came to DC as a young teenager in the 1980s to escape violence in El Salvador, is another outspoken Washingtonian Latino. In a common theme for Salvadorans, who often had to flee quickly, he came alone, joining his mother and siblings who were already in DC. They settled in Columbia Heights, where he bore witness to the Mount Pleasant disturbances of 1991, when Latinx residents' protests against police violence erupted into nights of looting and a police lockdown of the neighborhood. Emanuel vividly remembers conflicts between Latinxs and African American youths in streets and schools—something frequently referenced by members of his generation in my ethnography—as immigrants were integrated into the city without support structures and became involved with youth activism to breach this divide. His wide and diverse social networks include local Latinxs as well as Black friends going back decades and friends of other backgrounds. A gifted and opinionated storyteller with an ear for language, Emanuel thinks a great deal about the local Salvadoran experience, which he explores through art, music, theater, and community involvement. In his interview and, as we grew to be friends, in many later conversations, Emanuel reflects on his generation's experiences and those of the youth of today as well as gentrification in the city. His stories are often irreverent but with a serious undertone.

The thoughts of "Gracia," a DC-born woman of Salvadoran parentage who was in her twenties when interviewed, revolved around her own ethnocultural positionality as she thought about language and identity. As she reflected on her journey of Latina identity from childhood through adulthood, she shared that despite her Salvadoran background, cultural connection, and fluent Spanish skills, her upper-middle-class background and educated way of speaking opened her up to accusations of being "White" or otherwise in disalignment with local understandings of Latinidad, which she came to understand as part of the broader racialized US class system. These and many other participant insights are presented in the chapters that follow.

This book takes the relationship between language and identity for Latinxs in the DC metropolitan area as a lens for developing new theoretical directions for sociolinguistics and related fields. I articulate a raciomultilingual perspective and argue for its necessity in understanding Latinidad and the sociolinguistics of minoritized immigrant groups more broadly.

Although I discuss linguistic features, I do not present a traditional sociolinguistic variation analysis that seeks to correlate particular language elements such as pronunciation with different social groups—for example, Latinxs versus White Americans, or young women versus old men. Instead, I unpack how local Latinxs' attitudes and ideologies about language and identity manifest through their "talk about language" and their language itself. I examine an extensive range of material: my original sociolinguistic data; material from the Smithsonian Institution archives, which I investigated through my research associate appointment; and ethnographic observation to theorize more deeply about how DC Latinxs' linguistic repertoires—their range of language behavior—and beliefs about language affect how they understand and construct ethnocultural identity. As I will show, new sociolinguistic meanings emerge that are specific to the local context but also still draw on broader US and Latin American ideology. As part of this exploration, I also examine tensions and consensus around Washington, DC, Latinx identity and its interaction with discourses of race, place, belonging, and diversity.

Latinidad in the Nation's Capital

Washington, DC, and its surrounding metropolitan region, colloquially known as the "DMV," exemplify some of the tensions and complexity of migration and diversity that characterize today's global cities—urban regions where international networks of migration, communication, finance, and labor create much diversity, social stratification, and transnationalism.[2] The DC metropolitan area is home to the nation's twelfth-largest Latinx population and unique circumstances of migration. Diversity characterizes DC Latinxs past and present, including people from all Latin American countries and having much socioeconomic and cultural diversity. The DC region is also the only place in the United States where Salvadorans are the largest Latinx group, a trend that dates from the 1980s, when political upheaval in Central America sparked widespread migration to the DC area.

DC Latinxs arrived to a complex, majority–African American city with a proud local culture but a city that also reflected much inequality and a legacy of racial segregation. Further, the region has experienced much change in recent years. DC proper was one of the most heavily gentrified areas of the country between 2000 and 2019 and still today is among the top-twenty most-gentrified US metropolitan areas, with residential displacement disproportionally affecting African Americans and Latinxs.[3] This changing social landscape has led to much local debate and concomitant discourses of privilege, discrimination, and residency rights.

As we will see, language attitudes in the Washington, DC, metropolitan area stigmatize Salvadoran Spanish and African American English (AAE) for a complex combination of sociohistorical reasons that continue to hold weight, but new facets of identity pride that push back against these discourses emerge in relationship to DC's unique social context and identity as a place.

While the topic is evergreen, my research also coincides with a period of community self-searching as a generation of elders and activists reflect on their legacies. Diversity and representation within the community have been an important part of this debate. The drumming and call-and-response in the Nationals celebration that open the introduction to this book are part of the African tradition embedded in many Latin American cultures. Similarly, Afro-Latinxs helped found the DC community. But activists contend that their stories are often overlooked. This ongoing discussion is a sign of richness—no community is homogenous, and there doesn't need to be a single "official" narrative. Communities are living things that are created through discussions such as these. At the same time, underlying dynamics that lead to privilege and exclusion cannot be ignored. The DC Latinx community contains many stories, and which ones you hear depend on who you talk to. Nevertheless, there are common themes that I trace in the following chapters.

How You Speak Defines You . . . or Does It?

"*Dime cómo hablas, y te diré quién eres*" (Tell [show] me how you speak, and I'll tell you who you are). This adaption of the idiomatic phrase "Dime con quién andas, y te diré quién eres" (Tell me who you walk with, and I'll tell you who you are) emphasizes the role of language in identity while reminding us of the original significance—that who we are does not exist in a vacuum but is constructed in relationship to others. Language is foundational to how we understand ourselves, others, and the world. Our identities—who we consider ourselves to be and how we are viewed by others—depend on how we speak, in combination with other social factors.

The questions of "Who am I?" and of social perception are actively relevant to social understanding and social justice. As of this writing, the United States is undergoing a period of soul-searching and public outrage not seen since the civil rights era of the 1960s over who we are as a nation in response to egregious incidents of racial injustice and emboldened White supremacy. Against a broader backdrop of historical and ongoing discourses about race/ethnicity, rights, and belonging, minority groups are misunderstood, misrepresented, and vulnerable to discriminatory rhetoric and attacks. These discourses have real-world consequences, as we can see in the United States' history of discriminatory legislation toward immigrants and people of color. However, questions of representation and discrimination extend beyond the United States. Europe continues to debate migration and refugee issues, and public discourse is growing around race relations and colorism within Latin America (a factor that also affects diasporic Latinxs). In short, language and identity are powerfully symbolic as well as practical in understanding social relations and dynamics of diversity and tension. While I conducted my study in the United States, its themes are relevant to an international audience. Throughout the book I contend that language must always be analyzed in context in order to be understood. Ultimately, I go beyond language and identity to tell a story about Latinx settlement in the region and the ways in which communities are continually self-defining.

Toward a Raciomultilingual Perspective

My raciomultilingual perspective centers the complex multilingual repertoires and identities of immigrant and diasporic groups whose racialization and associated intersectional positionalities relate to numerous local, broader, and ultimately postcolonial ideologies. The framework extends raciolinguistic theory and research on language ideology, linguistic embodiment, and authenticity as well as bilingualism, heritage languages, and the sociolinguistics of globalization.[4] I build on Jonathan Rosa and Nelson Flores's definition of raciolinguistic perspectives as not only the study of language and race but a project that strives to theorize how race and language have come to be seen as naturally connected symbols of each other both historically and in the present day.[5] Raciolinguistic ideologies account for the ways in which language and race have historically been, and continue to be, stereotypically intertwined and inscribed on the bodies of racialized speakers. Further, these ideologies and their practical consequences are an inherent part of the lived language experiences of US Latinxs and other minorities as individuals and collectives.[6] This concept resonates with Mary Bucholtz and Kira Hall's observation that identity-related semiotic processes are "simultaneously embodied and linguistic processes."[7] This perspective is different from simply working on race-related language in that it is specifically a critical social and historical perspective that considers how these concepts came to be and their continued relevance in everyday life and social thought. Or, as H. Samy Alim stated in 2016, it is a perspective that uses diverse methods of linguistic analysis to ask what it means to speak as a racialized subject at the intersection of language, race, and power in contemporary America and more broadly.[8]

A raciomultilingual framework centers multilingualism within a raciolinguistic perspective. It posits that raciolinguistic perceptions of minoritized speakers transcend language boundaries. Given this, and since—as Ofelia García and Li Wei note—multilinguals do not experience their languages in isolation, multilingual repertoires must also be examined holistically.[9] This perspective brings together ideologies about language and people that suffuse sociolinguistic thought in a systemic social way and that affect the entire linguistic repertoire despite manifestations that may be specific to a particular language, dialect, or feature. The paradigm acknowledges named languages such as "English" and "Spanish" as abstractions that are themselves socially constructed. However, it also recognizes that their relevance to speakers gives them power in how identity is conceived.[10]

By centering multilingualism, a raciomultilingual approach considers how racial categories and notions of languages and language varieties are co-constructed compared to normative ideologies of monolingualism and prescriptivism. For example, Sarah Benor's notion of the ethnolinguistic repertoire addresses ethnic-associated features without emphasizing abstract varietal boundaries but engages less with active multilingualism—an area that is essential for understanding racialized immigrants.[11] Fluid multilingual approaches move away from deficit ideas that explicitly or implicitly compare multilinguals' language production with monolingual norms—a comparison still implied in concepts such as Jan Blommaert's "truncated competence"[12]—in favor of the idea that speakers use the totality of languages and linguistic elements at their disposal to achieve communicative goals.

My raciomultilingual perspective is inherently multiscalar. This structure allows for the coexistence of multiple, sometimes contradictory discourses around Latinx identity as well as the evolution of new ideologies with their own referential ideological centers of authenticity and the racialization of place-related linguistic identity. Ambiguity and simultaneous discourses are important aspects of understanding diversity.

Sociolinguistic scales as defined by Blommaert operate on different levels of space and time, with implications for ideologies' mutability and stability such that ideologies at higher-level scales are more likely to be considered natural or universal and, hence, enjoy more permanence.[13] This distance is semiotic rather than geographic, although these dimensions sometimes overlap. Further, there can be more than one center of reference, a phenomenon known as polycentricity.

A multiscalar model sheds new light into how linguistic ideology both circulates widely and is reinterpreted at the local level in immigrant and diasporic contexts. This perspective is necessary as sociolinguistic research increasingly moves away from assumptions of homogeneity, stability, and boundedness in language and communication in favor of emphasizing "mobility, mixing, political dynamics and historical embedding."[14] At the same time, resilient stereotypes about languages and speakers endure.

In figure 1.1, I present a model that accounts for the reach and intersection of different sociolinguistic ideologies and related indexical meanings that I observed in my research. The model represents how ideological systems operate and interact at different time/space scales and, in the case of Latin American immigrants and their descendants, integrate systems from both sides of the diaspora (United States and Latin America) as well as specifically local meanings. As such, it accounts for how ideologies of race, class, and education that manifest in both Latin America and the United States due to a common—yet different—history of European colonization intersect and overlap. At the same time, it accounts for the emergence of local meanings that simultaneously challenge and reference these broader beliefs. This lens is particularly important in immigrant and diasporic contexts, where multiple languages and sets of beliefs are in play.

Both the United States and Latin America have color-related social hierarchies rooted in their colonial histories, where Europeans and their descendants were privileged over Indigenous peoples, people of African descent, and later non-White immigrants. However, there are also particularities of classism and colorism. For example,

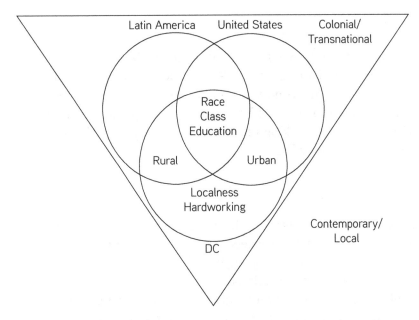

Figure 1.1. Multiscalar model of interacting sociolinguistic ideologies and emerging new meanings in diaspora

in Latin America, rural areas tend to be viewed as less White and associated with indigeneity, and cities are associated with elites and prestige speech, as opposed to US discourses about urban areas that tend to portray them as crime-ridden, non-White "inner cities."

A certain flattening takes place at higher scales such that locally relevant nuances are obscured and simplified into stereotypes that are assumed to be natural or "common sense." For example, my Salvadoran participants had a more nuanced perspective on Salvadoran language and social diversity than had non-Salvadorans, who held a simplified and stereotypical view. Further, my research shows the enduring power of anti-Black ideologies, despite DC Latinxs seeing African American language and culture as a defining aspect of the city's identity and despite their firsthand knowledge of diversity among local African Americans. Finally, identities are also negotiated locally, and new sociolinguistic meanings emerge that are legible only in the local DC context.

The Bigger Picture

A raciomultilingual perspective has much to offer our understanding of language and identity and the construction of race and ethnicity under the dynamic conditions offered by mobility under globalization and late modernity. These issues are important in linguistics and for scholars working on issues of language, culture, race, and ethnicity more broadly.

Language and Identity

Language is not a passive index of identity but an active means of identity construction. Speakers use a wide range of discourse strategies—such as storytelling, stylistic language use, taking stances toward different conversational topics, and positioning themselves in alignment or opposition to others[15]—to construct their own identities as individuals and as members of different groups and to project identities onto others. This quotidian speech relates to broader existing indexicalities and ideological associations between language and identity but through habitual use can perpetuate or transform existing meanings and give rise to others.[16]

Language and identity are intimately connected. I understand identity, or speakers' senses of self, as a combination of who we think we are and how others perceive us.[17] Identities are multifaceted and can be immediate or abstracted, intimate or impersonal, ephemeral or with aspects that many consider more permanent. Such identities can, for example, be grounded in families, communities of practice, or ethnic and national groups. Further, these identities are continuously constructed through social interaction rather than being static or inherent to the individual.

Language is a key means by which identity is enacted in relationship to others and through socialization. Without language, society is not possible. Language is strongly associated with social groups: it is part of who we imagine ourselves to be.[18] For example, heritage languages are often associated with ethnic identity, such as Spanish for US Latinxs. This symbolic relationship is known as social indexicality, or the ways in which language serves as an indicator of social group membership and related social qualities.[19] While these identity associations can help maintain language and culture, they can also be used to delegitimize those who do not speak "correctly" or in accordance with expectations.[20] However, "covert" pride can also attach to nonprestige language as part of in-group identities. And while popular perception often stigmatizes hybrid and innovative linguistic practices such as translanguaging as "incorrect," new identities associated with these practices often arise in later generations, as amply demonstrated by literature on migrant and diasporic youth identities.[21]

Translanguaging is similar to code-switching, or the use of two or more languages in a single interaction, but is more encompassing, emphasizing how bilinguals use the full range of their linguistic resources to navigate and make sense of the world. Translanguaging puts the focus on people who grow up bilingually as holistic individuals with unified bilingual repertoires, which they learn to call by different names such as "English" and "Spanish," rather than starting with "English" and "Spanish" as de facto separate categories that speakers "switch" between—a model in which bilinguals are often compared to monolingual native speakers and seen as lacking.[22] Hybridity refers to new forms and practices that draw on resources from more than one language or culture, bearing in mind that cultural and linguistic boundaries—though often believed to be clear and permanent—are themselves inherently porous and dynamic. Today's hybrid language forms—implicitly contrasted with convention when described as "innovative" and often stigmatized as "incorrect"—are often tomorrow's norms, as with "Spanglish" in the United States.[23] Hybridity also gives rise to "third space" practices and ideologies that are more than the sum of their parts.[24] However, hybridity is not the same as parity, as Frances Aparicio notes in her work on constructing Latinidad, nor is it reflective of a homogenous experience. Privilege and discrimination are still reflected within hybridity, and hybridity can be strongly stigmatized even as it becomes normalized or takes on covert prestige within a community.

Language functions both as an index of social membership and of authenticity such as "real" culture or ethnic identity. Sometimes language itself is transformed into a social image or icon.[25] Similarly, inadequate language (variously determined as impure, non-native, stigmatized, or otherwise nonnormative for the community in question) can be used as a means of deauthenticating speakers and challenging their identities. As this predicament demonstrates, authenticity itself is constructed and ideological: rather than being an innate quality, it is constructed through discourse and other semiotic practices.[26] Notions of authenticity nevertheless have real-life consequences for identity and social perception.

Race and Ethnicity

A raciomultilingual framework examines the ways in which bilingual repertoires are understood in terms of the monoracial and monolingual ideologies that surround them. Social perception of language does not exist in a vacuum but is discursively linked to speaker physicalities. Language is not only spoken but also embodied in the sense that our ways of speaking, through their iconic indexical social meanings, locate our embodied selves as particular kinds of people in hegemonic social space.[27] In this book, I examine how race and ethnicity are salient to how DC Latinxs perceive themselves and others in terms of language.

Race and ethnicity are social constructions that are often assumed to be "commonsense" natural fact.[28] This naturalization erases contradictory evidence, such as diversity within ethnoracial groups, in favor of essentializing views of homogenous identity, while also imposing false divisions. Despite being abstractions, however, these labels have real social consequences. Since race and ethnicity are often used as a means of justifying the privilege or oppression of different groups, they affect all of society but disproportionately impact minoritized groups.

Language is an important part of this discrimination. Systemic prejudice against minoritized peoples was historically endemic in the United States and continues in the present day.[29] Linguistic discrimination against Latinxs and other minoritized groups is widespread, from accent discrimination to English-only legislation.[30]

A succinct example of sociolinguistic indexicality in action is the assumption that each person speaks one language related to their "real" self, that English and minority languages are thus incompatible, and that speaking English therefore represents Americanness. This xenophobic discourse is racialized: the non-English-speaking, un-American "immigrant other" is conceived of as non-White. As this example demonstrates, linguistic ideologies do not merely target language but operate within broader ideological bundles that James Gee calls "big-D Discourses": "ways of being in the world, or forms of life which integrate words, acts, values, beliefs, attitudes, social identities."[31] Resting on the same underlying beliefs, speaking English at the perceived expense of the heritage language makes immigrants' children vulnerable to accusations of cultural rejection.[32]

Social thought can also take on a life of its own. Ideological proliferation (in what Gal and Irvine call "fractal recursivity"[33]) gives rise to ideological constellations of related meanings. In terms of race, for example, non-Whiteness is typically stigmatized in the United States. Stereotypes targeting racial minorities abound. For example, Latinxs and African Americans are often associated with urbanness and toughness, among other stereotypical qualities; these representations are also gendered.[34] This widespread perception contributes to discrimination but can also cause non-Whiteness to function as an index of authenticity, with Whiteness seen as inauthentic. A relevant example of this is Latinxs' mockery of the White-associated "Valley Girl" accent and other linguistic features as *"la voz gringa"* (the White voice).[35]

My raciomultilingual perspective incorporates a broad and critical look at the social context in which language functions and is understood to enhance constructivist perspectives on the ways in which race is associated with language and vice versa. It also provides a mechanism for looking deeply into the social meaning of language via ideologies that accrete around race in modern societies. While race is a construct, its social weight and effect on racialized people are impactful. The ways in which race and ethnicity are investigated and theorized in language studies are in an exciting moment of growth, where the models we use and their implications for the field are being challenged, opening new directions for linguistics' contributions to knowledge and to society.

The Sociolinguistics of Migration

Migration shines a spotlight on the reciprocal relationship between language and identity. Linguistic identity is particularly complex for immigrants and their children. Speakers must simultaneously navigate their desire for cultural continuity and the pressures they face in a new country. For example, while heritage languages are often an important source of identity and pride, minoritized groups often face linguistic discrimination, among other forms of prejudice. Further, language and identity change over time as new practices emerge in response to the new environment. Later generations often have different language profiles and attitudes than do their immigrant parents and ancestors.

Changing urbanities challenge us to examine new investigative directions. As loci for migration, cities are ideal locations to study sociolinguistic diversity and identity.[36] Recent research moves beyond the neighborhood-grounded social studies tradition—which, however, remains productive—to account for more complexity in the relationship between physical places, lived social spaces, and language.[37]

Further, cities themselves are changing. In traditional immigrant gateways such as New York City, immigrants tended to live in tightly clustered enclaves, then move to the suburbs as they grew wealthier. In more recent "emergent" gateways such as Washington, DC, and its suburbs, immigrants of different languages and backgrounds intermingle in diverse global neighborhoods, although more homogenous ethnic enclaves, such as Latinx neighborhoods, also persist.[38]

Globalization, neoliberal economics, and climate change cause mass migration and increase social stratification.[39] Researchers in the past two decades have theorized "global cities," a globalization-induced phenomenon whereby cities are characterized by "super-diversity": highly diverse migration from all over the world, where immigrant communities are internally diverse socioeconomically as well as in terms of legal status and histories of migration.[40] The proliferation of this complex diversity includes social stratification, mobility, and transnationalism related to international networks of migration, communication, finance, and labor. The dynamic and stratified sociolinguistic contact and "organized heterogeneity" in global cities such as Washington, DC, emphasize inhabitants' social understandings of language and lead to the reconfiguration of these meanings.[41]

The notion of superdiversity, or the diversification of diversity under new conditions of contact and mobility, arose in a similar tradition in linguistics to account for the multiplicity of language repertoires, practices, and social meanings caused by globalization.[42] While the term has been criticized as Eurocentric, its emphasis on the many dimensions of diversity among members of a single "group" as well as among people of different backgrounds and on the challenge that this multidimensionality presents for traditional notions of "one language, one people" is well taken.[43] However, while a growing body of research addresses these more nuanced understandings of diversity among Latinxs in global cities and in the Latin American diaspora, much remains to be done on the topic in the United States.[44]

Theorizing Latinidad

Latinxs are a strong and growing presence in the United States. They are the largest US immigrant group and represent a wide range of origins and experiences. However, the ways in which diversity among Latinos ("intraLatinx/a diversity"[45])—and within racialized immigrant communities more broadly—intersect with language and identity are not yet fully understood. This book extends theorization in this direction.

Dina Okamoto and G. Cristina Mora define panethnicity as identity formation across ethnic boundaries through both imposed social organization and subgroups' own interactions, organization, and institution building.[46] The former often happens in colonial situations;

the latter, through immigration. Both are relevant to US Latinx identity. The dominant US gaze and institutional positioning group Latinxs into a single category, while Latinx activism and media have created solidarity.[47]

The term "Latino/a/x/e/u" contains much diversity: national origin, immigration histories, race, gender, sexual orientation, socioeconomic status, language, and more.[48] Rosalyn Negrón notes that US Latinxs encompass "sociohistorical roots in nearly every continent, distinct immigration histories within the US, and at least nineteen dialects of Spanish" as well as diversity among Latinxs of the same national origin.[49] While Spanish is generally seen as a shared cultural marker, it is also a site of identity negotiation due to this diversity and due to differences in proficiency and usage that emerge among US-born Latinxs and that contrast with Latin American norms.[50]

Panethnic terms such as "Latinx," "Latino," and "Latinidad" have been criticized for masking diversity and tension among Latinxs, including differences in power and privilege, by Aparicio and other scholars.[51] Aparicio also notes, however, that the terms are fluid, situational, and strategic and that people of Latin American descent can identify with multiple terms at the same time: "The term 'Latino' then does not necessarily displace the significance of the national identifiers, but is used to signal the multiple and relational selves of colonized subjects."[52] Rather than being a static identity category, "Latinidad" is a site of dynamic negotiation between similarity and difference and of shared placemaking and knowledge production. Further, since the term inherently operates in relationship to dominant White US society, it can be used to navigate power dynamics and create a sense of shared affinity and practices.[53] This indeed was the motivation for the panethnic term "Hispanic," which Latinx activists sought in order to increase the group's visibility and access to resources from the 1960s on.[54]

Further, Rosa argues that "Latinx" is also seen as a racial category in the United States.[55] He notes that the United States' ideological Black/White race binary gives rise to a "spectrum" ideology in which Latinxs are positioned as Brown in relationship to these two reference points despite their broad range of ancestries and phenotypes:

"Insofar as Latinx identities are produced as part of a US settler colonial history and broader histories of European colonialism, we must continually attend to the ways that these forms of coloniality shape perceptions of Latinx bodies in relation to an imagined phenotypic spectrum from Blackness to Whiteness, and Latinx communicative practices in relation to an imagined linguistic spectrum from Spanish to English."[56]

Within this framework, further complexities exist. Negrón notes that "Latinidad" can be understood as "a constellation of differences rooted in a common colonial past with ripple effects that continue to this day in ways that bind US Latina/os. While ancient in its impulses, ethnoracial categorization and the marking of status are part of the colonial legacy."[57] Rosa observes that colorism in Latinx communities is a colonially patterned racial logic that interacts with historical and contemporary historical, political, and economic positionalities, and Rubén Rumbaut argues that "Hispanic elites historically asserted white identities for themselves and their communities."[58] These ideologies operate within and across US Latinx communities and in Latin America.

Defining Terms

So far I have used some terms that may or may not be familiar to the reader. Before continuing, I would like to define some of the principal ones that will reoccur in these pages.

Languaging

Language does not simply consist of sets of linguistic features and grammatical rules but is a lived social practice: a continual, dynamic process of "languaging," or "using language to make meaning."[59] Languaging is a social practice that is learned and reproduced through interaction. As part of this process, the social meanings attached to language are crucial for how speakers perceive, interpret, and construct their social worlds. These habits and beliefs in turn affect language behavior with immediate-time consequences, such as language use or avoidance, and long-term consequences, such as systemic language change and language maintenance or loss.[60]

Named Languages

The names we give to languages, such as "Spanish" or "English," are abstractions. Bilingualism highlights this, as it often gives rise to forms that are difficult to categorize neatly as belonging to one or the other. Take, for example, the words *"lonchar"* (to eat lunch) in Spanish, or "taco" in English. While speakers may still be aware of the words' origins, can the words really be said to belong only to one or the other language? Recent linguistic research explores the nuances of this discussion for how we understand and study language.[61] However, named languages remain useful for ease of discussion. Further, naming languages remains important to speakers, even as their own fluid bilingual practices may challenge and be challenged by these language labels.[62] The idea of separate languages is meaningful to people for the very reasons I seek to unpack: their indexical connections to identity and culture. Exploring these attitudes and ideologies helps us understand how linguistic identities and language itself are imagined.

Community

Communities are social groups that gain their identities and cohesion not though homogeneity but through interaction, imagination, and process.[63] Their construction and imagination are inherently social processes "reproduced in the interactions of social networks, and represented by signs and symbols in the imaginings of individuals internal and external to the community," although not all community members will know each other or interact personally.[64] "Community" in this sense extends to all types of groups that possess a sense of shared identity and history based on material or social constructs such as geography, ethnicity, or gender. Such a community's collective values, beliefs, and practices are expressed through the creation and retention of particular narratives about the past: its social memory.[65]

Communities play an important role in the transmission of language, norms, and ideologies and are sites of cross-generational language maintenance and change. Speech communities—or groups of people with shared language practices, norms of interpretation, and communicative expectations—operate on multiple scales, from the national level to local communities of practice.[66] However, communities are not limited to geographical place; they take place in social space.

Bilingual and multilingual communities display a wide range of characteristics depending on their sociohistorical contexts and cultural norms. A common cause for bilingualism is migration, in which people move to another region or country for a variety of purposes and under a range of circumstances. Migrants' social circumstances and conditions of migration affect their migration experience and language outcomes, as does the nature of their co-ethnic community in the host country, their reception by dominant groups in the new country, and the structures available to support or inhibit their majority-language learning and minority-language maintenance.

Multilingual Repertoires

Linguistic repertoires refer to the range of linguistic behaviors at a speaker's disposal and how they are used.[67] Scholar John Gumperz defines linguistic repertoires as "the totality of distinct language varieties, dialects and styles employed in a community" as well as communicative norms and frames of interpretation.[68] Further, repertoires are not static but encompass trajectories of language learning related to experiences of migration.[69]

In a bilingual community, the repertoire may range through varied Spanish and English competencies and through mixed practices and different dialects. A particular individual's repertoire will consist of these elements in line with their personal contexts and learning conditions. New linguistic repertoires that contain elements of both cultures and languages but are more than the sum of their parts also emerge across generations. These linguistic repertoires allow speakers to express new aspects of identity and culture that reflect their lived realities.

Repertoires are often linked to ethnocultural identity, as expressed by Benor's definition of ethnolinguistic repertoires: "fluid set[s] of linguistic resources that members of an ethnic group may use variably as they index their ethnic identities."[70] While heritage languages often retain traditional identity associations, such as the belief that "if you're Latinx you should speak Spanish," different aspects of the linguistic repertoire can be used to display and construct new aspects of identity.[71] For example, dialects can be used to express identity, and later Latinx immigrant generations often make extensive use of hybrid bilingual practices such as translanguaging. However, these innovations are often unfavorably viewed by native speakers. Indeed, as scholars have noted, US Latinxs' language is often stigmatized on both sides of their bilingual repertoires—both Spanish and English.[72]

While repertoires contain languages and varieties, they underscore that these labels are convenient abstractions; there is much fluid language use and hybrid forms that may not neatly fit into the category of one language or another. The idea of repertoires and ranges of bilingualism aligns with recent research that challenges the idea that languages are separate and bounded entities in which multilinguals achieve separate proficiencies. Rather, they emphasize that speakers use the totality of their language repertoires to achieve communication in daily life.[73]

Heritage Languages

The term "heritage languages" emerged in North American bilingualism debates to acknowledge speakers with a cultural and familial connection to a nondominant language who consider themselves learners of their languages and cultures, who primarily learned them in a nonacademic setting, or who have some proficiency in the language.[74] Heritage languages are similar to the notion of "home language" or "mother tongue," which are more current outside of the US context.[75] The idea of heritage languages and heritage learners arose to expand narrow understandings of bilingualism that implicitly or explicitly equate it with native-like proficiency in two languages.[76] These understandings—and ongoing prejudice against heritage speakers that stigmatizes their language abilities as "incomplete acquisition"[77]—are based in the normalization of monolingual language behavior as the ideal in language proficiency and "commonsense" notions of "native speaker-ism," which are themselves social and ideological constructs that draw as much on essentialist ideas of race and culture as on language.[78]

The United States has always been multilingual. Indigenous multilingualism was present during precolonization and continued alongside European colonial languages (English, Dutch, French, Spanish). Multilingualism continues today via surviving Indigenous languages and the languages brought by migrants from all over the world. Spanish, the second-most-spoken language in the United States, is both an immigrant language and a substratum language in the former Spanish territories of the US Southwest and Puerto Rico. However, US language policy is largely assimilationist, a tendency exacerbated by racism and xenophobia during times of heightened national anxiety.[79]

Under these circumstances, heritage languages tend to be lost across generations, a pattern that has been well documented since Joshua Fishman's seminal research on US minorities.[80] Spanish tends to be retained longer than other immigrant languages, due to continuous Latin American migration.[81] However, Latinx language use contains more complex patterns of heritage language maintenance and loss that relate to the specifics of different communities—differences that are masked by large-scale data such as census reporting.[82] It remains to be seen what effect formal education may have on this trend in the future. Spanish is the second-most widely studied language in the United States, and additive bilingual education such as dual language immersion is increasing in popularity, although serious questions about access and privilege remain.[83] These questions are germane to Washington, DC, due to its diverse Latinx population, generally tolerant climate, and flourishing bilingual education programs.

Hispanic? Latino? Latin@? Latinx? Latine?

Names have power to shape reality, and power is implied by who does the naming.[84] "Latino" and "Hispanic" are terms borrowed from Spanish *"hispano"* and *"latino,"* having their origins in "América Hispánica" from the Spanish colonial period, and "Latinoamérica" from the period of independence. The terms took on relevance among Latinxs in California in the second half of the nineteenth century following its US acquisition through the Treaty of Guadalupe Hidalgo but declined in usage before being popularized through Latinx activism and media and institutional usage in the late twentieth century.[85]

The term "Hispanic" was first used by the US Census in 1980 following activism for a panethnic term to represent the interests of Latin American–origin populations in the United States.[86] Later, "Latino" rose in popularity as a means of distinguishing origins in Latin America from those in Spain and was first included in the census in 2000.[87] Individual preferences vary, though "Hispanic" is generally perceived as a governmentally imposed term.[88] Regional understandings also exist, such as in the border state of New Mexico, where the historic *nuevomexicano* community, which traces its descent to the Spanish colonial period, uses the term "Hispanic" to distinguish itself from the Mexican identity of newer arrivals.[89] In general, panethnic terms are used in conjunction with national origin as a more salient identifier, but panethnic identification comes to take precedence in later generations of US-born Latinxs.[90] More recently, queer, gender, and feminist activists in the United States and Latin America have proposed -x, -e, -u as gender-neutral alternatives to the neutral-masculine ending -o, with the -x favored in the United States and the -e and -u easier to pronounce in Spanish.[91] Debate around the term continues. The Real Academia de la Lengua Española (Royal Academy of the Spanish Language), the largest prescriptive body, does not recognize the new terms. Nevertheless, "Latinx" and "Latine" are gaining popularity among younger, college-educated Latinxs and progressives.[92] Despite criticism of "Latinx" as a form of US cultural and linguistic imperialism, it—like "Latine"—originated in queer and activist Latinx spaces in the United States and Latin America; however, "Latine" tends to be preferred in Spanish due to ease of pronunciation.[93] By the time this book is published, preferences may well have shifted further as terminology continues to evolve and be debated.

Naming can be controversial precisely because it encodes representation. In terms of group identities, there is not always consensus around naming, and popular adaption may lag that of activists and intellectuals.[94] Part of the issue is the idea that there can and should be only one "right" term. Another is that the terms may have different implications, although not everyone who might identify with the term is necessarily aware of them all. These implications themselves change over time.[95] The debate over "Latinx" is controversial precisely because it engages with questions of identity, which are polemic in our time. Understandings of gender continue to evolve in all communities. The structure of Spanish, with its grammatical gender, brings this debate to the forefront, but Latinxs are not alone in struggling with these questions. The debate itself is a healthy sign of vitality, and not all will identify in the same way or prefer to use the same terms. Finally, the naming of minority groups is often politicized beyond their communities in ways that serve outsider interests. A community's desire for representational self-determination is often dismissed as "political correctness run amok," as in pushback against Native Americans' attempts to have racist sports team names changed.[96] Similarly, public debate over "Latinx" in the United States ties into broader debates about gender and sexuality, which have been strongly polemicized in recent years.[97] The debate is similar to that over personal pronouns in English but is more intense because Spanish grammatical morphology carries through the noun phrase (e.g., *una mujer bonita*).[98] As in English, however, a person's individual identification can coexist with broader attempts at inclusivity that may not affect them directly, such as using the gender-neutral term for the collective and when addressing an unknown audience and using whatever term one personally identifies with in self-reference.

I use participants' own words (e.g., Latino/a, Hispanic) when quoting their speech. Since "Latinx" had not yet risen to the level of popular consciousness when I conducted the bulk of my fieldwork, it does not appear in the interview transcripts in this book. I struggled deciding which term to use in general, since the terminological debate is real among the participants I am still in touch with. Some, particularly younger people, use "Latinx" for its inclusive meanings; some, particularly older people, find it unnecessary or incorrect; and some feel that "Latino" is a term that was fought for, so they do not want to see it altered or "taken away." In the end, I decided to use the "–x" in line with the current inclusivity movement when speaking in general. Language is always changing, and the controversial uses of today are the established conventions of tomorrow. While "Latinx" may give way to, for example, "Latine," I feel that it is important to recognize this community conversation, although gender in itself is not the focus of this book. Further, "Latinx" is a term I increasingly hear used by younger people in the community, and this book is aimed at the future generation of scholars. In these cases, the "–x" is used in general to be inclusive, and the "–o/a/x" depending on how the person themself identifies. Apart from this, I generally hear "Latino" rather than "Hispanic," and I sometimes hear people refer to themselves as "Spanish," a working-class way of referring to Latinxs, not people from Spain.[99] I rarely hear locals refer to themselves as "Hispanic" in casual conversation, and I have heard it described as a "census term," so its use by some participants in my study may be due to a perception of interviews as an "official" genre.

Having set the stage, in the next chapter we take a closer look at Latinxs in the Washington, DC, metropolitan area. In addition to current demographic information, I describe how Latinxs migrated and put down roots amid the broader picture of DC demographics and culture. We also consider intersectional complexities of race, social class, and national origin that reflect US and Latin American hierarchies but are influenced by the particularities of the DC area as a global metropolis.

2

"Empanadas, pupusas, and greens on the side"

DC Latinidad

The DC metropolitan area is unique in a number of ways. As the seat of the US government, power and privilege are ever present while at the same time deep-seated inequalities thrive. The Latinx community is highly diverse, as is the DC region in general. Moreover, Washington, DC, historically has had a strong Black presence and culture. For much of the twentieth century the city was majority Black, and the region remains home to many African Americans. It is a major site in the African diaspora; for example, it has the largest Ethiopian community outside of Africa.[1] DC's Black majority led to its iconic status as "Chocolate City" and to unique cultural forms such as "go-go," a percussive African American funk genre with Latin influences that evolved in the 1960s and 1970s and is unique to DC.[2] Go-go is so important to local identity that the city legislated it as DC's official music in 2020, and a go-go museum recently opened. Go-go played at the ceremony when Marion Barry Avenue—a street named in honor of the legendary, if controversial, DC mayor—was unveiled intersecting Martin Luther King Jr. Avenue in the Anacostia neighborhood, an important site in local Black history that retains its culture and identity despite changes in the city.[3] While the Black majority was lost in 2011, DC remains a majority-minority city where Black history and culture are a strong presence. At the same time, DC is a city of neighborhoods reflecting wealth inequality and the legacy of racial segregation as well as current changes.

43

Given the city's demographics, many Latinx immigrants to DC have been in extended contact with African Americans, creating a mix of friendship, assimilation, and tension. The most visible wave of immigrants was a massive Central American migration in the 1980s, making DC the only area of the United States with a Salvadoran majority among Latinx. However, Latinx of all backgrounds are present. DC's unique fusion culture can be seen in Latinxs' celebration of go-go's recognition at the Grammy Awards and in comments such as those by "Marcos," a Washington native: "That's the DC we remember, had, cultural food. You know making, *empanada pupusas* but also having cauliflower green—and greens on the side too. That's DC. A fusion. . . . that was DC Chocolate City. It was an infusion of whatever culture you had with, the [Black] culture." As local oral historian José Centeno-Meléndez, shared in conversation, DC is different from what he learned about Central American studies and Latinx studies in college. In this, he specifically mentioned a working-class Black and Latinx context in which he felt diversity of "Spanish" backgrounds—including Latinx of all racial backgrounds—as well as a sense of Salvadoran identity, which contrasted with the more homogenous perspective he was presented with in his academic studies.

Washington, DC

The city of Washington, DC, is the federal capital of the United States. DC is organized in a system of four quadrants radiating out from the Capitol Building, the seat of Congress (see figure 2.1). Within these quadrants, it is also a city of wards (smaller administrative units) and of neighborhoods with distinct histories, demographics, and characteristics.

DC sits between Maryland and Virginia on land originally inhabited by the Nacotchtank, also known as the Anacostans, which is where the name for the Anacostia River derives.[4] The region was founded as the site of the federal government in 1790 on land donated by both states as part of a political compromise to relocate the capital nearer the powerful slaveholding southern states, which

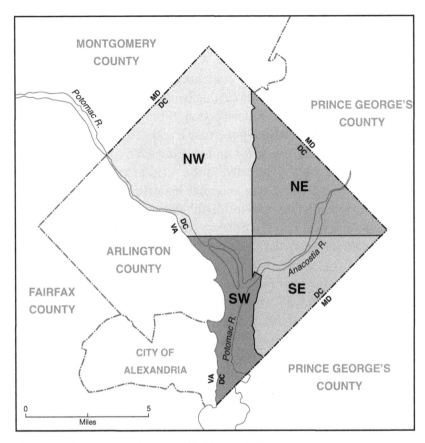

Figure 2.1. The four quadrants of Washington, DC.

feared that the original capital, Philadelphia, was too closely aligned with abolitionists, since Pennsylvania was one of the northern states that abolished slavery in the second half of the eighteenth century.[5] Virginia took back the land west of the Potomac River in 1846 in order to have access to its ports for the slave trade, which is why the map today is asymmetrical.[6]

DC sits between two major US cultural regions, the north and the south, and is difficult to characterize as a northern or southern city.[7] President John F. Kennedy famously described Washington as "a city of Southern efficiency and Northern charm,"[8] which, pithy but not necessarily accurate, neatly represents this ambiguity. Its intermediary location was a deliberate political compromise due to historic competition between the regions—tensions that ultimately culminated in the American Civil War of 1861–65. Washington, DC, is a federal district, not a state or territory. Politically, it is liberal, with 92 percent of voting residents casting ballots for the Democratic candidate in the 2020 presidential election. While over the years DC has gained the right to local self-governance and casts three votes in the Electoral College for president and vice president of the country, its residents' votes are not included in the popular vote.[9] The quest for DC self-governance and statehood has historically been opposed by conservative politicians due to this liberal bent and its history as a Black city, a debate that continues to this day.[10] Indeed, locals often differentiate between "DC" the city, with its own local culture, and "Washington" as a culture of politics and nonlocal, transient politicians. In the late twentieth century, DC faced issues of poverty and violence, which are still very much present in local memory, but it was also a city of neighborhoods, where—as numerous study participants commented—people said hello to each other and elders kept watch from porches. There is still a deep affection for the city and a sense that it is misunderstood by outsiders. As Marcos said, speaking to imaginary gentrifiers, "Don't be so judgmental. Try to stop comparing it to home. It's DC, it's not home to you. See us from here, we love it. We don't complain . . . [except] about not being able to live, where our grandparents are from, where my mom's from. . . . We were kicked out [by gentrification]."

DC as African American City

DC has historically been the site of much wealth and privilege but also inequality and disenfranchisement.[11] Ironically, in a nation founded on the premise of freedom for all, slave labor built the capital.[12] DC was also home to a substantial free African American population.[13]

DC has been a city with a substantial Black population since its inception. At the time of its founding, 25 percent of the city's population were enslaved or free African Americans; this trend held true in 1800, with enslaved persons significantly outnumbering free

African Americans.[14] Still, Washington, DC, was one of the earliest sites of emancipation from slavery in the United States (in 1862, three years before the Thirteenth Amendment outlawed slavery in all states) and had a thriving Black population and relatively more freedom than the South. For example, DC had more liberal rules governing free Blacks than neighboring Virginia had, leading to an influx of Black population after the retrocession in which Virginia took back District territory west of the Anacostia River. Other notable waves of Black migration to the District of Columbia came after the Civil War, leading, for example, to the important community of Barry Farm, an independent Black community for resettled former slaves associated with Frederick Douglass that became a hub of Black middle-class life and activism.[15] Much Black migration to DC also occurred during the Great Migration of African Americans away from the Deep South during a large part of the twentieth century.[16]

This population encompassed diverse social classes.[17] While DC's large African American population historically enjoyed more freedom and rights than African Americans in neighboring Maryland and Virginia, they still experienced much discrimination. Post–Civil War and into the twentieth century, Jim Crow laws segregated education, recreation, and public spaces, and workforce discrimination and residential exclusion were pervasive[18]—a legacy that continues to impact wealth and residency today.[19]

At the same time, DC was a hub of Black activism, both local and national;[20] for example, Black DC was closely involved with Martin Luther King Jr. in the civil rights movement, and landmark lawsuits in DC weakened Jim Crow laws in 1953 a year before *Brown v. Board of Education* led to their repeal.[21] DC also was, and continues to be, a mecca of African American arts and culture. Howard University, the premier Black university in the country, was an intellectual hub.[22] The arts thrived, with iconic jazz musicians such as native son Duke Ellington, whose legacy continues in the Duke Ellington School of the Arts, and many others.[23]

DC became the first majority–African American city in 1957.[24] Its symbolic importance can be seen in the funk band Parliament's iconic 1975 album that names DC as "Chocolate City." At the same time, the city remained affected by race-based housing practices that maintained residential segregation—with the west side of the city predominantly White and the east side predominantly Black—and that division encouraged White suburbanization.[25] Emanuel recalled, "White people always lived on the other side of 16th Street. 16th Street was the dividing line so no . . . White person was . . . seen on this side," a comment consistent with commentary in Jessica Grieser's study of DC African American language and identity.[26] The consequences of segregation persist in de facto residential segregation to this day.[27] Suburbanization, both White and Black, increased after the 1968 riots that followed the assassination of Martin Luther King Jr., when many Black neighborhoods were destroyed.[28] In general, racial inequality and urban disinvestment continued to grow, leading to an increase in crime and other poverty-related issues during the 1970s and 1980s.[29]

This historic presence and identity make African American English (AAE) a strong presence in the city. The Language and Community in the Washington, DC, Metropolitan Area Project at Georgetown University has been documenting DC-area AAE for years.[30] While DC AAE is not a monolith—for example, Grammy-nominated Christylez Bacon, a local musician with an exquisite ear for language and sound, told me in a Smithsonian interview that DC AAE varies by quadrant and even by neighborhood—Black English is indexically associated with "DC," as amply attested in my data and as can be seen by media focus on Black English in pieces tracing "DC language."[31]

Gentrification

DC is one of the most heavily gentrified areas of the United States.[32] Economic revitalization, spearheaded by former mayor Anthony Williams's (1999–2007) commitment to encouraging business, unfortunately exacerbated inequity by sparking intense gentrification and a sharp increase in housing prices, with working- and middle-class residents being displaced by wealthier, primarily White new residents—many in traditionally Black and Latinx neighborhoods.[33] This pattern resonates with broader US patterns whereby

Table 2.1. Race/Ethnicity in the DC Metropolitan Area, 2022

Race/Ethnicity	DC (%)	Metropolitan Area (%)
White	45	42
Black	45	24
Hispanic	11.7	17
Asian	4.7	11
Islander	>0.1	>0.1
Native American	>0.1	>0.1
Two or more	3.21	5

Sources: US Census Bureau, Quick Facts District of Columbia, "Population Estimates, July 1, 2022," https://www.census.gov/quickfacts/fact/table/DC/PST045222; U.S. Census Bureau, American Community Survey 1-Year Estimates, 2022, Census Reporter Profile page for Washington-Arlington-Alexandria, DC-VA-MD-WV Metro Area, http://censusreporter.org/profiles/31000US47900-washington-arlington-alexandria-dc-va-md-wv-metro-area/.

gentrification is concretely and discursively understood along race lines due to long-standing residential and economic segregation in which wealthier White newcomers displace poorer residents who are often African American, Latinx, or other people of color and immigrants.[34]

This residential and economic pressure, together with the local history of race relations, keeps race salient in local discourses about gentrification. Gentrification is commonly seen as a primarily White phenomenon, and its displacement of less-wealthy, long-established residents of color out of the city is resented, with racial displacement foregrounded in these debates.[35] Further, the city lost its Black majority in 2011 (see table 2.1). While African Americans remain the largest racial/ethnic group in a "majority-minority" city, they are no longer the overall majority.[36] Together, these trends highlight racialized claims to belonging in which a binary is seen between Whiteness and African American language and culture and non-White identity more generally.[37]

Gentrification is not only an economic and residential phenomenon but an identity work that manifests through struggle over place and residency and in which different gentrifiers and displacees have different resources and, hence, power.[38] Numerous headlines reflect the racial overtones of the gentrification debate and competing claims to the city, such as "Farewell to Chocolate City."[39] Recently, a Twitter (now X) controversy over a Washingtonian magazine ad campaign—"I'm not a tourist, I live here"—pointed out that the campaign portrayed many affluent young Whites but not a single African American.[40] Another conflict erupted around new residents' attempts to ban public playing of go-go music in a Black neighborhood, which critics saw as emblematic of cultural displacement.[41]

Immigrant Destination

In its 1975 album, Parliament contrasted DC as "Chocolate City" with its White-majority "vanilla suburbs."[42] However, the suburbs are now much more diverse. While Whites are still the majority in the metropolitan area outside the city, there are also large African American and Latinx populations, and the metropolitan area has diversified rapidly with immigration from around the world.

The Washington, DC, metropolitan area is considered a "newly established immigrant gateway," meaning urban areas that received much immigration, typically from Latin America, Asia, and Africa, in the latter half of the twentieth century and where immigrant settlement tends to be in diverse suburbs as well as in the city proper.[43] DC internationalized as the United States increased its global role after World War II, which led to more diversity in the city and, particularly, in the suburbs.[44]

> Its evolution into a consensus top 15 global city since the 1950s (primarily over the past two decades) is largely due to the broadened reach of the United States into global affairs and its increasing role as a business and economic powerhouse.... [After World War II], there was a growing diplomatic base, and infrastructure to support it, such as international schools, began to grow.... DC became more cosmopolitan, urban, affluent, and diverse.... Greater Washington provides a strong example of the shifting role of national capitals into top networking and decision-making centers for politics, as well as economy and business.[45]

As a consequence, DC and its metropolitan region today are hyperdiverse, in Marie Price and Lisa Benton-Short's term (developed in research on Washington, DC). In cities with more than 1 million people, Price and Benton-Short write, a city is hyperdiverse when "at least 9.5% of the total population is foreign-born, no one country of origin accounts for 25% or more of the immigrant stock, and immigrants come from all regions of the world."[46]

As of 2021, 13.5 percent of Washingtonians and 23 percent of metropolitan residents were foreign-born, primarily from Latin America and Asia, followed by Africa. In DC proper, European immigrants were also a large presence, slightly outnumbering African immigrants, but in the metropolitan area overall European immigration was low.[47] Another characteristic of hyperdiversity is that ethnocultural groups are internally diverse along class, political, and national lines, in keeping with Steven Vertovec's understanding of "superdiversity."[48] For example, Salvadorans are the largest Latinx group in the DC area, but the Latinx population overall contains a wide range of national backgrounds as well as differences in socioeconomic status, education, histories of migration, and race.

While it is well documented that contact between social groups can cause material and ideological tension, it is also known that residential mixing can increase tolerance for diversity, as Michael Bader discovered in DC's metropolitan suburbs.[49] In general, DC and the metropolitan region embrace a discourse of diversity and tolerance, albeit imperfectly.[50] At the same time, contact between different groups leads to the highlighting of different identities, which is typical of contact situations and negotiation of discourses about what different aspects of identity mean on individual and group levels, and for being Washingtonian.[51]

DC as a Global City

The Washington, DC, metropolitan area is a global-city region. Global cities are associated with transnationalism, economic stratification, immigration, and diversity and are understood as large, densely populated urban areas with specialized service, financial, and cultural markets linked to the global economy.[52] DC's role as the seat of the US federal government and the high presence of international organizations, with corresponding sectors and labor forces, sets it apart from other large, diverse US cities. Indeed, it is regarded as the most politically vital global city in the world.[53] Its stratification is typical of global cities: locals often distinguish between the "Washington" of power and prestige and "DC," the local city of permanent residents and workers, which coexist with numerous other communities and economies. The imagination of social space in terms of language, identity, and interaction—for example, between long-term residents and recent arrivals—is foregrounded in DC as in other global cities, with specific discourses related to particularities of the local environment.[54] DC is characterized by international and local processes of mobility and stratification: migration from other countries and different areas of the United States, transnationalism, and intensive gentrification. Its political importance means that international flows of people, commerce, and communication permeate the local environment.[55] These flows give rise to new, intersecting "glocal" phenomena in which global and local processes influence each other and create new ways of being and thinking.[56] At the same time, local discourses deeply rooted in DC's historical context and that of the United States more broadly continue to hold sway.

While much social diversity is present, DC is a highly stratified city. The metropolitan area has an overall higher annual household income than the rest of the United States ($110,355 versus $67,521), but a closer look reveals unequal distribution.[57] The median DC household income is lower than that of the metro area ($93,547).[58] Washington, DC, has the highest level of income inequality in the country, and the metropolitan region is also very unequal in terms of income.[59] Race and ethnicity significantly affect wealth. White residents earn more than other groups throughout the area. Latinx and African Americans overall have lower incomes, but within this trend, patterns vary. In DC, for example, African Americans have lower incomes than Latinx but are more likely to own businesses.[60] In majority-Black Prince George's County, Maryland, African Americans outearn Latinxs and Asians but are much more likely to be unemployed, reflecting wealth gaps within as well as across demographic groups. Latinxs overall earn less than African Americans.[61] Social stratification can also be seen in terminal levels of education. The metropolitan area overall is highly educated: 61.4 percent and 53.4 percent of DC and metropolitan-area residents, respectively, have undergraduate degrees, compared with the national average of 23.5 percent. Level of education is also stratified, however, with people of color less likely to hold a high school diploma than Whites. In this respect Latinx are across the board the group least likely to hold a high school degree.[62] These social differences manifest ideologically in discourses that, in addition to local divisions, contrast the "international" professional sector with less-privileged local residents.

Latinxs in DC

Latinx are a significant presence in the District of Columbia and its metropolitan area. The top ten areas by Latinx population in 2021 were Los Angeles, New York, Miami, Houston, Riverside (California), Dallas–Fort Worth, Chicago, Phoenix, San Antonio, San Diego. The DC metropolitan area sits just behind San Diego, with 1,021,386 reported Latinx residents.[63] The number is likely higher given that official reporting of Latinx and immigrants is known to be underestimated.[64]

The roots of DC's Latinx community were established in the early twentieth century near the Latin American and Spanish embassies, where many residents worked.[65] The community grew after World War II, as professionals, students, and waves of immigrants and political exiles arrived in the area. The Adams Morgan, Mount Pleasant, and Columbia Heights neighborhoods became known as Latinx neighborhoods—El Barrio—and became hubs of art, culture, and activism.[66] These neighborhoods were a social place, not merely a residential location. El Barrio was established as a public Latinx cultural place through community activism in the 1960s–80s, including a community newspaper named *El Barrio* and institutions such as the Latino Festival, in which Latinx cultures were celebrated in a parade, and cultural practices such as music, dancing, and the

Figure 2.2. Salsa legends Celia Cruz and Tito Puente with DC organizer Willy Vásquez at the Latino Festival, 1985. Photograph by Nancy Shia.

buying and selling of traditional foods dominated the streets. Olivia Cadaval points out that this activity is related to Latin American use of plazas and public spaces for social life, a tradition carried over to El Barrio and continuing to this day.[67] Lamont Park, in the heart of Mount Pleasant, remains a site for public community events such as an annual Día de los Muertos celebration—a cultural tradition that syncretizes pre-Columbian and Catholic beliefs and rituals—complete with community-constructed ancestor altars, street theater, and general social congregation. Indeed, the name "*La Manplesa*" (Mount Pleasant) is iconic locally, evoking a sense of community solidarity and El Barrio's formative years. This association is clear through the use of this name in the 2021 movie *La Manplesa*, made by a local filmmaker via interviews with Latinx residents who lived through the formative Mount Pleasant riots of 1991, in which the community rose up in resistance to neglect and abuse to win increased visibility and civil rights.[68] El Barrio's symbolic role as the heart of DC Latinidad continues even as gentrification has priced

Figure 2.3. March for El Salvador going down Columbia Road NW, Washington, DC, 1982. Photograph by Nancy Shia.

many Latinx residents out of the area. People return for community events. At a Lamont Park street theater production in 2020 and the 2021 Día de los Muertos event, working- and middle-class Latinx families from the neighborhood and those living in Maryland and Virginia were in attendance, as well as neighborhood activists, families of different backgrounds, local musicians, artists, neighborhood figures, and community members selling traditional Central American foods and *La Manplesa* movie memorabilia. Traditional foods as well as vegan foods were available, indicating the interests and involvement of a younger generation of community members and activists. At the same time, Lamont Park is also the site of a weekly farmer's market catering to a largely non-Latinx clientele, which reflects changes in the neighborhood's residents.

DC Latinxs have always been diverse, and intermarriage between Latinx of different origins is common. In the small, early community, Latinx of different backgrounds intermingled and shared a sense of common identity.[69] Activism in the 1960s and 1970s by leaders such as Carlos Rosario, Reverend Antonio Welty, Casilda Luna, and many others formalized a sense of local Latinx community through demands for better social services and representation, aided by the growth of the Latino Festival and community organizations such as the Latin American Youth Center, Gala Hispanic Theatre, and Teatro de la Luna, along with bilingual schools and Sacred Heart Catholic Church's Spanish masses.[70]

The personal, professional, and familial connections thus created channels for large-scale Central American migration due to political upheaval in the 1980s.[71] This immigration exponentially increased the Latinx population and established Salvadorans as the largest Latinx group in the DC area (see figure 2.2).[72] However, despite the United States' alleged role in destabilizing El Salvador and other Central American countries, immigrants from the region were not granted refugee status, making their situation increasingly precarious even as they became an essential part of the region's culture and workforce.[73] Further, many of the new populations' needs were overlooked until dissatisfaction with political apathy, discrimination, and lack of access to resources and social services culminated in the 1991 Mount Pleasant disturbances, after which more supportive policies and greater Latinx political representation were established.[74]

As the Latinx community grew, satellite communities developed, such as Salvadorans in northern Virginia and the Maryland corridor and substantial Bolivian and Peruvian populations in northern Virginia.[75] Regional associations that maintain home-country cultural and economic ties and other transnational cultural and religious organizations also proliferated.[76] However, a sense of cohesion as well as diversity remains.[77] There is still a significant Latinx population in the city, and the original neighborhoods retain their symbolic importance in DC Latinx identity despite displacement and gentrification.

Latinx neighborhoods have been extensively affected by gentrification.[78] This is a topic of consternation and reflection for DC Latinxs: for example, performance artist Quique Avilés's show *Los Treinta*, dedicated to thirty years of Salvadoran settlement in DC, describes Columbia Heights' transformation from the heart of the DC Latinx community to a "center of gentrification." Rising housing prices have caused Latinx movement further into historically African American neighborhoods and expansion of existing satellite communities in Maryland and Virginia, which are increasingly the primary sites of immigrant settlement rather than the city.[79]

This displacement feels intensely personal. Numerous people I spoke with mentioned being made to feel out of place—for example, being questioned by new residents in the very doorways of buildings they have lived in for years. Marcos, who had much to say on the subject of changes in the city, commented, "Before, it was an honor to be who I was; now I have to pretend to be someone I'm not [hipster, more upper class] just to have fun in my city." He and others referenced a lost sense of belonging and community. "Alonso" settled in Columbia Heights upon arrival from El Salvador as a teenager; when asked if he thinks there used to be more of a sense of neighborhood or community in Columbia Heights, he stated,

> There definitely was. Cause everybody, say you're walking down the street this way and I'm walking this way. And I would be like "Good morning" and it would be like, "How you doing, good morning" and that was our interaction right, and that would be with everybody.... now it's all completely just, no one looks each other in the eye. Looking each other in the eye is like such an intimate thing for human beings.... I don't like it. I mean I appreciate the stores and everything, that's, you know it's all right there, but nobody—but everybody just feels like this is just a mall. Like the Heights is just a mall. Like we're a full neighborhood man, we you know, there used to be all these people here and houses and (taps table), you know and there was that actual, look you in the eye and say what's up. You know but now there's none of that. That's, disappeared.... [He is asked why he thinks this happened.] It has to do a lot with the community that's here now [sighs]. You know. The—that's it and I hate to be racial but it's really, it's a lot of White people doing it. I hate to be racial I don't like it, but really it's, you know, what was happening. With them, they don't want to look me in the eye and say what's going on, what's up, and, like "Hey you're shopping here, I'm shopping here with you" [claps hands]. That was the big difference. But now you don't get that at all. Like I don't know why, these people just don't

talk to you. Nobody—like I'm always saying "Good morning, how you doing," blah blah blah. They don't even, talk to you.

Alonso's commentary clearly portrays a sense of loss—the erasure of the close-knit Columbia Heights community and literally feeling unseen and unheard by White gentrifiers—centered on the lack of public courtesy and greetings. I heard this type of comment extensively in interviews and in conversations and ethnography; it is also part of a broader public discourse about displacement and culture erasure.[80] Saying hello to people is seen as a shared pragmatic norm—part of DC culture—and its loss was a loss of manners and community. I have personally observed this change in Columbia Heights, for example, with older residents of color holding doors open when entering a store and saying hello and good morning to strangers. They are often ignored by newer—usually younger, often White—residents.

Gentrification-related displacement has changed the composition of the traditional Latinx center-city barrios. Tension over residential rights is often couched in discourses of race, identity, and social qualities, such as morality. For example, Gabriella Modan found that Latinxs perceived gentrification to be an invasion of White suburbanites, while White gentrifiers used moral stances around public hygiene and sexual harassment to justify displacing Latinx men from public spaces.[81] More recently, a public exhibition of photos from the La Esquina photo project documenting a longtime street corner community of practice in a historic Latinx neighborhood sparked debate.[82] New residents angrily commented in online forums that the photo exhibit was attacking them, and they invoked similar tropes to those found by Modan to defend their presence and delegitimize the *esquineros*.[83]

African American Contact

As might be expected in a heavily African American city and region, Latinx were and are in extended contact with African Americans. Since DC had such a middle-class Black presence, Blacks were the local power structure that Latinx workers interacted with. Further, in the 1980s and 1990s, at the height of Central American migration to the region, there was much contact as Black and Latinx youth adjusted to each other in schools. For example, José Benítez found that local Salvadorans reported job discrimination by African Americans and youth clashes between the two groups but also reported that second-generation Salvadoran Washingtonians and those who immigrated as children felt connections with African Americans as part of the local culture, a situation of conflict and assimilation that Ana Patricia Rodríguez also noted in DC Salvadorans' self-examination of identity through theater.[84] This contact led to cultural influence and linguistic assimilation, as has been found in many areas of the United States.[85] This facet of the linguistic repertoire is due to social contact that made AAE the contact/assimilation variety for many Latinxs and due to a shared sense of non-White identity, an observation also noted by Ana Zentella and by Phillip Carter.[86] Since DC was a majority Black city, where much of the local culture and society of all classes was Black, Blackness's normalization and local prestige may have further encouraged assimilation.[87] There is also a significant Afro-Latinx history in DC, from early community leaders to current activism.[88]

My participants did reference clashes between Latinx and African Americans. These narratives largely depicted African Americans as the aggressors and themselves as the aggrieved parties, as might be expected, but my participants also sometimes expressed anti-Black racism. For example, the following quote expresses a sense of grievance based on language discrimination but also attributes negative qualities to African Americans: "*Los morenos nos discriminan de hablar español; dicen que uno le viene a quitar el trabajo a ellos, pero ellos son unos haraganes, uno no le va quitar el trabajo a ellos*" (Blacks discriminate against us for speaking Spanish; they say that we come here to take their jobs away, but they are lazy, we are not going to take jobs away from them). This sentiment speaks to material circumstances of contact and competition between the two groups in working-class settings as well as ideological sources of tension and resonates with previous research on conflict narratives between Latinx and African Americans, as documented by Kendall King and Anna De Fina.[89]

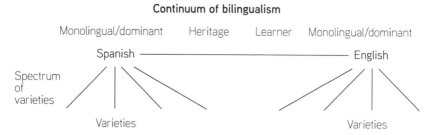

Figure 2.4. Latinx multilingual repertoires

However, my participants also described close social contact and relationships with African Americans and a general sense of solidarity as minoritized groups. Overall, while my participants did report incidents of social and linguistic discrimination between themselves, African Americans, and unmarked "Americans" (whom they conceived of as White), they generally perceived the DC region as accepting due to its multiculturalism. As one commented, "I think since this area is really diverse, especially in this country, it's not much of a problem just because of the diversity everywhere you know, uh now with the election, who knows. I guess it's like people are more accepting, but there is always the other half that stays the same you know. Inside the bubble." They contrasted this to areas they perceived as less tolerant, such as Virginia and Maryland outside the metropolitan area, and the southern United States more generally.

Multilingual Repertoires

DC-area Latinxs' linguistic repertoires encompass a wide spectrum of language diversity. Figure 2.3 is my model of this abstraction. While not all DC-area Latinxs have the same linguistic repertoire, certain elements are common, and the social meanings of different repertoire elements are widely shared.

DC-area Latinx Spanish ranges from Spanish dominance to heritage Spanish and encompasses dialects from all over the Spanish-speaking world. English ranges from English dominance to non-native-learner English and encompasses varieties such as general American English, AAE, and Latinx English, which I discuss in more

Table 2.2. Local versus Nonlocal *Washington Post* Items by Latino/Hispanic versus Salvadoran, 1990–2012

Topic	Local % (n)	Other % (n)	Total % (n)
Latino/Hispanic	46.8 (88)	53.2 (100)	100 (188)
Salvadoran	58.7 (37)	41.3 (26)	100 (63)

Table 2.3. El Salvador/Salvadoran versus Mexico/Mexican in *Washington Hispanic* and *El Tiempo Latino*, 2017–2019

Periodical	El Salvador % (n)	Mexico % (n)	Total % (n)
El Tiempo Latino	90.8 (819)	9.2 (83)	100 (902)
Washington Hispanic	35.2 (113)	64.8 (208)	100 (321)

detail in the chapters that follow. Individual repertoires vary based on personal experiences, including country of origin, immigrant generation, time in the United States, and interconnected factors such as social networks, language exposure, and educational opportunity—experiences of immigration that affect all of the above, and more.

This model uses terms such as "language" and "variety" since it is difficult to talk about languages without imposing names. However, it is important to recognize that these terms are constructed abstractions and that repertoire elements are not mutually exclusive. Rather, they work together in hybrid and dynamic ways.

Salvadorans

The DC area has the second-largest Salvadoran population in the United States and is the only area where Salvadorans are the majority.[90] Salvadorans consistently make up approximately one-third of DC-area Latinxs, followed by Mexicans and Latinxs of a wide range of national origins, such as Central America, Bolivia, and Peru.[91] While there are numerically larger Salvadoran populations in California and Texas, they are relatively small percentages of the total Latinx population in those regions and are invisibilized within the dominant Mexican American culture.[92]

To give an example of Salvadorans' importance in the region, a corpus search of *Washington Post* items from 1990 to 2012 that contained the words "Latino" or "Hispanic" returned 188 items, and a separate search for "Salvador" or "Salvadoran" returned 63 items, or 25 percent of the combined total (table 2.2). Of the Salvadoran hits, the majority (~59 percent) were locally focused, such as substantial human-interest pieces focused on community issues and interests. Nonlocal items were typically international news and soccer.

A similar focus on Salvadorans was observed in the Latinx newspapers *El Tiempo Latino* and *Washington Hispanic*. *El Tiempo Latino* had 819 entries tagged "Salvador" (returning "*El Salvador, salvadoreño*") between January 1, 2017, and December 20, 2019 (table 2.3). The tagged items included local news, such as local events and organizations; national news, such as immigration policy; and international news, such as coverage of sports and El Salvador current events. This news often transcended different scales, as in the case of transnational events and "*ciudades hermanas*" (sister cities) such as San Miguel, El Salvador, and Arlington, Virginia.

In contrast, "Mexico" received only eighty-three tagged items in *El Tiempo Latino*. This is notable given that Mexicans are the largest US Latinx population. *Washington Hispanic* also had many "Salvador" hits but more items tagged "Mexico." This outcome is likely due to Mexico's larger role in US international affairs and trade, as most of these hits were international news.

Due to their strong local presence, Salvadorans have a special referential role in local Latinx identity. Salvadorans are so prominent in DC that even the mariachi groups that used to play in the streets of Mount Pleasant played primarily Salvadoran music, in keeping with the band members' origins.[93]

Many Salvadorans were and are working class, but many have also become middle class since the major migration wave of the 1980s.[94] Particular concerns related to immigration history also affect the Salvadoran community, such as the lack of a permanent pathway to citizenship for many due to the US government's refusal to grant them refugee status, creating vulnerability.

Salvadorans' local prominence gives them a central role in DC Latinx identity. However, they also face discrimination. An interesting example of these perceptions is a short *Washington Post* piece about the DC soccer team, which the opinion responses showed was resented by some Salvadorans who perceived it to degrade them as "uneducated and low-class"; at the same time, they acknowledged that many Salvadorans did have working-class jobs in cleaning, hospitality, and restaurants.[95] Stereotypes of Salvadorans range from positive labels of "hard-working" to associations with poverty, low education, and gang activity.[96] When two Salvadorans were asked how others perceived local Salvadorans, they responded: "*Que son humildes, sencillos*" (that they are humble, simple), reflecting local Salvadoran's class status, and "*malcriados porque la mayoría aquí anda en la calle; no pero de los salvadoreños también dicen que son trabajadores*" (ill-bred because the majority here hang out in the streets; no but they also say that Salvadorans are hard workers). An example from a conversation with Emanuel demonstrates this neatly. As he spoke about DC Salvadorans doing well for themselves, he mentioned Edwin Aparicio, a DC Salvadoran who is one of the most recognized flamenco artists in the United States and has been awarded the Cross of the Order of Civil Merit by the king of Spain. I noticed that he repeated the phrase "A fucking Salvadorian from DC" over and over, in disbelief at his acclaim: "A fucking Salvadorian from DC has been recognized with like the key at the White House by the king of Spain." This amazement and pride underscore the surprise at the contrast between the high-society honor—by the colonial *madre patria* no less!—and the idea of DC Salvadorans as humble.

However, because of their local strength, Salvadorans in DC have better cultural visibility and more pride than in other areas of the United States. In general, Salvadorans are invisibilized in discourses of US Latinx identity.[97] Mexican Americans' numerical dominance often means that they, as with other Latinx groups, are assumed to be "all the same" (as many of my participants noted), and Salvadorans' small numbers and material precarity in the United States often dictated that they "pass" as Mexican for reasons of security.[98] In the DC area, they are visible and proud.[99] Salvadorans are aware that they are the largest Latinx group in the DC metropolitan area. This majority status helps them maintain their culture, something they specifically contrast with assimilating to Mexican customs in California.[100]

Diversity, Divisions, and Cohesion

"Superdiversity" is a controversial term because its Eurocentric perspective implies that the flourishing of diversity is something new, which is not the case.[101] Its emphasis on multiple aspects of diversity, however, is useful for capturing the proliferation of diversity within group categories such as race and ethnicity and for recognizing the differences brought about by dimensions such as national origin, race, gender, immigrant trajectories, socioeconomic status, and more within macrocategories. In terms of DC Latinxs, these dimensions are all attested. DC-area Latinx encompass every national origin and race, from White to mestizo to Afro-Latinx and Asian. Motivations for migration include economic, educational, and familial reasons as well as violence and political oppression. Some Latinx are economically precarious and politically vulnerable, whereas some are middle class and some are wealthy. This diversity interacts with a sense of cultural and linguistic commonality and shared US Othering to create opportunities and barriers to cohesive Latinx identity formation.

Internal diversity and panethnic identity interact in complex ways for Latinxs. Research in Chicago, for example, found that Mexican and Puerto Rican identities (although reinterpreted in the local context) contributed to a fragile sense of pan-Latinx identity but tended to be overshadowed by national differences that were reinforced through discourses and cultural practices that contrasted the two groups with each other.[102] Differences between the two national groups were supported by stereotypes and discourses about race, such as Blackness and Indigeneity, gender, and language. However, social stereotypes tended to diminish in later generations as mixed residency patterns become more common, along with mixed marriages.[103] Research in Florida similarly found that living in a diverse Latinx neighborhood reduced or "flattened" national identities in favor of panethnic identity.[104]

In previous research on Washington, DC, Lucinda Hart-González found that first-generation Latinx primarily identified by national origin but also shared attitudes of belonging to a Latinx commonality.[105] Mixed Latinx social organizations contributed to panethnic identity, while family and relocated social networks supported national identity. Hart-González also found that participants of different backgrounds reported largely interacting with co-nationals. National-origin social networks are now frequently transnational, with business, nonprofit, and sister-city associations as well as personal social and economic networks and digital communication.

DC-area Latinx are also socioeconomically diverse. Latinxs in the metropolitan area overall enjoy higher incomes and more education than in other areas of the country.[106] However, Latinxs still earn less than Whites, and there are differences among Latinx in terms of income, employment, and education. The highest proportion of DC Latinx households either earned less than $10,000 annually or earned from $50,000 to more than $200,000.[107] Similarly, large numbers of DC Latinxs are employed either in service or in management/professional jobs. A comparable division can be seen in levels of education: 44 percent of DC Latinxs have college degrees, but 29 percent have less than a high school education. In Maryland and Virginia, the majority of Latinx hold less than high school degrees, although 21–24 percent hold college degrees. And in Virginia there is also a split among Latinxs between US citizens and noncitizens, where 43 percent of noncitizens have less than a high school degree.[108]

Taken together, these statistics indicate a social divide, mirroring the region's divisions between an upper-middle-class to elite Latinx sector that is better off than the national average, on the one hand, and an underprivileged sector, on the other. This difference—typical of global cities' increased socioeconomic disparity—also reflects Latin American hierarchies of privilege, as the many international political entities and organizations in DC's specialized economy draw on home-country elite populations.[109] The class difference between privileged elites and a working-class local population, including nonelite immigrants, is ideologically marked; for example, I have heard the term "World Bank Latinos" used to distinguish international-sector elites from the local community. This distinction is long-standing: in a 1980s study on DC Latinxs' dialect attitudes, Hart-González noted the difference between the two groups and excluded "international"

Latinxs from her study.[110] In DC, being "international" carries locally relevant associations of social class, since in the "international" Latinxs there are more elites than locals: they tend to be from higher social classes in Latin America, be more educated, and work in more white-collar and transnational jobs. "The more-elite, transient sector" in DC is opposed to "local," so, for example, "international" Latinxs—often transnational, working in the international sector—are seen as different from the local Latinx community, a distinction that plays out along lines of social class and a host of other factors. DC is also home to a substantial US-based Latinx civil servant sector, through federal jobs and national organizations, creating another layer of complexity in the local environment.

Different groups' relative opportunities in the United States are tied to histories of migration. Immigrants migrate for a host of reasons, ranging from the political to the economic—all of which affect the characteristics and opportunities of different waves of immigrants from different countries at particular times. While social class is malleable in migration, where a middle-class professional may not be able to find similar work upon migration, home-country class differences and education broadly translate, and these factors in turn are inherently tied to colonial legacies of privilege and marginalization. This influence is particularly relevant in DC, given that its international sector is accessible only to highly skilled migrants. Home-country and international relations privilege also manifests in terms of residency status, where middle-class and elite migrants are more likely to be able to access legal residency, and in terms of international relations, such as policies giving preference to Cubans and excluding Central Americans from refugee status. Immigration status affects different groups' security and opportunity in the United States as well as their ability to travel between the United States and their homelands. For example, Deferred Action for Childhood Arrivals (DACA) and Temporary Protected Status (TPS) debates about whether citizenship should be granted to undocumented immigrants, including those who arrived as children, are highly relevant to Latinx in the DC region, since many Salvadorans are affected by this legal limbo.

Latin American social hegemonies reflect a colonial legacy of colorism and class divisions.[111] These histories manifest in issues of discrimination and stereotyping and in differences in economic opportunities, education, and urban versus rural divisions.[112] These tensions carry over to migration contexts. In the United States, darker Latinxs receive fewer opportunities than lighter-skinned Latinxs.[113] Samantha Prado Robledo found that colorism affected attitudes toward assimilation, with self-identified light-skinned Latinx more likely to view themselves as American and to believe in the importance of assimilation and the idea of the United States as a meritocracy.[114] Furthermore, Latinxs in the United States are aware of discrimination among themselves: the majority report that discrimination by Latinxs toward other Latinxs is a problem, with more assimilated Latinxs discriminating against the more vulnerable (undocumented, less wealthy, less proficient in English) and with Afro-Latinx also experiencing discrimination.[115] In New York City, Negrón demonstrated that Whiteness and nationalities associated with Whiteness (e.g., Colombianness) were preferred by Latinx study participants over Blackness and Indigeneity.[116] Elizabeth Aranda, Sallie Hughes, and Elena Sabogal found in Miami that Central Americans tend to be looked down on by South American and Caribbean Latinxs due to race and class stereotypes.[117]

These ideologies are borne out in linguistic research. Negrón has shown that in New York, a city with a diverse Latinx population and a Caribbean (mainly Puerto Rican) majority, Latinxs of different national and racial backgrounds orient to Puerto Rican identity as they use their linguistic repertoires to negotiate the social landscape.[118] While Caribbean Spanish has many features in common, Puerto Ricans and Dominicans were disadvantaged in New York's Latinx hierarchy due to race and poverty, with Puerto Ricans occupying an ambiguous position due to their local prominence. These social hierarchies were reflected in sociolinguistic attitudes as New York City Dominicans' Spanish was accordingly viewed as having little prestige.[119] Moreover, these hierarchies can be said to stem from intersectional raciolinguistic attitudes and colorism, where Blackness is stigmatized in both the United States and Latin America. In Puerto

Rico, for instance, Dominicans are considered Black as a means of distinguishing them, even though the Caribbean region as a whole has much African influence.[120] These Latin American ideologies persist in immigrant communities but also adapt to the US racial binary.[121]

For another example, consider Miami. Cubans are locally dominant politically and tend to be better off than other Latinx groups owing to a combination of circumstances of migration and US immigration policies that, until 2017, granted citizenship to all Cubans who reached US soil. This local status is reflected in Miami language attitudes, echoing Ana Celia Zentella's findings that local social position determines positive or negative evaluation of dialects.[122] However, Phillip Carter and Salvatore Callesano found that Miami Latinxs still ranked Cuban Spanish lower than Peninsular Spanish despite Cubans' local presence and prominence.[123] Further, Caribbean Spanish and Central American Spanish are generally stigmatized in Miami compared to South American and Peninsular Spanish.[124] Race is also salient in Miami Latinxs' perceptions of Spanish, with Blackness stigmatized, as is common in Latin America and the United States.[125] This finding is echoed in many Latinx communities in the United States, including in Chicago and New Jersey.[126] In both these examples, local context and relative positioning of Latinx social groups along hierarchies of prestige related to race and social class, with roots in historical-colonial and contemporary hierarchies, affect social and linguistic perception.

In the DC area, Salvadorans occupy an ambiguous position of being a visible and proud majority but also facing discrimination by other Latin American groups.[127] José Benítez notes that this attitude was particularly common among South Americans, a situation that may relate to local and more general circumstances of migration, in which South Americans tend to have higher socioeconomic status in the United States than that of Central Americans, who often migrated due to civil unrest or economic instability, coming from rural areas, in the case of El Salvador, and often without legal residency.[128] Central Americans also tend to be looked down on by South American and Caribbean Latinxs due to race and class stereotypes, and South Americans, such as Argentinians, are often seen as more

White.[129] These stereotypes hold true in DC: one participant in my study commented that a blond, blue-eyed Uruguayan friend was surprised to be taken for a non-Latinx and was regarded with suspicion when seeking immigrant-serving social services. In contrast, the stereotype of Central Americans is that they are non-White—Brown and mestizo. In conversation with a Salvadoran friend, for example, I noticed that he would consistently comment if a Salvadoran person was "White passing"—a discursive foregrounding of race that points to its relevance and that Whiteness was not the norm.[130] The friend also clearly drew class associations with European-descent Salvadorans, specifically noting that the White Salvadoran in question came from a professional, financially comfortable background.

All this said, it bears repeating that there is a high degree of mixing and conviviality in the DC region. There is much interest and acceptance of different Latinx backgrounds, as expressed in the typical question "¿Qué país?" (What country [are you from]?), in line with a general interest in multiculturalism in the DC area. There is also friendly jostling about different Latin American countries, which is very common in Latin America. But the jokes can also have teeth owing to stereotypes and hierarchies of prestige, class, race, region, and more. While a great deal of identity negotiation takes place, DC-area Latinx report generally getting along and view intra-Latinx diversity as a positive thing "because you learn about others' cultures." Class differences between local and "international" Latinx, which mirror Latin American social stratification, are in some ways more relevant to socialization and division or cohesion than are differences of national origin between local Latinxs.

Multiple Discourses

There is more history—and more histories—in DC than any one chapter or multiple books can describe. This polyphony is one of the things that make it DC. Multiple stories and voices and discourses cohabit and do not necessarily move toward a single, more homogenous narrative.

In the next chapters I explore a Salvadoran-normed notion of "local Latinidad" that coexists with discourses of diversity, showing that neither narrative is fully dominant but rather both are part of understanding of local identity. If you ask someone in DC, "What are DC Latinx like? What do they sound like?" they will tell you Salvadoran, or Central American more broadly. But they will also point to diversity among Latinx as a defining characteristic of the DC area. Similarly, as I found in survey results, a large group of people (Salvadorans and non-Salvadorans alike) will say local Spanish is Salvadoran, but others will say that diversity itself is what characterizes the Spanish of the area—that local Spanish is too diverse to be characterized by a single dialect. I also present extensive evidence of contradictory attitudes toward Salvadoran Spanish and AAE as iconic yet ambiguously evaluated in the area.

This dynamic tension also relates to broader questions of community narrative. DC Latinx represent many different experiences and waves of migration, and the communal sense of self has evolved over past decades as its composition changes. DC Latinidad has been very diverse since the beginning, and there was a great deal of initial representation from Caribbean leaders in terms of grassroots community support for jobs and housing as well as in terms of developing more formal structures with DC city government and the institutionalization of the Latino Festival (figure 2.4).

The wave of Salvadoran and Central American migration in the 1980s brought with it a new population and a new generation of youth who grew up facing similar challenges of war-torn trauma and integration into a city experiencing urban poverty and violence, and this influx spurred a new generation of activists and a new kind of community building and solidarity centered on the Central American experience. The community is currently going through another moment of reflection as several generations of activists consider their legacies and reflect on questions of representation. Undoubtedly, the community narrative and narratives will continue to develop through both the reflection of elders and the efforts of a new generation of local Latinx scholars and activists.

3

"En la viña de Dios hay de todo"

Spanish and Identity

What role does Spanish play in DC-area Latinidad? Spanish is the second language of the United States, and it links the identities of US Latinxs in complex ways. The United States has the second-largest total number of Spanish speakers in the world, after Mexico; the fourth-largest number of native speakers; and the most second-language speakers.[1] Nevertheless, Spanish use tends to diminish with time as subsequent generations shift to English. Further, Spanish has rich dialectal variation. The ways in which it is spoken and what this means for identity vary in different communities in the United States, as they do in Latin America, with new practices and meanings that emerge in the US context.

As we have seen, Washington, DC, and its metropolitan area are home to a diverse Latinx population. This raises a multitude of questions for how Spanish forms part of local Latinx identity. Do DC Latinxs see Spanish as an essential part of ethnocultural identity? What are the implications of this identity association for their bilingual children? Do they believe that there is a distinct "DC Spanish," and, if so, is it Salvadoran? As we will see, these are nuanced questions that reflect the social landscape of DC as well as the broader US and Latin American contexts.

Spanish in the DC Metropolitan Area

Spanish in the Washington, DC, metropolitan area is more robust than in many areas of the country. DC-area Latinxs report less Spanish loss across generations than in the United States in general:

only 2 percent between 2006 and 2015 versus the US average of 5 percent.[2]

In general, Latinxs in DC and the metropolitan area report as much or more Spanish home use than in the surrounding states of Virginia and Maryland as a whole. Among DC Latinxs, 74.6 percent report speaking Spanish at home, as do 79 percent of metropolitan-area Latinxs.[3] Overall, Spanish in the DC area experiences less decline across generations than in most of the United States.[4]

These patterns may speak to the DC region's global-city diversity and welcoming multicultural environment. Participants perceived the DC area as a multicultural area with little discrimination in contrast to other areas of the country. DC and its surrounding suburbs are immigrant welcoming, to the point that Texas governor Greg Abbott performatively bused Latinx migrants apprehended at the Mexican border to DC as well as to other liberal areas of the country—a move quickly echoed by other right-wing governors.[5] DC's international political climate leads to prestigious Latin American institutional presences, such as embassies, and the city has Spanish-language arts and cultural events and a thriving dual-language immersion bilingual education sector. In general, bilingualism is supported as part of culture and is also seen as valuable for work and travel. This interest is not limited to the elite: most of my mainly working-class survey participants (66 percent, or 29 of 44 who answered the question) said they sent their children to a bilingual school, and those who did not said they would like to have the opportunity to do so (91 percent; 10 of the 11 follow-up responses). Bilingual education initiatives are also present and growing in the greater DC metropolitan area.

This environment contrasts with Virginia and Maryland "outside the Beltway." In participants' comparisons between the DC area's tolerant multiculturalism and the rest of the country, "the South" and "further out in Virginia" were specifically mentioned as more racist. English is designated as the official language of the state of Virginia and in several Maryland counties—a nativist raciolinguistic ideology that resurged across the country in the wake of California's Proposition 227 (1998), which eliminated bilingual education out of a sense of cultural grievance more than an actual threat to English.[6]

In my data, all survey participants spoke Spanish, and almost all (97 percent) reported speaking it well or very well (see table 3.1). This includes most 1.5- and second-generation speakers (G1.5 and G2, respectively), although the second generation reported less proficiency (more "well" and less "very well").

Beyond raw numbers, who speaks what language to whom and in what circumstances are together essential to understanding language in a community. Much research shows that domains of heritage languages tend to be restricted to the family, community, and informal settings but that this same language use, and the strong social ties and identity connections it fosters, can keep the language alive in the face of pressure to shift to English.[7]

My G1.5 and G2 survey participants—the generations where language practices typically differ from those of their elders—reported using Spanish with family, such as at weddings and parties and when talking to the older generation (see table 3.2). Spanish thus appears to be sustained within family networks. In talking to family of their own generation, such as siblings and cousins, they reported bilingualism ("equal parts Spanish and English")—with a few indicating "mostly Spanish" or "mostly English"—and two G2 participants reported using only English.

Social networks outside of the family also have an important impact on language use, whether bilingualism, which I am discussing here, or the dialect diversity that we will see later in this chapter. Most of the G1.5 and G2 participants reported having mostly Latinx friends.[8] Both generations tended to use both Spanish and English with close friends (see table 3.3). However, while three G1.5 participants reported using all or mostly Spanish with close friends, no G2 participants did, and more G2 participants reported using only English with friends. I observed a similar trend in their self-reported language use at parties with friends, where G1.5 reported "all Spanish" to "equal Spanish and English," but the reverse was true for G2 ("equal Spanish and English" to "all English") (see table 3.4).

Opportunities to use Spanish outside of intimate spheres are also

Table 3.1. Spanish Proficiency: Survey Self-Reporting

Generation	Very well % (n)	Well % (n)	Not very well % (n)	Not at all % (n)	Total % (n)
G1	58.1 (36)	6.5 (4)	3.2 (2)	0	67.8 (42)
G1.5	12.9 (8)	3.2 (2)	0	0	16.1 (10)
G2	9.7 (6)	6.5 (4)	0	0	16.2 (10)
Total	80.7 (50)	16.2 (10)	3.2 (2)	0	100.1 (62)

Table 3.2. Spanish Spoken with Family of the Same Generation

Generation	All Spanish % (n)	Mostly Spanish % (n)	Equal Span/Eng % (n)	Mostly English % (n)	All English % (n)	Total % (n)
G1.5	0 (0)	10 (2)	35 (7)	5 (1)	0 (0)	50 (10)
G2	0 (0)	10 (2)	25 (5)	5 (1)	10 (2)	50 (10)
Total	0 (0)	20 (4)	60 (12)	10 (2)	10 (2)	100 (20)

Table 3.3. Use of Spanish with Close Friends

Generation	All Spanish % (n)	Mostly Spanish % (n)	Equal Span/Eng % (n)	Mostly English % (n)	All English % (n)	Total % (n)
G1.5	5 (1)	10 (2)	20 (4)	5 (1)	10 (2)	50 (10)
G2	0 (0)	0 (0)	25 (5)	5 (1)	20 (4)	50 (10)
Total	5 (1)	10 (2)	45 (9)	10 (2)	30 (6)	100 (20)

Table 3.4. Use of Spanish at Parties with Friends

Generation	All Spanish % (n)	Mostly Spanish % (n)	Equal Span/Eng % (n)	Mostly English % (n)	All English % (n)	Total % (n)
G1.5	10 (2)	10 (2)	10 (2)	0 (0)	20 (4)	50 (10)
G2	0 (0)	0 (0)	20 (4)	15 (3)	15 (3)	50 (10)
Total	10 (2)	10 (2)	30 (6)	15 (3)	35 (7)	100 (20)

important for Spanish maintenance. Participants reported using it at work: 66 percent reported using all Spanish, mostly Spanish, or equal Spanish and English in the workplace, and many mentioned bilingualism as a future professional asset for their children. While most survey respondents were working class, their vision of bilingual opportunities for their children were broader.

Translanguaging in Bilingual Communication

Variously known as code-switching, language mixing, and translanguaging—different terms invoke different theoretical frameworks that I will not get into here—the use of features considered to be from different languages has always been an important aspect of bilingual communication and identity. In my survey 79 percent of participants reported using both Spanish and English in the same interactions, sometimes referring to this as "Spanglish." A major reason for blending the languages was communication across family generations. G1 participants reported mixing Spanish and English when speaking with their bilingual children, and G1.5 and G2 participants reported using to Spanish to speak with parents and older relatives, inserting English words as needed. English was typically spoken in less-intimate settings: G1 participants reported that they needed to speak English at work, in medical encounters, when shopping, and in school, while the younger generations largely used Spanish and code-switching with family, with Latinx friends, and at community events such as church. These generations perceived translanguaging to be informal—something that would not be done in a professional setting.

Participants in their feedback also reported more extensive discourse functions than simple communicative necessity. For example, a young G2 Salvadoran woman commented, "It happens with my friends who are Latino/Hispanic. We use Spanglish when we know that it has more meaning in Spanish, so it refers to that. We use them interchangeably. It gives more understanding and more sense to understand the situation or the thing I am talking about. I feel like it is more descriptive because they know what it translates to and the definition, and they know the meaning." Another G2 Salvadoran young woman, who completed her survey in Spanish, mentioned using words such as discourse marker "like"—a contact-induced habit. The sociolinguistic interview participants also reported using "Spanglish." While they tended to see it as informal or a sign of low proficiency, they also reported discursive and identity-related functions. For example, a young woman born in Washington, DC, described code-switching as a Latinx language practice.

The translanguaging that occurred in the sociolinguistic interviews typically took place when discussing Latinx identity, such as culturally specific mentions or when voicing the self and others. Overall, little code-switching took place, although people were encouraged to speak in whatever language they felt most comfortable or to code-switch if they preferred. While this is not surprising in the interviews, since I am not Latina and am unmistakably East Asian in appearance, I was surprised that there was also little translanguaging in the surveys conducted by young Latina student interviewers with participants of their own age. I noticed that while one young Latina student interviewer from Miami translanguaged (for example, with discourse markers), the young woman she was interviewing did not follow her lead and switch languages. This could have been a function of not knowing each other well or could also have been a genre effect. The knowledge that they are being "interviewed" is a context in which people do not feel fully colloquial.

Self-recordings made by "Héctor," in his thirties at the time of recording, and "Cándida," a G2 Mexican American woman in her twenties, paint a truer though still limited picture of Spanish and code-switching in the community.[9] While only representing these two participants, the self-recordings lend credence to the idea that speakers tend to keep the languages separate. Both used Spanish when talking to older family members and with Spanish speakers. Translanguaging did appear to have cultural and identity connections. It was used when explaining specific cultural items such as a *"milpa"*—a small cornfield—to friends. It was also used among the younger generation to voice their parents but not for peer conversation. In another example, translanguaging was used to address the audience on a bilingual radio show to engage the audience and transmit a bilingual identity.

Spanish as a Marker of Latinx Identity

Spanish also functioned as part of my participants' Latinx identity. Much research in the United States and internationally has demonstrated that speaking Spanish is associated with Latinx identity, although the connection may weaken for later generations.[10] Spanish has long been a unifying factor and a marker of group identity and solidarity for the DC Latinx community.[11] However, this connection also complicates identity and belonging for later generations. This existential debate is echoed in the arts: Rodríguez, looking at DC Salvadoran issues in local theater and music, noted a preoccupation with Spanish loss in the younger generation, along with dialect variation in Spanish and English—themes that I return to in this and the following chapter.[12]

Participants overwhelmingly expressed pride in their Spanish and their identities. Survey respondents categorically believed that Spanish was an important part of cultural identity and wanted to transmit Spanish to their children. However, the relationship between heritage language and ethnocultural identity is more complicated than this finding might imply. Ideologies linking Spanish with ethnocultural identity make the heritage language a site of identity negotiation and gatekeeping. Heritage speakers, whose bilingualism can take many forms, are vulnerable to accusations of inauthenticity. "If you are Latino and you don't speak the language, you don't get the discount": you can't be in the group. "Viviana" is a young woman who immigrated to the DC area from Guatemala as a child. Thinking about Spanish and Latinx identity, she commented, "Some Latinos look at other Latinos and you're like wait a minute, you look Latino but you're not speaking to me in Spanish—what's wrong with you [laughs]?" While she first expresses the censuring group gaze through third-person referents ("some Latinos"), her pronominal shift to the second person makes it clear that she shares the attitude being voiced. The shift from collective to individual voicing positions her in the gatekeeping in-group that judges non-Spanish-speaking Latinxs as having something "wrong" with them for not speaking in Spanish, even though she softens this evaluation through laughter. Meanwhile, her own bilingualism is positively evaluated by her family and community: she shared a story about an interview in which she surprised an immigration lawyer by speaking fluent Spanish. This ability flew in the face of expectations of "young" Latinxs, assumed to be G2 and nonfluent.[13] Viviana's mother, proud of her, spread the word through the family, and collectively they were proud of her achievement.

Sometimes the ideology equating Spanish with ethnoracial identity takes the form of actual exclusion. "Celia" came as a child to the northern Virginia area, where her family—middle class in Bolivia—struggled economically and moved frequently. She later married a Salvadoran man. Celia is a caring mother who does her best to provide her children with a good education and upbringing as well as inculcating Bolivian culture and the Spanish language in them. She is proud and generous; at the time of our interview she was struggling financially but still treated me to a *salteña* (the national savory pastry) at a Bolivian restaurant that is well known in the community. Perhaps due to an ugly incident in which her daughter was endangered by Latinx gangs, Celia had a certain ambivalence toward Latinx immigration at the time of our interview, which manifested in her "law and order" stance.

Celia reminisced about the migration experience and balancing out different aspects of her identity. Having learned to speak English and to socialize with non-Latinx friends, she recalled an incident in which she was excluded from a friend group in elementary school for not speaking in Spanish. While traumatic, the incident pushed her back toward the Spanish-speaking side of her identity.

Excerpt 3.1

CELIA: Growing up there [in a Latinx-dominated housing project] was, was interesting. Um (.) That- they WERE more accepting but the Latinas wanted, they wanted to be exclusive Latina group. Like ev- everyone had their own clique. (laughs) And, the Hispanic girls acCEPted me, you know, I- I (.) got along better with the AMErican crowd (taps table) because I spoke English really well (.) And the Latinos were a little, you know, cocky (laughs).

INTERVIEWER: (laughs)

CELIA: And they're like "YOU, are HISP-" you know *latina*, you know, why do act like you're, a *gringa* (laughs) I'm like, "I'm just, [ME" (laughs)

INTERVIEWER: (laughs)

CELIA: But um, in order to get me out of that shell they invited me to go PRAY. For one of our GUY friends. That had gotten HURT. At uh, Saint Anthony's, is a, famous Catholic, church. Over there near- near Route Seven and Culmore. [clicks tongue] And uh, when we get- when we got to the door and they're like "Oh. We forgot you can't come in, you're not *latina*." (laughs)

INTERVIEWER: OH (sympathetically)

CELIA: And I was BAWLing and I'm like "I can't belIEVE you guys," you know? And they're like "Well, START speaking SPANISH, you know you need to pray in Spanish" and, the priest comes out and he was like "What's the matter" and I, told him and he's like "Oh, well, I guess you have something, you know, you, should DO it." So that FORCed me, I'm like, OKAY (laughs)

While Celia did speak Spanish, her Latina friend group perceived her to be someone who rejected the language and, hence, her Latina identity. They in turn gate-kept her "Latinaness" along this dimension, calling her a *"gringa"* (White girl). This designation justified excluding her from an important personal, social, and cultural event—praying for an injured friend—with the support of the priest, an important authority figure. Celia had to conform to the expected ethnolinguistic behavior in order to be accepted. While at the time this treatment was traumatic, she later also expressed gratitude for it, since it obliged her to reconnect with the language. However, similar pressure on her young sons from members of the community seems to be largely negative.

The shame attached to not speaking Spanish—a collective expectation that is reinforced in the community—is one that I have explored in previous research.[14] Celia shared a further anecdote of her young sons being shamed for not speaking Spanish: "When we are in an all-Hispanic setting, they [her sons] feel embarrassed. Because they—because the Hispanics aren't very—they're like '¡Qué barbaridad! ¿No, no me entiendes el español?' (laughs) And my sons turn red, and they're like, 'Sí entiendo' (laughs). 'Pero no hablo.'" In these interactions, her sons are positioned as "not speaking Spanish" despite being able to understand it and respond in a conversationally appropriate way (they also attended a bilingual school). Since their speech is not the same as that of native speakers, their bilingual abilities are dismissed.

Part of this shame rests in the perceived cultural rejection associated with not speaking Spanish. Identity discourses that associate Spanish with being Latinx and English with being "American" mean that not speaking Spanish is often seen as choosing to abandon the home culture in favor of Americanization. Celia's young friends perceived her as resisting Spanish and therefore "not Latina." "Diana," a young Paraguayan woman who also immigrated to DC as a child, described her younger sister as having better English than her, framing this as Americanization: "Yeah. She's just more Americanized than I am. I like to keep to my roots." Meanwhile, she herself remains oriented to Paraguayan and, more broadly, Latinx culture. She prefers Latin music, she practices traditional dance, and her friend group is mainly Latinx. Her boyfriend is Central American (Honduran)—something that caused her to reflect on different types of Spanish.

While the ideology that not speaking Spanish deauthenticates ethnic identity is strong, some participants pushed back. Héctor, a DC-born Central American man, commented, "I know a lot of Latinos that, don't speak, Spanish, and they don't want to get close to Latinos because they're—they're scared of being made fun of. You know what I'm saying? But they look Latino and they are Latinos," an attitude consistent with other research on intergenerational US Latinx language and identity change.[15]

Discourses of language inadequacy tend to center on the youth, in particular the figure of the G2 immigrant. As "Ángel," who immigrated from South America as a child and works extensively with urban youth, commented, "First-generation born-here kids you know? One, they all speak English. All of them. They might speak Spanish, they might speak Spanish very well, not so good, whatever, but they all speak English. First language."[16] The perception of G2 Latinxs as inadequate Spanish speakers can have detrimental effects on their self-esteem, community connections, and desire to speak the language. Washington-born "Noemí" used herself as an example of "bad Spanish" despite using it regularly (sometimes exclusively) with family members. "Ricardo," a middle-class Ecuadorian man who arrived in DC as an infant, stated, "My Spanish is not as good as it should be"; the modal "should" indicates his awareness of an expectation or standard that he fails to achieve.

G2 interviewees also reported linguistic insecurity in interactions with family and other Latinxs. As Héctor commented, Latinxs who do not speak Spanish (or who don't speak it well enough to "count") may avoid other Latinxs to avoid censure and teasing. "Rico" is a Washingtonian of Salvadoran background who is trying to get on his feet and "stay out of trouble" after becoming involved in drugs and violence as a teenager. At the time of our interview he was working at a grocery store after dabbling in construction. He described his parents teasing him about his nonnative Spanish pronunciation, which they attribute to his American birth: "Man, you were born here." While he portrays this criticism as playful, it clearly connects negative evaluation of his speech with his G2 identity.

Other participants specifically described how linguistic insecurity contributes to language avoidance. "Maureen" is a DC-born Latina of mixed Caribbean and other Latinx heritage who has moved into the middle class through education and holds strong ideologies about linguistic correctness. She felt pressure to speak "proper" Spanish or face criticism by other Latinxs, and she expressed accent-related shame. Even though she speaks Spanish fluently, she reported that an occasional nonnative accent will slip out, revealing that she is second generation (conflated with "speaking badly") and that she doesn't speak Spanish as she "should." This embarrassment causes her to avoid speaking Spanish ("It's [her accent] very embarrassing to me, which is why I don't speak as often as I should now").

The ideologies of language purity that Maureen has internalized contribute to her linguistic insecurity and heritage language avoidance. These expectations are based in monolingual norms that privilege the language of idealized native speakers over the realities of bilingualism. In the case of Celia's sons, they were shamed for not speaking Spanish when they do understand it and are able to respond in the language. The shaming they face from adult community members illuminates the tension between the boys' assumed lack of Spanish and their actual bilingual abilities. Further, deficit discourses about youth often hold them to the standard of educated native speakers—something that is impossible to achieve without growing up and being educated in a Spanish-speaking country. Emanuel, the G1.5 Salvadoran I introduced in chapter 1, has worked extensively with Latinx youth for decades. He commented that many of the youth speak colloquial Spanish with their families but lack literacy and more sophisticated repertoires. While this pattern is typical of people raised abroad who were not primarily educated in their heritage language, he interprets it as a sign of general language loss.

Excerpt 3.2

EMANUEL: And then, it's going the other way too, cause, *latinos* are losing their language. So the same thing that has happened to, the Irish an, you know an (.) you know all those, children of- great grandchildren of, WHITE immigrants, you know, a LOT of- most people didn't keep their language. So that's beginning to happen with us.

INTERVIEWER: Is it happening very strongly in the=

EMANUEL: =Yeah. Cause I mean, like, you give HALF of the kids in a our group, you give em a, a Spanish-language newspaper and (.) it's TORture for them to read. Especially if you ask them to read out LOUD. So if you, you know if you give em an- and that's a newspaper. Now if you give em like a, a book? A NOVel, or a POEM you know?

INTERVIEWER: So the arts are really, like, harder

EMANUEL: Because you know is more sophisticated you know. Like if you- if you read a García Márquez text, I mean it's, DENSE. Very dense. You know?

INTERVIEWER: So like people like maybe they can still talk at home or whatever [but they can't like

EMANUEL: [Yeah!
uh huh yea:h. It's like uh hu::uh *a qué horas* you know. *(te) voy a recoger* yeah
                             at what time   I'm going to pick you up
yo, tengo hambre you know, simple things
I'm hungry

INTERVIEWER: Or, like, talking with grandma kinda thing.

EMANUEL: ↑Right. You know. *Tienes que ir a lavar la ropa* you know.
                         You have to go wash the clothes
Limpia tu cuarto. You know. *No vas a venir tarde* you know, this is like the
Clean your room.   You're not going to be late
simple- you know, mundane daily, routine things you know of ↑course they can say that

---

These prescriptive discourses of language correctness obscure later generations' actual bilingual abilities. While they often coexist with a strong desire for heritage language transmission and are seen as "helping children learn to speak correctly," ironically, they can discourage children from speaking Spanish.

My participants viewed Spanish as an important part of Latinx identity. Spanish has a comparatively high degree of linguistic vitality in the DC metropolitan area in comparison to the United States as a whole. This may pertain to the region's social and cultural environment, where, in addition to personal and community motivations, multiculturalism is normalized at different levels of society, supported through bilingual education, and incentivized by an international work environment. However, deficit discourses that can cause linguistic insecurity and avoidance by later generations persisted, even within families and the co-ethnic community—sites that are typically seen as bastions of language maintenance. Participants' comments reveal the identity tensions that individuals experience as they navigate their bilingual worlds. Monolingual-normed ideologies of language proficiency and purity conflict with their actual bilingualism and interact with discourses of ethnocultural authenticity, creating insecurities that heritage speakers internalize and that can cause their "Latinxness" to be questioned by themselves and others.

"Normal" versus "muy vulgar": Many Spanishes and Their Meanings

"*Dime cómo hablas y te diré quién eres*" (Tell [show] me how you speak and I'll tell you who you are). As much as what language you speak, how you speak it matters. Spanish dialect diversity is broad, varying along regional lines—associated with but not necessarily correlating with national boundaries—and, as with English or any other language, along social groupings such as class, education, region, gender, and more, leading to cultural pride but also stereotypes and "dialect dissing."[17]

DC Latinxs' rich diversity is reflected in their Spanishes and related language attitudes. When asked to describe the Spanish spoken in the DC area, Latinxs commonly respond in one of two ways. Many, pointing to the large Salvadoran population, will respond that it is Salvadoran or, more broadly, Central American. Others will respond that DC Latinxs are diverse, as is their Spanish, so there is no one single dialect. These two coexisting discourses reflect the tension inherent in a sense of cohesion—the belief that there is a community with certain shared characteristics—that is defined by diversity, yet within which a particular group—Salvadorans—has come to carry a particular weight in the imagining of local Latinidad.

Forty-eight percent of my survey participants reported that DC Spanish is Salvadoran or Central American; 31 percent reported DC Spanish is diverse, representing different countries; and 21 percent gave responses that did not fit either category (i.e., "*bien*") (see table 3.5). Two sample responses: (1) "*[Es centroamericano] como lo mayoría somos de Centroamérica. Salvadoreño creo que mucho más.*" ([It's Central American] as the majority we are from Central America. Salvadoran I think much more.) (2) "*Acá diferentes países tienen diferentes*

Table 3.5. Descriptions of DC Spanish

	Salvadoran/ Central American % (n)	Diverse % (n)	Other % (n)	Total % (n)
Survey participants	48.4 (30)	30.7 (19)	21 (13)	100.1 (62)

españoles" (Here different countries have different Spanishes). When asked to describe their own Spanish, participants specified countries, for instance, *"el acento salvadoreño"* (the Salvadorean accent), or simply responded, *"de mi país"* (of my country).

The following quote by a Salvadoran woman in her thirties, employed as a cook, shows participants' awareness of specific aspects of dialect diversity.

Excerpt 3.3

Los salvadoreños se conocen po:r, por el acento de hablar, como "ey vos, ey vos," eh o la forma de llamar a un ↑niño "cipote." (. . .) Sí, en México es "chamaco," nosotros le decimos "cipote," y en Honduras les dicen "guiro, guiros"

(Salvadorans know each other by, by their accent in speaking, like "hey you, hey you" *eh* or the form of calling a child *"cipote."* (. . .) Yes, in Mexico it is *"chamaco,"* we call them *"cipote,"* and in Honduras they call them *"guiro, guiros."*)

In this quote, which is one of many such examples, the speaker identified the informal second-person pronoun *"vos"* and the manner of its phrasing as a marker of Salvadoran identity. She also identified lexical variation, making a comparison between the words that Salvadorans and those from surrounding countries use to refer to children.

Throughout the surveys, participants referred to lexical, morphological, and phonetic variation when asked to describe their own Spanish and that of others. They commented on vocabulary differences between their own and other dialects and gave examples of regional vocabulary, as above. They also named household items, foods, and many other items: for example, *molcajete*, a Mexican word for a traditional hand mortar used to grind spices and make sauces, and *pupusas* and *baleadas*, typical foods of El Salvador and Honduras, which are thick corn or flour tortillas, respectively, stuffed with a variety of savory fillings.

Voseo was a major feature that Salvadorans commented on as part of their dialect. *Voseo,* or the use of the nonstandard second-person singular pronoun *"vos"* and verb conjugation—*"vos sos"* ("you are"; general Spanish *"tú eres"*), *"vos comé"* ("you eat"; general Spanish *"tú comes"*), and so on is an archaic Spanish form that survived in areas of Latin America that were geographically isolated during the colonial period, such as much of Central America.[18] It is a well-known feature of Salvadoran Spanish, among other dialects, and one that has been shown to be a salient part of Salvadoran linguistic identity elsewhere in the United States and in theatrical representations of Latinx identity in Washington, DC.[19]

Salvadoran participants reported *voseo* as a salient dialect feature along with other characteristics such as rising inflection: "*Sí, nosotros- es el tono así, nosotros, de 'vos,'*" "Yes, we—it is the tone like this, (that) we (use with) *"vos."* They voiced examples of *voseo* to represent Salvadoran linguistic identity. In excerpt 3.3 above, the speaker pointed to *voseo* as a key linguistic index of Salvadoran identity—a verbal signal by which Salvadorans recognize each other. Similarly, in another example a stay-at-home mother from El Salvador used *voseo* when voicing a conversation with her husband to show dialect differences between them:

Excerpt 3.4

Sí, hay palabras que él dice, "¿Vos conocé tal cosa así?" "No," le digo yo, "no sé qué es." Y él se me lo enseña por el teléfono y, "Ay sí lo conozco por este nombre," le digo yo, y "Sí vaya" me dice él, son cosas que son iguales pero lo conocen por distinto nombre. Y nos referimos a lo mismo.

(Yes, there are words that he says, "Do you know this thing like this?" "No," I tell him, "I don't know what that is." And he shows it to me on the phone and, "Oh yes I know it by this name," I tell him, and "Yes go on!" he tells me, they are things that are the same but they are known by a different name. And we are referring to the same [thing].)

Salvadoran survey participants also reported on the pragmatics of *"vos"* where it is used with intimates, such as family members, but not with outsiders, an observation borne out by my Salvadoran American research assistants. In a different conversation with me, Emanuel used *voseo*—*"Cuidála, cuidála"* (Take care of her, take care of her)—when voicing his family, a situation in which *voseo* would be appropriate along lines of familiarity as well as varietal solidarity. In general, he uses *voseo* when talking with me in Spanish, which I interpret as a reflection of our friendly relationship as well as his down-to-earth personality and perhaps as his own habitual dialect use or pride.

Unsurprisingly, given *voseo*'s register associations (informality) and relational connotations (intimacy), while Salvadoran participants of all immigrant generations reported it in daily life, described it as an identity marker, and gave examples of its use in different contexts, they did not use it to address the interviewers. In one of the self-recordings, however, I note *voseo* in a naturalistic setting. In Héctor's recording of a family dinner, he used *voseo* toward elders. This observation, when put together with participants' self-reported *voseo*, contrasts with research conducted elsewhere in the United States, where Salvadoran immigrants—particularly the second generation—tend to avoid *voseo* and accommodate to the local majority (Mexican) *tuteo* norms.[20] Travis Sorenson also found that Salvadorans maintained *voseo* more in DC than in Houston, Texas, a city with a large Salvadoran population but where the majority group is Mexican American.[21] The difference is likely due to Salvadorans' local majority in the DC area—a dynamic that leads to prominence and pride. This interpretation resonates with Sorenson's observation that DC Salvadorans associated *voseo* with pride and culture and with other research showing that Salvadoran *voseo* maintenance in the United States relates to identity pride.[22]

"Se come la s"

The colloquial term *"se come la 's'"* (the s is eaten) refers to /s/ weakening, a common feature in the Spanish-speaking world and one that tends to be heavily stigmatized.[23] The term refers to the elision or aspiration of /s/ in certain positions—at the end of words or syllables ("*la' persona'/lah personah*" [*las personas*]), or less commonly at the beginning of words or syllables. It is a common feature of Salvadoran Spanish and most Central American Spanishes, although it is not exclusive to the region.

In the words of one working-class Salvadoran mother in her thirties who has lived in DC's Columbia Heights neighborhood for three years: "*En México chocan con la zeta, pero nosotros no*" (In Mexico they emphasize the "z," but we don't). This quote makes clear that the Salvadoran pronunciation, and its contrast with other Spanishes that do not follow this pattern, such as Mexican Spanish, is salient as part of her linguistic identity.

The Salvadoran participants consistently showed /s/ elision in their Spanish (see table 3.6). To dig deeper, I compared their speech with that of speakers of other dialects. I examined /s/ realizations for a sample of Salvadoran G1 speakers and all the G1.5 and G2 speakers who chose to do their surveys in Spanish compared with /s/ realizations of Mexican, Peruvian, and Puerto Rican participants—three countries whose /s/ patterns differ from those of El Salvador. I also note attention to regional diversity among Salvadorans. Most Salvadorans in the DC area come from the rural region of Oriente, but one participant proudly came from the capitol.[24] I draw on participants' language attitudes to explain the patterns that I found.

"Adela," "Beatriz," "Clara," "Delma," and "Elsa" are all women between the ages of thirty-three and forty-seven who immigrated to DC as adults. They work in fields such as cleaning and food service; one is a stay-at-home mother. Their highest level of education, conducted in El Salvador, is high school or less, and they report being more comfortable in Spanish than in English. Beatriz, Clara, and Delma have each been in the DC area for more than a decade; Elsa has been in DC for three years and Adela, the most recently arrived, for five months.

"Ángela," "Belén," and "Carina" were younger—twenty-one, nineteen, and thirty-five years old, respectively. Ángela and Belén immigrated to the DC area at age fourteen; Carina arrived at age seven.

Table 3.6. Salvadoran /s/ Realization by Generation

	Generation	0 % (n)	H % (n)	s % (n)	Total % (n)
Adela	1	19.7 (59)	7 (21)	73.3 (220)	100 (300)
Beatriz	1	26.6 (25)	19.1(18)	54.3 (51)	100 (94)
Clara	1	27.2 (125)	12 (55)	60.8 (279)	100 (459)
Delma	1	38.1 (151)	14.1 (56)	47.7 (189)	99.9 (396)
Elsa	1	44.6 (71)	14.5 (23)	40.9 (65)	100 (159)
Ángela	1.5	1.2 (1)	0	98.8 (81)	100 (82)
Belén	1.5	33.6 (40)	12.6 (15)	53.8 (64)	100 (119)
Carina	1.5	36.8 (42)	14 (16)	49.1 (56)	99.9 (114)
Alicia	2	32.7 (108)	3 (10)	64.2 (212)	99.9 (330)

Note: I coded /s/ impressionistically as sibilants [s], aspirated [h], or elided [0], verifying my coding visually in Praat.

Ángela is a student, Belén did not state her occupation, and Carina is a cashier. All completed high school; Ángela had begun college, and Belén was studying for a professional certificate. They reported speaking both Spanish and English well or very well but being more comfortable in Spanish. Carina and Belén also felt they did not read or write English well, whereas Ángela felt she read and spoke both languages very well. Finally, "Alicia," born in DC to Salvadoran parents, was nineteen years old and had begun college. She reported speaking both languages well or very well but being more comfortable speaking Spanish.

I coded /s/ impressionistically as sibilants [s], aspirated [h], or elided [0], verifying my coding visually in Praat.[25] Following John Lipski, I examined tokens in word- and syllable-initial and final environments before consonants, vowels, and pauses.[26] I focused on stretches of conversation beginning a few minutes into the survey, when responses became longer and more conversational.[27]

All of the Salvadoran participants sampled, with the exception of Ángela, whom I discuss below, showed Salvadoran patterns of /s/ weakening. Notably, DC-born Alicia fell within the rest of the group's ranges, although on the high side for sibilant /s/ and the low side for elision /o/. These results suggest that in DC, where Salvadorans are the largest Latinx group and there are many other /s/ eliding

Central Americans, young Salvadorans may not experience the same kind of sociolinguistic pressure to change their Spanish as they do elsewhere in the United States.[28] Combined with the *voseo* findings above, Salvadoran dialect seems to remain vital across generations, likely due to Salvadoran's majority presence and cultural pride.

Sociolinguistic attitudes, however, are complicated. Within the group, linguistic attitudes are a likely explanation for variation. Elision of /s/ is typically stigmatized in the Spanish-speaking world.[29] Adela, the G1 speaker with the least amount of /s/ weakening, expressed concerns about Salvadoran Spanish as informal or "slangy." In this she differentiated her speech from that of others, including family members, by giving examples of how she uses standard vocabulary such as "*dinero*" and "*niño*" rather than Salvadoran regional terms such as "*pisto*" or "*cipote*." Her use of relatively unweakened /s/ may reflect this desire for linguistic correctness.

This interpretation is supported by the style-shifting I noted during the conversations. Speakers used more sibilant [s] at the beginning of interviews, when they were using more careful speech and answering demographic information, than later in the interviews and in conversational stretches, when they used more elision and aspiration. This style-shifting is consistent with many years of research on how formality affects the use of colloquial speech in sociolinguistic interviews as well as recent research by Ana Iraheta showing that Salvadorans weaken /s/ more in casual speech and less in professional settings.[30] The style-shifting suggests that participants see stereotypically Salvadoran language features as colloquial or even incorrect and that these attitudes affect their linguistic behavior.

Ángela is a G1.5 speaker who almost categorically used unelided /s/. Identity and prestige norms may well play a part in her speech. Ángela is from the capital, San Salvador, which is known for pronouncing the /s/. However, San Salvador Spanish still has a high rate of elision; Lipski found that unweakened /s/ production was only 40.05 percent.[31] It seems likely that language attitudes—where the language of the capital, and full pronunciation of /s/ in general, is considered "better, more refined, more educated, [and] more civilized"[32]—also encouraged Ángela to avoid /s/ weakening. This interpretation is borne out by her metalinguistic commentary, in which she distanced herself from the stereotypical Salvadoran accent. Ángela drew attention to the fact that she is from the capital and commented that although in DC the perception is that all Salvadorans speak like they are from Oriente, different regions of El Salvador speak differently. The Oriente dialect is common in DC but also considered uneducated, lower class, and rural.[33] As someone with her roots in the national capital, Ángela may be particularly oriented toward prestige speech and away from association with this regional—and, more broadly, national—stereotype.

Excerpt 3.5

ÁNGELA: *Hay [muchas personas] que hablan con [acento] de El [Salvador] porque*
         [s] [s] [s]   [s]   [s]
Vienen de um, de la parte oriental, y [los] de la parte de occidental [hablamos],
                                        [s]   [s]
diferente. [Incluso siendo] el [mismo país].
            [s][s]   [s]   [s]

INTERVIEWER: *Y que son los estereotipos, o, like, uno de,*

ÁNGELA: *(laughs) [Sólo] el [acento] del habla. [Se escucha] la [diferencia] entre*
                  [s]   [s]   [s] [s]   [s]
[las dos], las [dos] diferentes partes
 [s] [s]   [s]

INTERVIEWER: *Bueno*

ÁNGELA: *Que [todos hablamos] igual. Igual. Como- Yeah. Como, [si usted es], yo [soy],*
             [s]   [s]   [s] [s] [s]   [s]
yo [soy] de la parte um, de la capital,
    [s]

INTERVIEWER: *Aha*

ÁNGELA: *[Todos piensan], que, [si] yo [soy] de El [Salvador], hablo como la gente de la*
         [s]   [s]   [s]   [s]   [s]
parte de Oriente, y en [veces todos me dicen], ¿Y [estás segura] que [eres] de
                        [s,s] [s]   [s]   [s, s] [s]   [s]

continued

Excerpt 3.5 *continued*

> El [**Salvador**]? Porque no [**hablas**] como [**ellos. Sí, sí**] *(laughs)*
> [s]   [s]   [s] [s] [s]

INTERVIEWER: Oh

ÁNGELA: Y [**eso**] me [**pasa muchas veces**]. Que todos [**somos iguales**] *(laughs)*
           [s]   [s]   [s] [s,s]   [s]   [s]

ÁNGELA: There are many people that speak with the accent of El Salvador because they come from the eastern part, and those from the western part we speak, differently. Even though it is the same country.

INTERVIEWER: And what are the stereotypes, or, like, one of [them],

ÁNGELA: Some. (laughs) Only the accent when speaking. One hears the difference between the two, the two different parts

INTERVIEWER: Okay

ÁNGELA: That we all speak the same. The same. Like- Yeah. Like, if you are, I am, I am from the part um, of the capital,

INTERVIEWER: Aha

ÁNGELA: Everyone thinks, that, if I am from El Salvador, I speak like the people from the part of Oriente [region], and sometimes they all tell me, "And are you sure that you are from El Salvador? Because you don't speak like them." "Yes, yes" (laughs)

INTERVIEWER: Oh

ÁNGELA: And this happens to me a lot. That we are all the same (laughs)

"Hablan con el acento de su mamá" (They speak with their mother's accent): Dialect Contact

Given Salvadorans' local prominence, it might be expected that other Latinxs would accommodate to Salvadoran speech norms. My examination shows that this is not the case. I compared the Salvadoran /s/ case study with the ways Mexican, Peruvian, and Puerto Rican participants spoke Spanish. These Spanishes provide a point of contrast, since Mexican and Peruvian Spanish do not generally /s/ weaken and since Puerto Rican Spanish /s/ weakens more extensively and along different phonetic patterns than Salvadoran Spanish.[34]

"María," a thirty-three-year-old Mexican housewife with a high school education, has been in the DC area for eleven years. "Perla," from Peru, is a thirty-one-year-old full-time student with a high school education and degree in therapy; she has been in DC for three years. Both are Spanish-dominant and reported not speaking English very well. María had only three elisions and one aspiration in her entire interaction, and she reported that other Latinxs can tell she is from Mexico when they hear her speak. Perla, who considered Salvadoran Spanish to be *"muy vulgar"* (very vulgar), showed 27 elisions and 6 aspirations of 219 total /s/ tokens, or 15 percent overall.[35] These patterns suggest that these speakers, who arrived in the DC area as adults, have not accommodated to Salvadoran Spanish.

G1.5 "Pía," who emigrated from Peru at age six, and DC-born "Rebeca," of Puerto Rican parentage, are both nineteen-year-old college students who speak both languages well or very well. Pía reported feeling equally comfortable in both languages, while Rebeca feels more comfortable speaking English. Pía arrived in DC as a child and has a strong Peruvian identity. In her metalinguistic commentary, she expressed that she does not accommodate to Salvadoran Spanish because she prefers her own variety:

Excerpt 3.6

> *No lo cambio. Porque me gusta más mi español sudamericano de Perú que el español centroamericano. Siento que es un poco más formal a lo que los centroamericanos siempre hablan. Sí, tengo amigas dominicanas y su español es muy confuso. Prefiero que me hablen en inglés que en español, porque siento que es más fácil entenderlos así.*

> (I don't change it. Because I like my South American Spanish from Peru more than the Central American Spanish. I feel that it is a little more formal than what the Central Americans always speak. Yes, I have Dominican friends and their Spanish is very confused. I prefer that they speak to me in English than in Spanish because I think it is easier to understand them like this.)

She states that her lack of assimilation to Salvadoran Spanish relates to identity associations as a Peruvian but also to valuing Peruvian Spanish over Salvadoran Spanish in terms of correctness. Her stance of dedication to linguistic correctness is deepened by her comments about Dominican Spanish, which she considers "confused" and "hard to understand" to the point that she prefers to speak English with these friends. Notably, she had no /s/ elision in her survey recording. Meanwhile, Rebeca, born to Puerto Rican parents in Washington, DC, followed Puerto Rican aspiration and deletion patterns (49 percent and 22 percent) rather than the Salvadoran patterns I observed.

While the purpose of this study is not to generalize about the speech of all Latinxs in the DC area's large and diverse population, /s/ findings appear to support my participants' overall perception that heritage dialects tend to be maintained (*"hablan con el acento de su mamá"*: [they] speak with their mother's accent). Salvadorans in DC do not seem to be losing their dialect features as in other areas of the country, and Latinxs of other backgrounds do not seem to be acquiring Salvadoran features. This lack of acquisition of Salvadoran /s/ patterns might seem surprising, particularly in the later generations, since much research indicates that smaller groups accommodate to the dialect of the largest group in an area.[36] However, stigma attached to Salvadoran Spanish as a variety may inhibit dialect acquisition, along with simple pride in national origins, evidenced by 31 percent of survey respondents who reported they did not adapt their regional Spanish when talking to others. One Salvadoran participant commented that she categorically uses Salvadoran Spanish, while a South American participant commented that he does not shift since he views his Spanish as more correct than Central American Spanish. This metalinguistic commentary lends weight to the interpretation that Spanish dialects not only are maintained as part of distinctive national identities but also are related to more generalized prestige evaluations.

The reasons for this pattern likely lie in the DC social environment. Salvadorans are the Latinx majority group but only around a third of the population, rather than an overwhelming majority, as Mexican Americans are in California and Texas. A wide variety of Spanishes are spoken in DC by Latinxs who are of different backgrounds and who maintain a sense of their own identities, community events and organizations, and transnational ties, despite much local socializing and mixing. For example, "Samuel," a young Peruvian man who immigrated to the DC area at the age of three, commented, "Well, from the people I hear at my church, I go to Spanish Mass, they all talk in their own ways, I guess, their own slang, people will get into a group, from what I see, their own country and they make their own group and they talk, they all speak in their own slangs, from where you're coming from, where your roots are." This sustained diversity means there is not a single local target variety, as opposed to Mexican-based Los Angeles Vernacular Spanish in California.[37] Further, as research in New York City has shown, a majority presence is not enough to make a group's Spanish an acquisition target if they have relatively low prestige in the local social hierarchy.[38] This finding may be germane to the DC area since, as I discuss later (see especially chapter 5), Salvadorans and their language occupy a somewhat ambivalent position.

While participants appear to maintain their home Spanishes rather than acquiring those of others, they do report shifting their own dialectal features to more neutral ones in order to accommodate their interlocutors, an action I call "dialect downgrading." Approximately half of survey participants reported using different kinds of Spanish depending on the person they are speaking with or where they are speaking. The lack of evaluative comments around this languaging practice indicated that they viewed it as normal.

Participants often reported using more "general" Spanish to facilitate communication with Latinxs of other backgrounds. I refer to this as dialect downgrading rather than dialect shifting, as they report downgrading regional features that might cause misunderstandings in mixed groups rather than shifting between dialectal features (although Marcos reported being able to shift between his mother's Salvadoran Spanish and his father's Mexican Spanish, and one Mexican woman stated that after prolonged contact with Guatemalans, she acquired some pronunciations and lexicon that can cause her to be misidentified).

Style and dialect perceptions often overlapped, with regional usages considered inappropriate in formal contexts. For example, Salvadorans gave the example of *voseo* as something used only with intimates and not with unknown interlocutors or in formal settings *"de respeto"* (out of respect). A Dominican participant stated that Dominican Spanish is "ghetto" and "slangy" and that in office settings she uses a more neutral Spanish, which she considers professionally appropriate. And "Spanglish" was mentioned as informal and inappropriate for situations where respect and formality were needed.

"Como deberíamos hablarlo" (The way we should speak it): Dialect Attitudes

Now to the whys and wherefores of dialect perception. Dialects are powerful indices of national origin. But their social meaning does not stop there.

Latinxs are a hugely diverse population, with differences tied to material and historical circumstances inscribed on markers such as race and social class in Latin America and the United States. These differences among groups lead to different stereotypes and ideologies that carry over into language perceptions and that share general commonalities as well as manifestations specific to local contexts. The ways in which diversity and dynamics among Latinxs affect language attitudes in the DC area is a theme that will carry over into following chapters.

Discourses of diversity and tolerance have circulated in the DC Latinx community since its inception.[39] Spanish sociolinguistic diversity is celebrated as an opportunity for sharing and as part of the local culture. Participants commented favorably on the diversity among Latinxs: *"Pues bien, como los países son diferentes nosotros tenemos nuestra cultura cada país tiene su cultura"* (It's good, as countries are different, we have our culture, each country has its culture). Another participant commented favorably that *"uno aprende de otras culturas*" (you learn from other cultures) through speaking with Latinxs of different backgrounds. This discourse of diversity resonates with DC's discourse of diversity as part of the city's identity and with the normalization and celebration of multilingualism and multiculturalism in the metropolitan area more broadly.[40] However, just as both diversity and social stratification intensify in global cities, material conditions of inequality are present among Latinxs, and ideologies of stigma and privilege are also present.[41]

Table 3.7 summarizes my participants' dialect attitudes based on qualitative commentary that arose spontaneously or in response to questions about participants' own Spanish and the Spanish spoken in the DC area. The dialects were evaluated independently unless the participant offered a comparison; that is, while Spain, Peru, and Colombia were perceived as better or having more correct Spanish than Central American Spanish, Peninsular and Colombian dialects were not evaluated in comparison to each other.

Peninsular, Peruvian, and Colombian Spanish were viewed most positively. As Alicia commented, "*Como yo quisiera hablar al acento que tienen los colombianos los españoles es bien bonito. Yo pienso que es bien bonito.*" (Like, I would like to speak with the accent of the Colombians or the Spaniards. It is very beautiful.) A Honduran stay-at-home mother in her thirties unfavorably compared Honduran and Peninsular Spanish. "*Ellos [los españoles] lo hablan perfecto el español ya nosotros hablamos español pero siempre no lo hablamos como deberíamos hablarlo, pronunciando bien todas las palabras*" (They [the Spaniards] speak Spanish perfectly, and we speak Spanish but we never speak it as we should, pronouncing all the words well). Samuel, an eighteen-year-old Peruvian man, commented, "Our [Peruvian] Spanish is really formal." His comment resonates with Pía's preference for "South American Spanish," which she and other participants viewed as "more formal" than Central American Spanish.

These quotes express several sociolinguistic attitudes and ideologies. One is the notion of "*hablando bien*" (speaking well), focusing on the element of pronunciation, where fully pronouncing sounds ("*como deberíamos hablarlo*") is seen as correct, and changes such as the elision common in Central American and Caribbean Spanish

Table 3.7. DC Dialect Attitudes Hierarchy

	Spain	Peru	Colombia
Well spoken	Hablan bien Lo hablan perfecto	Formal	Su acento bonito
	El Salvador	Dominican Republic	
Badly spoken	humilde, sencillo, rural, vulgar, callejero, malas palabras, no formal, ghetto	Difficult to understand, rapid	

are seen as incorrect. This attitude ties into broader sociolinguistic ideologies that privilege the speech of certain regions based on race and class associations dating to colonial times. As one young man, a community organizer from Mexico who has been in DC for five years, commented, *"Bueno, personas me identifican de una manera rápida cuando me oigan hablar en español. O creen que soy de ciertos países porque soy más moreno."* (Well, people identify me quickly when they hear me speak Spanish. Or they think I am from certain countries because I am darker.) Language attitudes also tend to assign correctness to dialects with "faithful" sound pronunciations (i.e., not eliding or aspirating /s/, not interchanging /l/ and /r/), a preference that relates to social attitudes that disprivilege poorer, less-White areas of Latin America where these tendencies are common, as well as reflecting the idea that proper speech has fidelity with the written word and is not "informal" or slangy.[42] The attitude that Spain, as the colonizing *"madre patria"* (motherland) speaks the most correct Spanish is more social ideology than linguistic fact, as Spain contains many dialects, many of which share "informal" characteristics such as /s/ elision with Latin American Spanishes and in fact contributed these features to their development.[43] In tandem with this historical footprint, prescriptive institutions such as the Real Academia Española perpetuate the notion of correct ways of speaking at the expense of "nonstandard" linguistic diversity.[44] Peruvian Spanish is also considered to be well spoken in Latin America due to its perceived formality, clear pronunciation, and lingering prestige associations from being a colonial center.[45]

Sociolinguistic attitudes also relate to the US environment. In the United States, Colombians and South Americans in general tend to be more middle class than other Latinx groups and also enjoy a higher rate of naturalization.[46] This pattern holds true in the DC metropolitan area, where Colombian immigrants tend to be better educated and wealthier than Salvadoran immigrants.[47] This positionality, along with Colombian Spanish's reputation for correctness in Latin America, likely contributes to its high prestige in DC as in other areas of the United States.[48] As a young DC-born Colombian woman commented in her survey, apart from the stereotypical association between Colombia and cocaine, "[we're] perceived well . . . yeah just respected, pretty much respected."

Comments about Dominican Spanish portrayed it as nonprestigious. Numerous participants said that they found it hard to understand, and Peruvian Pía commented that she preferred to speak English rather than Spanish with her Dominican friends. The sole Dominican survey participant, a Washington-born woman in her thirties, joked with the Dominican American student interviewer that Dominican Spanish was "ghetto." These assessments are in line with other research showing that Dominican Spanish—a dialect with many nonstandard features and from a heavily Afro-Latinx area of Latin America—is not generally seen as prestigious.[49] Finally, in contrast to discourse in much of the United States, where Mexican Spanish is the major reference point, few participants discussed it, and their comments were largely descriptive rather than evaluative. This omission speaks to Mexicans' relatively low profile in the DC area compared to the United States as a whole.

The dialect attitudes I found show a continuity with attitudes documented in Washington, DC, in the 1980s—the initial period of massive Central American migration to the area. Lucinda Hart-González found that G1 Latinxs from all over Latin America rated Peninsular, Peruvian, and Argentinean Spanish highest, and Salvadoran and Puerto Rican Spanish lowest, out of eighteen national varieties of Spanish.[50] These perceptions support José Benítez's assertion that South Americans in the DC region display a certain sense of superiority over Salvadorans, although Hart-González's results were more generalized.[51] The similarity between the two studies suggests that dialect attitudes in the DC area have remained stable.

DC-area findings also resonate with dialect hierarchies elsewhere in the United States. In Miami, Phillip Carter and Salvatore Callesano noted that Peninsular Spanish was valued over the local majority dialect, Cuban Spanish. Peninsular voices were consistently rated highest despite Cubans' social and economic prominence in the Miami region and their general status as relatively well-off among US Latinxs. Carter and Callesano attribute this to "Eurocentric ideologies, colonialist ideologies that construct Spain as la madre patria, and the ideological workings of the Real Academia de la Lengua Española and other institutions that support 'purist' language ideologies."[52] Similarly, Rosalyn Negrón observes that Peninsular Spanish and Colombian Spanish were privileged, and Dominican and Mexican Spanish disparaged, in New York City.[53] She notes that this local hierarchy relates to the social and economic conditions of different Latinx groups in New York City itself, where Colombians are perceived as "White" due to their more middle-class status. However, the hierarchy she observed also draws on US and Latin American status hierarchies based on European colonial discourses of race and social class. Similar dynamics appear to be at play in DC Latinxs' dialect attitudes.

Negrón also noted that Puerto Ricans—historically the largest and most prominent New York City Latinx group—are ambiguously positioned.[54] Their cultural importance gives them an important symbolic role in New York Latinx identity, while at the same time they—and their language—are seen as nonprestigious since they are viewed as non-White and lower class. A similar dynamic appears to be at play with respect to Salvadorans in the DC area.

Salvadoran Spanish

Salvadoran Spanish is the most commonly spoken Spanish in the DC area and the one that was most commented on by participants. Numerous comments were made about Salvadorans' local presence.

Salvadorans were often described as "strong, hard-working" and "proud, united." Salvadorans portrayed themselves as hardworking pillars of the community who overcame difficult circumstances to make good: "*Bueno hay mucha gente que es dueño de restaurantes. Se ha superado. O sea de que, y eso es bueno. Hay muchos hay muchos negocios latinos.*" (Well, there are a lot of people who are restaurant owners. They have overcome. Or, and this is good. There are many there are many Latino businesses.) Latinxs of all backgrounds also commented on Salvadorans' local presence and pride.

As the language of the largest Latinx group, Salvadoran Spanish is normalized and, like its speakers, enjoys a certain symbolic prominence. Salvadoran participants reported that they spoke "normally," "like everyone else they knew," and "the same as in my country." However, negative attitudes toward Salvadoran Spanish were also common among Salvadorans and non-Salvadorans alike. The tension between these two discourses can be encapsulated by one young Latina of mixed Salvadoran and Peruvian heritage who told me anecdotally that she prefers to speak like a Peruvian both to be a little different from the norm and because Salvadoran Spanish is seen as "ghetto," adding that this attitude is shared by other mixed-origin Latinxs she knows. In another example, a South American participant mentioned being ostracized as a child for not speaking the Spanish as her Salvadoran peers but did not describe trying to change her way of speaking to fit in.

As we saw in the last section, some Salvadorans viewed Salvadoran Spanish as vulgar, and they distanced themselves from this way of speaking by saying that they themselves speak more formally. Adela commented, "*Esas son las vulgares o sea tipo callejero.... Así no hablo yo*" (These are the vulgar or street-type [words].... I don't speak this way). Clara specifically connected a negative evaluation of Salvadoran Spanish to local stereotypes of Salvadorans as street, or ghetto: "*[La gente piensa] que lo mal los salvadoreños son malcriados porque la mayoría aquí anda en la calle, aprende sólo malas palabras*" ("[People think] badly of Salvadorans; they are ill-bred because the majority here hang out in the streets, [they] only learn bad words). Non-Salvadoran participants overall characterized Salvadoran Spanish as "street-language Spanish," slangy, and "ghetto." Diana, the young South American interviewee with a Central American boyfriend, considered Central American Spanish to be incorrect and "ghetto," an intersectional linguistic ideology that she contrasted with "correct" Peninsular and South American Spanish. Other descriptions of Salvadorans and their language were less negative but not associated with high social class (*"humilde, sencillo y rural"*—humble, simple, and rural).

Stigmatization of Salvadoran Spanish rests in part on its nonstandard linguistic features, such as *voseo* and s-elision. Other dialects, such as Caribbean and Argentinian Spanish, share these features but are not equally stigmatized. Argentina is a large, relatively rich, and stable country with a White racial identity. Argentinian immigrants, as with South American immigrants in general, tend to be better educated and better off than other Latinxs.[55] Argentinian Spanish tends not to be stigmatized; my participants did not comment on it, and it was even regarded as prestigious in DC the past.[56] Meanwhile, Caribbean Spanish—covering a heavily Afro-Latinx region, although complex hierarchies of race also affect sociolinguistic perception among different Caribbean nations[57]—is generally stigmatized, as in my participants' commentary on Dominican Spanish. Spanish dialect attitudes are affected by material conditions linked to migration and home country factors, US and Latin American raciolinguistic discourses, and factors in the local environment—all of which contribute to identity negotiation among Latinxs.

DC Salvadorans overall are a working population or worked their way into the middle class after immigration, so they do not benefit from social class prestige. This status relates to their circumstances of immigration, where migrants (many from the rural province of Oriente) fled violence and, later, working-class migrants came both fleeing violence and seeking economic opportunities. Thanks to the United States' refusal to recognize their refugee status, many were caught in the limbo of undocumented immigration status, a precarious status that continues through the DACA debate today.[58] Salvadorans are also viewed as mestizo rather than White, a perception that in Latin America is often linked to class as well as race.[59] This notion resonates with Negrón's observation that low-prestige occupations, precarious immigration status, and apparent Indigenous heritage contribute to low-status perceptions of certain Latinxs, such as Mexicans and Ecuadorians, by other Latinxs in New York City.[60]

There were also negative stereotypes about Salvadorans. One Salvadoran woman's discomfort reflected awareness of this discrimination: "*Sí [la percepción de salvadoreños] de allá es complicado, yo prefiero [no contestar]*" (Yes, [the perception of Salvadorans] there is complicated; I prefer [not to answer]). Comments by many other participants fill in the gap. Salvadorans were described as being "street," "*picaro*" (untrustworthy), uneducated, and involved with gangs and violence. Adela—the Salvadoran woman who was very aware of prescriptive norms and used little /s/ weakening—stated that other Latinxs in the area have a negative perception of Salvadorans as "*picaros*," "*machistas*" (macho), and "*mujeriegos*" (womanizers). She pushes back against this reputation, which she distances herself from, but knows that it affects Salvadorans in general:

Excerpt 3.7

> *En la viña de Dios como dicen por allí hay de todo. Y por los malos pagamos los buenos así que ni modo. Sí se siente feo y por lo general descalifican al, al salvadoreño. . . . Pero yo me siento excepta de todo eso.*
>
> (In God's vineyard, as they say over there, there is everything. And we, the good ones, pay for the bad ones, so what can you do. Yes, one feels badly and in general [others] disparage the Salvadoran. . . . But I feel exempt from all that.)

Adela uses constructed dialogue to show the response she receives when she says she is from El Salvador, extending this to Salvadorans more broadly through the use of the universalizing third person: "*'Ah' le dicen así. '¿De dónde tú sos?' 'Del Salvador,' 'Ah' le dicen. Osea ese 'Ah' es como- yo lo siento así como, no sé algo feo para uno.*" ("Ah," they say like this. "Where are you from?" "From El Salvador," "Ah," they say. And this "Ah" is like—I take it as, I don't know something ugly for one.") She describes a general sense of disparagement when revealing her background (an "Ah" that makes her feel bad), connecting this to a general perception of Salvadorans as disreputable as well as specific stereotypes.

Samuel, the young Peruvian man who arrived in the DC area as a child, commented,

Excerpt 3.8

> Like um, like every time we see- well, I'm trying to put this in the most nicely way possible because my family they're really stereotypical. Um, like, every time we see someone from Central America, we assume they are following a bad path. Simply because they're- in my own family I see that.

This comment, that his family assumes that Central Americans "follow bad paths," resonates with general stereotypes that they are "street" or "ghetto" and uninterested in education, which many participants expressed.

Participants noted similarities between Central American dialects, as summarized by one middle-aged Salvadoran woman who works with bilingual children: "*Honduras, El Salvador, Nicaragua hablan casi igual*" (Honduras, El Salvador, Nicaragua speak almost the same). This perception lends itself to regional solidarity but also exposes generalized "Central American" Spanish to shared stigmatization. Central Americans overall were subject to the same class-based stereotypes, but there were fewer national stereotypes due to the groups being less well-known. Hondurans, for example, stated that there aren't many stereotypes of Honduras, specifically because many people are not aware of the country. As one Honduran immigrant in her thirties, a stay-at-home mother, commented, "*No que sólo que tal vez, porque tantos latinos que vemos no se sabe, si de Honduras del Salvador donde sea tal vez que alguien sepa en específico de tal país es así es asá pero de allí, no. Todo es igual.*" (No, it is only that sometimes, because many Latinos that we see one doesn't know, if [they are] from Honduras or El Salvador, wherever, maybe someone will know specifically from this country it's this, it's that, but from there, no. It is all the same.)

Participants' attitudes paint a picture of how different Latin American Spanish varieties are viewed in DC, a view that has remained consistent over time, indicating a continuity of local sociolinguistic perception.[61] The attitudes are related to different Latinx groups' social positions and perceptions locally, which also tend to reflect broader class and migration patterns among US Latinxs.[62] These views in turn relate to Latin American social hierarchies. In both contexts, class and privilege are also related to racial perception. Colonial ideologies of race and class linger, with material consequences for Latinxs of different backgrounds and physical appearances that in turn perpetuate status hierarchies.[63] However, local negotiation and contestation of these discourses also exist, as we will see in chapter 5.

Conclusions

Spanish is important to the participants' Latinx identity. Indeed, as a common language, it facilitates communication and solidarity—features that my participants commented on and that have been present since the community's inception.[64] In this, the ways in which one spoke Spanish—whether as a heritage language or a particular regional dialect—were strong but complicated indices of identity. Sociolinguistic attitudes tended to replicate Latin American prestige norms, which also related materially to diversity of national origins, socioeconomic status, and race among Latinxs in the DC metropolitan area.[65] However, multiple discourses about language and Latinx identity existed at the same time. These observations expand our understanding of diversity among Latinxs and panethnic groups in general and of how a sense of panethnicity can cohere and coexist with dynamic tensions.[66]

DC Latinxs' ways of speaking are as diverse as their origins. While this social and linguistic diversity is celebrated as part of local identity, divisions remain, and language judgments related to the local social environment and broader sociolinguistic discourses are current. The shared hierarchy of DC dialect attitudes reflects different aspects of relative local privilege that different groups enjoy locally and in terms of more widely shared ideologies. These ideologies are reproduced in the DC community but are also contested at the local level through normalization and covert prestige around Salvadoran Spanish—something I explore further in chapter 5. As such, language attitudes toward Spanishes in DC demonstrate tensions between commonalities and discourses of difference in the imagination of DC Latinx identity.

The dialect hierarchy, which stigmatized Salvadoran Spanish, existed in tension with Salvadorans' local prominence. It also coexisted with a narrative of multiculturalism as a defining characteristic of DC-area Latinxs. Sociolinguistic attitudes thus reflected broader discourses about identity, diversity, and cohesion—a conversation that has been going on in the local community since it first gained cohesion in the 1960s.

Meanwhile, Spanish's indexical role in identity creates tensions for younger generations targeted by deficit discourses. Their bilingualism is often misunderstood as lack of ability when compared to idealized native speaker norms—a widespread phenomenon that speaks to the strength of monolingual ideology in the United States and Latin America, not just Washington, DC. The younger generation's linguistic competence should be celebrated, not criticized, in order to support continued language use and self-esteem and identity connections.

A raciomultilingual lens shines a spotlight on how racial differences among Latinxs intersect with class and education and play into prejudice as well as the ways in which perceptions of Spanish are fundamentally based in social hierarchies, including racialization, grounded in colonial history. Here it is important to note that racialization is not the same as phenotype—it takes phenotype as an excuse but is a construct that justifies status-related social groupings. The same person's racial categorization can shift in different contexts, as Latinxs often report upon immigration to the United States.[67] DC Salvadorans, for example, encompass a broad range of physical appearances, including fair skin, but as a group they are not viewed as "White" Latin Americans in the same way that Argentinians are. Meanwhile, as Jonathan Rosa has convincingly argued, "Latinxs" as an ethnic group are racialized as non-White in the United States as a whole.[68] In this view, Spanish's racialization as an index of ethnocultural identity encourages language maintenance motivation but also intersects uneasily with changing repertoires for heritage speakers who might "look but not sound" the part. In the following chapters we will see how these dynamics intersect with participants' raciolinguistic attitudes about English and across languages and how raciomultilingual ideologies operate within the context of the DC region as a "majority-minority" city.

4

"Blacks and Latinos sort of roll in the same circles"
Sociolinguistic Socialization

> *You know Blacks and Latinos kind of roll in the same kind of circles, same kind of places and so I think somehow just like that kind of mixing . . . there's definitely like a Latino kind of DC [English], for sure and it's not a first-generation thing, it's a second-generation thing and beyond.*
> —Noemí

The previous chapter focuses on Spanish and Spanishes in the DC area and as part of the DC Latinx imagination. However, English is also a major—sometimes primary—part of US Latinx linguistic repertoires. For younger generations, it is often their dominant language and the one in which they live much of their social lives. The ways in which they speak it—or are perceived as speaking it—also contribute to their identities.

It seems there are as many local ways of speaking English as there are attitudes toward them. We'll examine some of them in this chapter, grounding them in the DC metropolitan area's social setting. How do DC Latinxs speak English, and how does this play into how they perceive their own identities and see themselves in relation to others? As we will see, the particularities of intersectional race and language that draw together factors in the local environment with broader raciolinguistic ideologies come into play.

Speaking English

Latinxs in the United States are often stereotyped as not speaking English—a discourse that, as with many perceptions of immigrants and minoritized groups, has more to do with mainstream social anxieties about "what it means to be American" and a diversifying society than with the reality of their sociolinguistic practices. The majority of US Latinxs are bilingual.[1]

Similarly, most Latinxs in DC and the metropolitan area report speaking English as well as Spanish, with 62.3 percent of DC Latinxs who speak Spanish at home reporting they speak English very well, as do the 52.3 percent of metropolitan-area Latinxs who speak Spanish at home. Furthermore, 25.3 percent of DC Latinxs also report speaking only English, compared with the approximately 21 percent of Latinxs in the metropolitan area as a whole who report speaking only English.[2] As might be expected, native-born Latinxs report greater English fluency and monolingualism than foreign-born Latinxs.[3]

My findings support these trends. G1.5 and G2 survey participants reported speaking English well or very well (see table 4.1). A lower percentage of G1 immigrants than in the census data (9.5 percent) reported speaking English very well or well, a pattern that may reflect data collection conditions and socioeconomic and educational diversity among DC Latinxs. In DC as a whole, there is a divide between working-class and more white-collar, educated Latinx immigrants, where higher-income Latinxs are more likely to speak English.[4] Since surveys were conducted at community organizations, G1 participants tended to come from lower socioeconomic classes

Table 4.1. Survey Participants' English

	Very Well, % (n)	Well, % (n)	Not Very Well, % (n)	Not at All, % (n)	Total, % (n)
G1	9.5 (4)	14.3 (6)	61.9 (26)	14.3 (6)	100 (42)
G1.5	75 (6)	25 (2)	0 (0)	0 (0)	100 (8)
G2	90 (9)	10 (1)	0 (0)	0 (0)	100 (10)
Total	31.7 (19)	15 (9)	43.3 (26)	10 (6)	100 (60)*

*Two missing G1.5 responses.

and have little formal education. Many of the organizations offered English classes, which could also have led to higher numbers of non-English-speaking participants.

Language Discrimination

Participants overall viewed the DC region as a tolerant and multicultural area. However, they were not exempt from the discrimination against "non-English speakers"—including those who speak English but with a nonnative accent—which has been amply documented throughout the United States.[5] A high percentage of G1 survey respondents (all but one of 43 percent who responded to the question) reported discrimination for "not speaking English." This discrimination took the form of negative attitudes, such as being shouted at for speaking Spanish and being told to learn English and more material discrimination such as difficulty finding jobs, a lack of service, translation problems, and poor treatment overall. Respondents also reported physical mistreatment, such as being pushed or being asked to give up seats on buses. Comments made it clear that many participants feel that "Americans" (whom they perceive as White but also African American) discriminate against them in general and when they hear them speaking Spanish.

G1.5 and G2 respondents also reported language discrimination. Although bilingual, they reported being told to "speak English" when customers heard them speaking Spanish, and people assuming they didn't speak English based on their Latinx appearance. In a narrative about college orientation, one young Salvadoran American woman described microaggressions when "a White man," assuming she did not speak English, attempted to answer her in broken Spanish. Still another respondent reported being pushed and belittled after Donald Trump won the 2016 US presidential election with an anti-immigrant and anti-Latinx platform—an event that many participants considered to have escalated discrimination.

In addition to their own experiences, later generations—more assimilated, more bilingual—were particularly aware of how discrimination affected their elders. For example, Samuel, from Peru, reported observing language discrimination when the tone of a traffic stop became unpleasant after the police officer heard his parents' accented English on the phone.

In terms of stereotypes, 63 percent of survey respondents believe there are stereotypes about Spanish speakers and those who speak accented English. For example, a G1 cook from El Salvador commented, "*Si hablas en inglés con un acento o no habla inglés te tratan diferente*" (If you speak English with an accent or don't speak English, they treat you differently). Some stereotypes were positive, such as Spanish speakers "getting along well because we speak Spanish," and some of the commentary revolved around different Spanish dialects. In terms of English, however, the majority of comments were negative, such as being unintelligent, lazy, "illegal" (lacking residency status), or un-American. A Colombian young woman who has been in the United States for twenty years commented, "People think that they [Latinxs] are stealing their jobs and that they're lazy and just don't know English because they don't want to. Or that they want to turn the US into a Spanish-speaking country. Especially now with the Trump presidency."

Participants noted that these stereotypes were racially oriented and were related to the US sociopolitical context: "*El estereotipo no tiene que ver con idioma, pero con como una persona se parece*" (The stereotype doesn't have to do with language but with how a person appears). Several reported that customers assume that they do not speak English. One young DC-born Salvadoran man, who reported that customers rudely tell him to speak English at work and treat him and other Latinx employees poorly, commented, "When I speak English well, people are surprised, as if Latino people can't speak English."

While participants noted linguistic discrimination, they also felt that the DC area was relatively tolerant compared to other areas of the country. In the words of one DC-born Salvadoran young woman, "Here it's very diverse so there's not much stereotyping. Some other places people think that Hispanics just mow the lawns and do housekeeping." This perception is consistent with the DC area's generally liberal culture and policies. For example, DC enacted the Language

Access Act to provide equal public-service access to non-English speakers in 2004, although with mixed results.[6] G1 participants in particular appreciated translation services, although they noted that translators were not always available. As this result indicates, much remains to be done.

Latinxs and Different Dialects of English

Latinxs speak English in many different ways beyond the question of a "nonnative accent." As with any group, the way in which Latinxs speak English reflects diversity as a function of the culture and peer groups that surround them.

One well-known feature of Latinx speech is Latinx English. Latinx English has its roots in Spanish influence and in contact phenomena. The bulk of this research has been conducted in the Chicano heartlands of California, Texas, and the Southwest, and New York City and Miami.[7] Research is growing in newer sites such as the Midwest and the South, but more remains to be done.[8] Very little information about this speech exists on Latinxs in the Washington, DC, area.[9]

While Latinx English shares some features with learner English, it is not the same thing. Latinx English is passed down through generations and is therefore spoken by native English speakers, including later generations who may not speak Spanish.[10] Some key aspects of Latinx English phonology are little unstressed vowel reduction, lack of vowel glides, and syllabification.[11] Some other features, and their difference from nonnative English, are presented in table 4.2.

As with Spanish varieties, I am using the term "Latinx English" (and, later, African American English, or AAE) as a convenience. Sarah Bunin Benor convincingly argues that ethnolinguistic repertoire, referring to a "fluid set of linguistic resources that members of an ethnic group may use variably as they index their ethnic identities," is a more accurate term, since linguistic features seen as typical of one group—such as the /s/ elision discussed in chapter 3—are actually usually found in more than one dialect but gain their "distinctiveness" through being associated with groups who are seen as somehow differing from the norm.[12]

Table 4.2. Latinx English versus Learner English

	Latinx English	Learner English
Vowels	/ɪ/ tensing before [ŋ] (-ing)	Low, backed /ae/ but also /ae/ /ɛ/ approximations;[c] lack of participation in local vowel system[d]
	Low, backed /ae/[a, b]	
Consonants	Interdental fortition (/ð/, "this")	More frequent fortition
	Consonant cluster reduction	More frequent final consonant deletion
	Rhotic /r/, as in general American English[c,e]; flapped or trilled[b]	/r/ as a flap;[f,d] devoicing and assibilation[f]
	Light apical /l/[g]	Not attested, although most varieties of Spanish have only light /l/[g]
	Not attested[h]	[sh] for /tʃ/[c]
	Not attested	Voiceless velar fricative [x] for [h][c]

[a] Fought, *Chicano English in Context*; Carter, López Valdez, and Sims, "New Dialect Formation."
[b] Tseng, "Vowel Variation, Style, and Identity Construction."
[c] Fought, *Chicano English in Context*.
[d] Poplack "Dialect Acquisition."
[e] Thomas, *Mexican American English*.
[f] Montanari et al., "The English Phonological Skills."
[g] Slomanson and Newman, "Peer Group Identification."
[h] Scholars such as Fought and Santa Ana note that early studies on Chicano English often conflated characteristics of nonnative English with features of Chicano English as a variety. Fought, *Chicano English in Context*; Santa Ana, "Chicano English."

AAE Influence in Latinx Linguistic Repertoires

Immigrants acquire the English to which they are exposed. Local varieties are learned, and new varieties can emerge. There is a long history of African American influence on Latinx language through peer social networks and school encounters in working-class urban areas.[13] Many Latinx youth who share spaces and economic similarities with African Americans "embraced African American culture, identity, and language."[14] Indeed, African American English can become integrated into Latinx repertoires to the point where it is no longer regarded as a Black ethnolect but simply as part of the English of the community.[15]

AAE has a long history in the United States, having developed from a combination of English dialects, African languages, and creolization due to racial segregation. Black English is not a monolith but contains much regional and class diversity.[16] However, it also has common features—such as /aɪ/ monophthongization, r-lessness, and /l/ vocalization—and has syntactic forms such as the absence of copular "be," which are found across regional and class lines.[17]

Latinxs in contact with African American peers tend to acquire features of AAE but not the entire system. This usage primarily takes the form of phonology. Weakening of the /aɪ/ glide and monophthongization, r-lessness, and consonant cluster simplification are well documented, as are /l/ vocalization, /th/ fronting (θ to f), /ð/ fortition, and final consonant deletion, although the last two phenomena may be also due to Spanish influence or interaction between language contact phenomena and AAE input.[18] It also takes the form of morphosyntax, particularly copular "be" absence, invariant "be," third-person singular -s, and deleted morphemic possessive -s.[19] Lexical and discourse/interactional influence are also attested.[20]

Black English as a Second Language

African American English is prominent in Washington, DC, and the metropolitan area. This degree varies, of course, such that neighborhoods in the wealthy Northwest quadrant have historically been, and remain, Whiter, while the Southeast quadrant continues to be majority Black.[21] However, there is a sense that "DC language"—the way folks speak locally—is Black English.[22] Within this category there is also diversity:[23] Grammy-winning musician Christylez Bacon—a DC native with an exquisite ear for language—commented in an interview conducted as part of my "You are what you speak" project at the 2017 Smithsonian Folklife Festival that DC language varies by which neighborhood you live in.

As a research associate at the Smithsonian Center for Folklife and Cultural Heritage, I was combing the archives for historical information about the DC Latinx community when I came across recordings made while planning the 1987 Folklife Festival, "Making a New Place Home." The 1980s were a formative period for the contemporary DC Latinx community, with massive Central American migration that increased the size of the community and that influences the community to this day. The field recordings I found proved to be a treasure trove. I found a recording of elementary school girls—Latina and Black—playing together, with AAE influence clearly evident in the Latinas' learner English.[24] As they spoke, they used /aɪ/ monophthongization, r-lessness, and other AAE features such as /l/ vocalization and consonant cluster reduction. Other features, such as /th/ fortition and final consonant deletion, could be due to learner English, AAE, or an interaction between the two.[25] The Latina children also used AAE morphosyntax such as future "gon" and the absence of copular "be."

This finding was compelling since it identifies the moments of cultural and linguistic socialization in which language learning takes place—the "smoking gun" of what Awad Ibrahim calls Black English as a Second Language, which is implied but not frequently documented in research (mostly on adolescent and adult speakers) on Black influence in Latinx English.[26] In the playground recordings, we hear the children playing and being socialized naturally into their peers' language and culture. This reminds us that DC immigrants arrived in a "common racialized space shared by ethnic minorities" where Whiteness was not the local norm that most encountered.[27]

Contemporary Latinx Repertoires

Fast-forward to the present day, where my investigation found that Latinx English (LE) and AAE features are still a part of the local Latinx linguistic repertoire. I identified LE or AAE features in fifteen of twenty-five interviews (nine G1.5 and six G2 participants; table 4.3). I also reviewed all thirteen surveys conducted in English (five G1.5 and eight G2 participants; table 4.4).

Table 4.3. Interviews: Latinx and African American English Features

Name	Generation	Age of Arrival	Current Age	Gender	Heritage	Current Class	City/ Suburbs	LE	AAE
Alonso	1.5	10	20s	M	El Salvador	Working	Suburbs	LE	AAE
Emanuel	1.5	14	40s	M	El Salvador	Middle	City	NNE/ LE	AAE
Marcos	2	n/a	30s	M	El Salvador/ Mexico	Middle	City	LE	AAE
Jose	1.5	12	30s	M	Colombia	Middle	City	LE	AAE
Rico	2	n/a	20s	M	El Salvador	Working	City	LE	AAE
Héctor	2	n/a	30s	M	El Salvador	Middle	City	LE	AAE
Pascual	2	n/a	30s	M	Peru/ Bolivia	Working	Suburbs	No	AAE
Viviana	1.5	8	20s	F	Venezuela	Working	Suburbs	Little LE	Little AAE
Candida	2	n/a	20s	F	Mexico	Working	Suburbs	Little LE	Little AAE
Sofia	2	n/a	40s	F	Paraguay/ Spain	Middle	City	Little LE	Little AAE
Bass	1.5	6	20s	M	Guatemala	Middle	Suburbs	Little LE	Little AAE
Carolina	1.5	9	20s	F	Bolivia	Middle	Suburbs	Little LE	No
Diana	1.5	6	20s	F	Paraguay	Working	Suburbs	Little LE	No
Celia	1.5	5	30s	F	Bolivia	Working	Suburbs	Little LE	No
Ángel	1.5	5	30s	M	Peru	Middle	Suburbs	Little LE	Little AAE/ SWE
Danielle	1.5	11	20s	F	Panama	Middle	Suburbs	Little NNE	SWE

Note: AAE, African American English; LE, Latinx English; NNE, Nonnative English; SWE, Southern White English.

As I listened to the recordings, I used auditory analysis to identify LE and AAE features, which I confirmed by visual analysis in Praat. I observed low and backed /ae/, syllabification, vowel shortening, and little unstressed vowel reduction, light intervocalic /l/ or Spanish denti-alveolar /l/ rather than American English alveolar /l/ in

Table 4.4. Surveys: Latinx and African American English Features

Generation	Age of Arrival	Current Age	Gender	Heritage	Class	City/Suburb	LE	AAE
G1.5	10	18	Male	Peru	Middle	Suburbs	NNE	No
G1.5	11	20	Female	El Salvador	Working	City	NNE	AAE
G1.5	11	19	Male	El Salvador	Working	City	NNE	AAE
G1.5	14	24	Female	El Salvador	Working	City	LE	AAE
G1.5	9	43	Female	Argentina	Middle	Suburbs	LE	Little AAE
G2	n/a	27	Female	El Salvador	Middle	City	LE	AAE
G2	n/a	30	Female	Dominican Republic	Middle	City	Little LE	AAE
G2	n/a	18	Male	El Salvador	Middle	City	Little LE	AAE
G2	n/a	18	Female	El Salvador	Working	City	No	AAE
G2	n/a	18	Female	Bolivia	Working	Suburbs	Little LE	Little AAE
G2	n/a	19	Female	El Salvador	Working	City	Little LE	No
G2	n/a	23	Male	Colombia	Middle	Suburbs	No	No
G2	n/a	18	Female	El Salvador	Middle	Suburbs	NNE	No

Note: AAE, African American English; LE, Latinx English; NNE, Nonnative English.

syllable-onset position, and some prenasal /ɪ/ (BIT) tensing.[28] In addition to these features, I found trilled /r/, which has not previously been discussed in research on G2 Latinxs. I also observed consonant cluster simplification and /θ/ fortition but have not focused on it, as it is also common in AAE. The /ae/ interpretation draws on my midpoint F1 and F2 analysis of tokens in prenasal and nonnasal position (BAT/BAN), excluding tokens following liquids and rhotics.[29] Other LE features were coded impressionistically and verified through visual formant inspection, as were the AAE features of /aɪ/ weakening in prevoiced and final phonetic contexts, postvocalic /r/ deletion or vocalization, and /l/ vocalization.[30] AAE influence also included morphology and syntax (see table 4.5). Examples include demonstrative "them" ("Where did you get them glasses"), double negation ("They didn't put me in no ESL or nothing"), and a lack of third-person verbal inflection ("There was three of them").[31]

A close look at the interviews showed that city residents tended to use more AAE and LE than suburb residents. The first six names

Table 4.5. African American English Morphology and Syntax

Example	Feature
He seen that video	Participle used for simple past tense
We was like huddled with my coach	Singular verb form used with plural subject
There was three of them	Lack of third-person verbal inflection
Y'all stay tryin' to put him on	Aspect marker "stay" for frequent or habitual action
You know you YOUNG, you know and it's easy to get caught up in relationships and forget about your ultimate goal	Zero copula
The girls be in the DMs like,	Invariant "be"; "be like"[a]
Where'd you get them glasses	Demonstrative use of the pronoun "them"[b]
They didn't put me in no ESL or nothing	Double negation

Source: Based on L. Green, *African American English*.

[a] Collins, "A Fresh Look at Habitual Be in AAVE."

[b] Bernstein, "Demonstrative Surprises!"

in table 4.3 (Alonso through Héctor) represent a core group of G1.5 and G2 men with LE and AAE features. All spent formative time in the Latinx Columbia Heights neighborhood; all but Alonso still live in the city. While several of the city residents are now middle class, all grew up in working-class families. However, one city resident—"Sofía"—although raised working class in Washington, DC, had little LE or AAE features. This may have been influenced by her high level of education (graduate study) and job in education.

Suburb residents, on the other hand, had little LE and little to no AAE features. In keeping with this pattern, the ten interviews that did not show any LE or AAE features (not shown) were all middle-class, suburb residents, or both, or had a strong orientation to education and linguistic correctness—an attitudinal finding that I unpack later in this chapter. Finally, two middle-class suburb dwellers, Ángel and Danielle, although largely standard English speakers, had traces of features that, while also common in AAE, appear to follow Southern White English patterns, such as a more extensive /aɪ/ monophthongization pattern.

The city/suburb pattern held for sociolinguistic surveys. All but one of the city dwellers, whether working or middle class, showed AAE features. Almost all also had LE or, in some cases, nonnative English features. One city resident had little LE or AAE, which may be due to her educational background as she was a student at an elite private university. As with the interviews, less LE and AAE were found in suburban speech.

Taken together, these findings suggest that city dwellers are more likely than suburb residents to have ethnic dialect features. Many of the participants live or lived in Latinx neighborhoods such as Columbia Heights or in newer areas of Latinx settlement in the Northeast and Southeast city quadrants. Their use of LE and AAE speaks to AAE's prominence in the city as well as to the continuing strength of Latinx social networks. Exceptions to these patterns were women with high levels of education. Further, the interviews group showed a core urban male group who had strong LE and AAE. These suggestive gender patterns are in line with previous research that finds women are more likely than men to avoid low-prestige features and that nonstandard features—particularly those associated with toughness, urbanity, and masculinity—may be more acceptable for men than for women.[32] I explore the discourses that attach to ethnic-associated English among DC Latinxs in the sections that follow.

Another example of language socialization and contemporary DC Latinx speech comes from Anna Mvze, formerly Aye Yo Smiley, a hip-hop artist of Peruvian descent. Born in Washington, DC, she was raised in Columbia Heights, where she attended diverse, predominantly Black schools with sizable Latinx populations. Anna's speech in eight publicly available interviews (not rap performances) reveals the same LE and AAE features I observed in my interviews and surveys as well as a range of AAE morphosyntax. There are participles used for simple past tense, "be" in only a single form in the past tense ("was"), the aspect marker "stay" indicating frequent or habitual action, invariant "be," zero copula "be," and grammar such as zero adverbs ("I take it really serious"; "It just happened natural") and double negation ("You can't trust nobody"), which are a feature of both LE and AAE as well as other nonprestige English dialects.[33] She also uses discourse marker "yo."

While Mvze's way of speaking may well relate to her hip-hop identity, it also seems to be consistent for her, not an act. Her morphosyntax is more consistent with AAE than with the limited forms that "wannabees" tend to use performatively or than non-Black Hip Hop Nation Language (HHNL). For example, she uses more extensive AAE forms than non-Black HHNL typically does, and she does not use equative copula "be."[34] Given the evidence that morphosyntactic influence needs more peer contact than phonology to develop, her patterns are likely the result of natural acquisition through socialization with her peers.[35]

Language goes beyond grammatical structure to be part of culture and identity, and AAE influence goes beyond pronunciation and grammar. Many people I spoke with mentioned the discourse-pragmatic norm of greeting others on the street, "saying hi," as an important part of local culture that is being lost with gentrification, as we will see shortly. In my own observation, these greetings were something I noticed when I moved to DC, particularly in Black neighborhoods, and it is striking that older residents in gentrifying neighborhoods still exchange greetings while new residents tend to ignore them.

What we can see in the evidence above is that contact features from the local sociolinguistic environment have coalesced into an enduring part of DC Latinxs' English that integrates both Spanish influence and African American features. Almost all speakers had some LE features. The coalescence of LE in the community, as opposed to nonnative English, is attested to by the kind of features present and their use by G1.5 and, especially, by English-dominant G2 speakers. Latinx English's maintenance in the community is likely due to the ongoing Latinx social networks that participants reported since LE is maintained by co-ethnic contact.

AAE influence was also much in evidence due to peer socialization. Even participants with mostly Latinx friends had significant AAE in their repertoires, supporting the theory that AAE was the primary variety to which immigrants and their children were exposed, particularly for working-class Latinxs in the city, and that it had become normalized in their speech. However, suburban Latinxs also showed LE and AAE influence, which speaks to the diversity of DC's suburbs.

Men used more of these features than did women, and wealthier and more educated Latinxs overall spoke in a more mainstream way. These findings echo much research on sociolinguistic variation, wherein less standard language, including ethnolectal forms, tends to be used be marginalized groups, and women are less likely to use nonprestigious forms. However, the centering of middle-class White English as "mainstream" and "normal" itself reflects raciomultilingual norms in which White Americans' language and culture are taken as the "default setting" and equated with appropriate language use.[36] Findings remind us that this assumption is often unwarranted. Latinxs in DC, past and present, arrived in a city where White Americans were not necessarily the main group with which they interacted, the primary input language for second-language learners, or the most prominent cultural referent. At the same time, White privilege still suffuses the local environment.

Contact, Conflict, and Community

> You know that whole concept of-of being amongst Black people and DC was (.) Chocolate City back in those days. It was 70 percent Black. It wasn't gentrified and it was very racially divided so:: you know and: I landed right here, 14th and Irving. A block from here. Whites. There was not one White person here. White people always lived on the other side of 16th Street. 16th Street was the dividing line so no no: no: (.) White person was (.) seen on this side. Especially on this area. If you talking about Columbia Hei:ghts. You know, Mt. Pleasant, Adams Morgan so (.) those were like (.) Mt. Pleasant an. so you saw White people over there. Over here you never saw White people, they were Black.
>
> —Emanuel

DC Latinx language evolved as Latinxs settled into the predominantly Black city. However, their integration was not necessarily smooth. Some participants felt that DC had been overall welcoming since local governance—specifically mentioned as Black—felt solidarity for others experiencing oppression. The city is also liberal, with a strong activist history, which contributed to this support. However, many participants mentioned tensions ranging from fights among youth in schools and in the streets, sometimes with fatal consequences, to overall municipal neglect and discrimination—systemic neglect that is well documented as leading to the three-day Mount Pleasant disturbances of 1991, which began after a rookie police officer shot a Salvadoran man. This event ultimately led to a report by the US Commission on Civil Rights and to better representation and services for the Latinx community.[37]

Regardless, participants agreed that Latinx youth integrated into the local culture. They viewed this connection as natural due to DC's demographics, residential segregation, and class similarities between Latinxs and Blacks. As Sofía, a bilingual therapist born in DC, commented, "I thought I was Black . . . because we were poor and all my White classmates were rich."

African American English was specifically identified as part of this cultural assimilation.

Excerpt 4.1

EMANUEL: It's completely different now. You know, because (.) you have, you know NOW like maybe the second generation? of kids that, *ahm*, have gone to:, elementary, school with Black kids? And the other way around as well? Um:, So they're- they're very much used to BEING with each other, as opposed to: you know teenagers being thrown into a room. And you know, and then if you were BORN here, as a LATINO or as a BLACK person, and if you go to that type of area you're very ↑likely to, PICK UP on language. So:, KIDS nowaDA:YS, you know like Latino kids, they sound like they're Black kids. You know if you're riding the metro or the bus and you listen to people talking, and you're not looking (.) you know (.) most of the times (.) kids tend to sound pretty much the same. You know with that whole street lingo and, "So:n ↑nah son I'm ↑sayin though you know no whoa man we was ↑waiting for you so what's up man this nigga (trails off)." So the other day I heard them say "NAWman we was at the ↑club man, and THIS nigga started beefin.'" "Was it a ↑Black nigga?" "NO man SPANish nigga." So, like it's THAT you know.

In this example, Emanuel describes young Latinxs' way of speaking—"they sound like Black kids"—as a consequence of their socialization with African American peers. He voices this through constructed dialogue, imitating a conversation he overheard on the bus. In this conversation the imagined participants use the term "Spanish n-word" to describe Latinxs. This usage is based on the "n-word with an a" as an endearment or simply a reference term among some African Americans as part of street language and hip-hop language, which has spread to be used by some in reference to Latinxs who are part of the same cultural circle.[38] The term combines this usage with "Spanish" as an ethnocultural term that is common among working-class Latinxs and Blacks.[39] "Spanish n-word" as part of urban vernacular is used in hip-hop generally and by Latinx hip-hoppers to describe themselves and others.[40] In Emanuel's constructed dialogue, the speakers' awareness of this expansion of the term can be seen by the need for clarification of the race of the person being spoken of, which is no longer encoded by the referent. In addition to Emanuel's comments, I have heard other working-class Latinxs in the DC area use it to describe themselves. However, the use of the n-word in any form remains controversial.[41]

The overall effect of this vocabulary in Emanuel's constructed dialogue is to position young DC Latinxs as speaking AAE and to present this as a natural part of how they speak due to their social environment. The example he uses also indexes street speech, a register to which the "n-word with an a" belongs. The perception of local English as AAE, described as "slang" or "ghetto," was widespread among participants. Let us now take a closer look at language attitudes.

Attitudes toward Black English

Participants viewed Black English's presence in Latinx linguistic repertoires as normal. This was amply attested by their comments about DC as a Black city in which sociolinguistic contact has led to Black English acquisition. Further, participants mentioned that Blacks, as the city's middle class and administrators, were often the local power structure—teachers, police officers, healthcare workers, and bureaucrats—that immigrants interacted with. Indeed, since 1975, when the Home Rule Act of 1973 allowed for DC's first popular elections, DC's mayors have been Black.[42] This context could potentially facilitate acceptance of Black influence on Latinx ways of speaking as part of a normal, local way of talking.

AAE's normalization did not mean that it was ideologically neutral, however. Black English, on its own and as part of Latinx linguistic repertoires, was still subject to sociolinguistic attitudes. There was still stigma associated with "sounding Black." Comments to this effect were made by participants, from immigrants to native Washingtonians, which indicates the widespread nature of this sentiment. For example, a G1 Salvadoran woman in her thirties, employed as a cook, commented,

Excerpt 4.2

> *El americano el blanco lo habla, bien, bien, este (.) educado bien claro? El moreno lo habla muy como* ghetto *entonces es muy rápido demasiado rápido habla el inglés.* Ghetto *que le llaman, como callejero. Sí, pero la mayoría de ellos se reconoce los que son de, alta educación verdad que lo habla como los blancos.*

(The White American speaks it [English] well, well, that is, [it is] educated very clear. The Black speaks it very ghetto; it is very fast, they speak English too fast. Ghetto is what they call it, like street. Yes, but the majority of them recognize those who are of high education who speak it like the Whites.)

In this excerpt she code-switches to use the English term "ghetto" to describe Black English, reinforcing her evaluative stance by reiterating its description as *"callejero"* (street). She characterizes White English as "good, educated, and clear"—a perspective reinforced by her perception that educated African Americans "speak English like Whites." These linguistic impressions clearly show that the speaker has internalized raciolinguistic ideologies linking color to linguistic correctness and prestige despite conducting most of her linguistic life in Spanish. Many participants voiced this attitude that AAE—"local language"—was "ghetto." These negative stereotypes of Blackness and of Black language indicate the persistence of negative US stereotypes about Blackness despite DC's strong African American history that may well intersect with colorism in Latinx cultures. As with Salvadoran Spanish, Black English was an ambiguous referent—simultaneously normalized and stigmatized—due to conflicting discourses about Blackness. African Americans were the largest Washingtonian population, with much cultural and linguistic presence and power in the city, but people of African descent as a whole still experience much stereotyping in the United States and the Americas.

From a raciomultilingual perspective, DC Latinxs' bilingualism is racialized in terms of the English they speak and the attitudes that surround it. The English they speak—influenced by both Spanish and AAE—is a normalized part of their linguistic repertoires, particularly for urban working-class speakers. Its social-semiotic meanings relate to raciolinguistic ideologies that intersect with social class in understandings of "localness" as well as broader abiding discourses, which unfortunately stigmatize Black language, as with AAE influence in Latinx English in general in the United States.[43]

A further raciomultilingual implication lies in the way that scholars assign "authentic" speech and label transgressive behavior. As Mary Bucholtz notes, the notion of sociolinguistic authenticity as grounded in a singular and unique social group—"one language, one people"—is a problematically essentializing construct that too often passes unremarked in linguistic research.[44] In DC and many other urban contexts, AAE is the majority English that immigrants are exposed to—"Black ESL."[45] Its use by Latinx youth is therefore not surprising, particularly given the long history of urban Latinx and Black contact and cultural blending. That is, frameworks such as "crossing," defined as "switching out of varieties not belonging to them," are not entirely adequate for understanding their speech. What English should immigrant youths be expected to learn, other than that of their peers? When Latinxs and other immigrants learn "mainstream" English, this is seen as unremarkable, yet this is not the English many immigrants are primarily exposed to. The paradigms we use to label and evaluate ethnic and immigrant language themselves reflect raciomultilingual assumptions.

That said, participants in my study also expressed complicated raciolinguistic ideologies. Blackness was seen as a normal and important—even primary—part of DC's identity as a city, and the participants shared a discourse about DC as a multicultural city in general. African Americans' role in many Latinxs' cultural and linguistic exposure was seen as a foundational part of the community's experience in DC. At the same time, I noted pervasive US stereotypes of Black language as "ghetto"—although, in a hyperlocal wrinkle, African immigrants were exempted. G1 survey participants, who often worked with both African Americans and immigrants from DC's large Ethiopian community, viewed Africans as fellow immigrants and did not place them within the same prejudicial paradigm.

Blackness is also widely stigmatized in Latin America, which may contribute to this dynamic—that is certainly the perception of Afro-Latinxs I spoke with and heard at events such as the "DC Afro-Latinos in Action" panel, where there is a feeling that Cuban, Puerto Rican, and other Afro-Caribbeans' key roles in founding the community have been ignored. Indeed, discussions about representation and "who controls the narrative" are very present in local conversation about community history and identity. Afro-Latinx activism has grown since I conducted my interviews, with organizations such as the DC Afro-Latino Caucus aiming to "bring visibility and improve the quality of life to Afro Latin@s in Washington DC," according to its LinkedIn mission statement. The DC Afro-Latinx Festival kicked off in 2022 in Malcom X Park—site of the drum circle I started this book with—celebrating Afro-Latinxs as well as local Latinx/Black cultural fusion, such as the iconic go-go music, which also has Latin roots.

Local and Broader Systems of Meaning Interact

Through the concepts of scale and polycentricity, the raciomultilingual model can account for the multiple beliefs and points of reference expressed by DC Latinxs.[46] Ideologies circulating at higher scalar levels—enjoying broader geographical reach, longer time-depth, greater institutional or state support, or a combination of the above—tend to be more powerful and less flexible than ideologies circulating at the local level. At higher levels, for example, abstracted "natural/commonsense" ideologies such as "one language, one people," native speakers as the ideal language model, and entrenched racism toward minoritized groups tend to persist and circulate broadly. At the local level, ideologies are more open to reconstitution and resistance. Local norms can evolve in relationship to the local setting, while broader discourses about race, prestige, and stigma continue to have an influence. Applied to my DC data, this model describes how participants could simultaneously feel that their nonstandard ways of speaking were normal in the community and even take pride in them while at the same time feeling a nagging sense of impropriety.

Polycentricity expresses that there are multiple centers of semiotic reference in diaspora. In the case of AAE, DC's local dynamics normalize it and make it the primary input variety for many Latinxs while broader racial hegemonic perceptions still endure, which are common in both the United States and Latin America but draw on shared colorist colonial legacies. Similarly, in chapter 3 we saw how Salvadoran Spanish is normalized locally but remains subject to broader dialect stigmatization. In both cases, ideologies of race, ethnicity, and class interact in complex ways in the formation and perception of an ethnolinguistic repertoire.

Conclusions

In this chapter we have examined ways in which DC Latinxs speak English as well as their attitudes about it. Most DC-area Latinxs are bilingual, and the ways they speak English are first and foremost affected by their peer groups and social environment. Mapping out features common to Spanish-influenced "Latinx Englishes" has demonstrated a strong influence of AAE. Interview commentary in this chapter shows that this was considered a local, "DC Latinx" way of speaking. Not everyone talks like this, of course; in the highly diverse metropolitan area, where neighborhood demographics are strongly segregated by socioeconomic status and often still reflect echoes of deliberate racial segregation, where you grew up matters. I noted an overall urban/suburban pattern, in which urban dwellers—particularly working-class men—show more of the ethnolectal repertoire features. DC's suburbs are also highly diverse, and some counties, such as Prince George's County, are majority Black. Latinx communities in the suburbs have grown since the 1980s, offering a productive direction for future linguistic research.

The raciomultilingual perspective applied in this chapter allows us to understand the multiple, sometimes contradictory attitudes and ideologies around the English and (as we saw in the previous chapter) Spanish that DC-area Latinxs speak. In chapter 5 we will see how local ways of speaking English and Spanish and their social meanings come together to construct the "social figure" of local Latinxs, and we will see how sociolinguistic ideologies cross language lines in the multilingual repertoire.

5

"¿Qué pasó vos?"

Voicing the Raciomultilingual Self and Other

So far we have seen some of the key sociolinguistic attitudes about DC-area Latinxs' Spanish and English. However, speakers do not experience their languages in isolation. Raciolinguistic ideologies cross language boundaries, and bilingualism itself becomes part of the construction of racialized identities. These ideologies are highlighted in the social figure of the local DC Latinxs—an image of what the stereotypical DC Latinx looks, acts, and sounds like. In this chapter we will see how participants discursively constructed this social figure through talk about language and identity. As they did so, they identified with, or distanced themselves from, the persona they created. This identity construction gives insight into how participants make sense of local dynamics and navigate tensions between diversity, cohesion, and ambivalence around understandings of Latinidad.

Raciolinguistic Ideologies Crossing Language Boundaries

We have seen how stigma and pride attach to common English and Spanish variants in DC Latinx repertoires and how these attitudes relate to both the local environment and broader social dynamics in the United States and Latin America. As I will show, these discourses are not restricted to one language or the other but are mutually referential. That is, they operate crosslinguistically in an inherently multilingual sense-making process such that a recognizable social figure is conjured up when this speech is heard or described.

Commentary by "Inés," a Guatemalan immigrant and mother in

her forties who has been active in the community for many years, illustrates this point. To the question, "Do you think it's [Spanish] important too as part of feeling Guatemalan or feeling Latino?" she responds,

Excerpt 5.1

INÉS: Yes, part of the- the identity. You will hear kids in the city that-you speak Spanish right? You know, you probably will hear them and will- you will hear them talking in English and, they talk just like an African American kid. You know? Uh if you hear their Spanish, it's WORSE, you know they talk (.) street language Spanish. And like I said you know it's all where they coming from, you know. We have a large, Salvadorian community, that, because of the war in El Salvador and Nicaragua and Guatemala, they, were not able to, get edu↑cation. So of course that's the way they speak to the kids and- and you know it's like, like a broken telephone

Inés describes prototypical DC Latinx youths' English as "sounding like an African American kid." Her immediate comparison with their Salvadoran Spanish, which she describes as "even worse," makes it clear that she does not regard either variety as prestigious. This interpretation is supported by her characterization of AAE and Salvadoran Spanish as "street language": informal and uneducated. She is sympathetic, attributing a lack of education to the turbulence that sparked major Central American migration to the DC area. Nevertheless, her linguistic evaluation still stands.

Ángel, a Bolivian/Argentinian who lived in primarily Salvadoran neighborhoods when he arrived in the DC area as a child, also used a crosslinguistic comparison to justify negative attitudes toward Salvadoran Spanish.

Excerpt 5.2

INTERVIEWER: So like where you were when you first came here was mostly like Bolivians?

ÁNGEL: In my family circle yes. Outside of that it was TONS of Salvadorians. My neighborhood was, ONLY I think Salvadorians, maybe a couple Guatemalans here and there I mean, preDOMinately Salvadoran. Um, and then, you know being around them, I've also learned why, they might get the stigma that they get. And it's- you know they use, I would say broken-down Spanish. And not what you would call, you know, um traditional, or- or- (.) They use words that you probably would not find in a dictionary. Um more kinda like, uh, what's that, kind of how the Jamaicans speak English, but it's not- it's like broken-down English you know, like=

INTERVIEWER: =Like pidginy kind of or=

ÁNGEL: =Yeah, I think that's also kind of another thing. And, so I think that has something to do with it, I don't know.

Ángel describes Jamaican English as "not real—it's like broken down English." This description delegitimizes Jamaican English as a variety—a discriminatory discourse that Caribbean Englishes and creole languages more broadly often face.[1] Its use as an example legitimizes his description of Salvadoran Spanish as likewise "broken," "not traditional," and nonstandard ("not what you would find in a dictionary").[2]

Social Figures

Social figures, or personae, are recognizable images of speakers conjured up by language and ways of speaking.[3] They link speech repertoires with different social groups via recognizable stereotypes.[4] To this point in the book we have seen that participants share a certain image of the prototypical "DC Latinx." While it is not the only way of imagining DC Latinidad—participants are well aware of the community's diversity, which is itself part of the local identity—this social figure has been repeatedly invoked by participants. The trend suggests that this image occupies a symbolic weight in local understandings of what it means to be Latinx in the DC area. Indeed, the participants' own alignment with or distancing of themselves from this image serves as evidence of its relevance.

Narrating the Self and the Other

Narratives are an effective medium for understanding identity construction. The stories we tell reveal much about our understanding of ourselves and others and the images we want to present to the world.[5] Storytelling is also a way of arguing for different points and achieving other local and interactional purposes.[6] Narratives can take many forms, with some following a conventional paradigm: "an active teller, highly tellable account, relatively detached from surrounding talk and activity, linear temporal and causal organization, and certain, constant moral stance."[7] These narratives often follow the classic structure established by William Labov and Joshua Waletzky:[8] an abstract introducing the story topic and an orientation that establishes the narrative's setting and participants, followed by complicating actions, resolution of the complications, evaluation of the narrative events, and a coda returning the speaker and listener to the here and now. Other narratives are less structured "tellings of ongoing events, future or hypothetical events, shared (known) events . . . allusions to tellings, deferrals of tellings, and refusals to tell."[9] These "small stories" are also valuable.

"Sounding local"

For social figures to exist, they need to be noticeable. This noticeability relies on a social figure and its voice being seen as somehow different from other figures and voices.[10] In other words, listeners need to perceive the recognizable voice as "sounding Latinx" as opposed to something else. Participants pointed to a recognizable way of speaking—an ethnolinguistic repertoire incorporating Spanish, Latinx English, AAE-influenced English, and translanguaging—which they associated with a local Latinx social figure. Héctor, a DC-born Latino of Salvadoran and other Central American heritage, used himself as an example of this way of speaking.

Excerpt 5.3

HÉCTOR: You know the- the way that you, you code-switch and the nuances of the way I speak, is not, in my opINion and my perCEPtion it isn't WHITE. I don't talk like a WHITE dude. But I don't talk like a Black guy either, and I- I think, so I, kind of have like a, a twang to my speech, I- I perCEIVE it as such . . . And so, I feel like I have my rhythm. And, it's a LATINO rhythm, it's a Spanish rhythm. And, it's despite it being, me speaking English, I feel like I have a pace.

Héctor distinguishes the Latinx way of speaking from "talk[ing] like a White dude . . . [or] a Black guy." In addition to referring to code-switching, he is aware that his pronunciation is different ("a twang in my speech") and mentions "a Latino rhythm . . . a Spanish rhythm" in his English. "José," a G1.5 Colombian immigrant and musician, also identified a "DC Latino accent." This accent had class associations: José reported that despite his middle-class background, he acquired the accent from other Latinxs through his employment in the working-class food industry.

Noemí, born in DC and having one Ecuadorian parent, shared a series of small stories that articulated her understanding of the "DC Latinx" voice and social figure.

Excerpt 5.4

INTERVIEWER: What did your family say when you went to middle school and you came back talking all like Southwest [quadrant]?

NOEMÍ: I didn't talk like that around them really.

INTERVIEWER: It would have been like (gasps) (laughs)

NOEMÍ: No. Yeah, I didn't. I did not. Be↑cause, there is a whole, there's this weird- like you know like Latino, kind of English, is the way ↑I've heard it (.) termed here at [university], but it's like just the way I knew, people even in my own ↑building, you know? But they didn't GO, like, I've always been kind of like into school and going to school and, you know my mom's REALLY prioritized education? Um, and I NOticed that other kids in the building, whose parents weren't so into that: you know they started getting into ↑gangs like, ALL of them were pregnant before eightee:n, you know,

continued

Excerpt 5.4 *continued*

and, they TALKed so: differently. So um, and it's funny it's this like distinct kind of like, I mean Salvadorian like kind of, I don't know but it like kind of mixes with, like you know?

INTERVIEWER: What does it sound like?

NOEMÍ: I ↑can't imitate it, [I can't imitate it,

INTERVIEWER: [Can you describe it?

NOEMÍ: Ah, gosh I'm trying to think because I was listening to this other interview in the [project] and I was like THAT'S it like, THAT'S the one. I can't remember which one it was, bu:t,

INTERVIEWER: You'll have to tell me which one it was [because I don't know what that sounds like.

NOEMÍ: [Yeah, yeah, yeah yeah, I'll TELL you I'll TELL you, because and I noticed my little ↑cousins talking kind of in that way too but I never ↑did. And my mom always just was like "Oh yeah that's how like those like, you know street children talk," like "That's- you're not a street kid," you know, yeah basically.

INTERVIEWER: Then you got to school and everyone was like you sound White (laughs).

NOEMÍ: Yeah.

INTERVIEWER: Basically.

NOEMÍ: Yeah. Bu:t, I mean, because ↑I always felt a little bit weird about those girls because I always felt like, I remember you know in middle school feeling like they were just kind of like trying, to be Black themselves? You know like the way they would do their hair like with the gel and like, you know like SMOO:TH it back in there so it's like so so down, and like um, and then they'd be like yeah, I'm ↑Spanish, I'm ↑Spanish. I'm like, girlfriend you are not Spanish.

INTERVIEWER: [(laughs)

NOEMÍ: [Like, we SPEAK Spanish. You know it's like we're *latinos*, you know, or like whatever if you want to say Hispa:nic or whatever, but like, NO like it's just really funny but, I wasn't- as close of friends with those people? Because um (.) ↑They just like, I feel like they were more recent? Like immigrants and stuff and like (cough) I didn't feel as like connected? So I don't know.

———

Noemí begins her story by describing the language she heard as a child in her apartment building and at school in the then-ungentrified Southwest quadrant of the city, which—like much of DC—was neglected and impoverished during her childhood in the 1990s. Her comments show that she considers the local Latinx voice to have Spanish and AAE influences and that she associates this voice with Salvadorans. Noemí evaluates this way of speaking as "street" or uneducated. Her explanation of why she herself does not speak this way—her mother's focus on education—reinforces this assessment. Her characterization of those who speak this way constructs a working-class, "street" social figure and resonates with stereotypical discourses about Latinxs as uninterested in education and prone to gang involvement and early pregnancy—an image that she distances herself from through language as a proxy for social identity.[11] Indeed, her own English does not show African American or Latinx English features, and she also makes frequent use of the White-associated feature "like."[12]

Gracia, the young DC Salvadoran whose journey and reflection on her Latina identity were introduced in chapter 1, shared a narrative about childhood encounters in which she was rejected by her Latinx peers because of the way she spoke.

Excerpt 5.5

1   GRACIA: In terms of you know of CULture, of identity, I think tha:t, coming
2   to TERMS with my Latino identity was, really difficult? Simply because (.) you know
3   like I had a really good grasp on the Spanish language, I, had gone down to El Salvador
4   all the time, and felt like, I was like "Yeah I'm Hispanic, I get it." And I just remember,
5   growing up I went to CCD in, like with a, predominantly Hispanic, parish? And I just
6   remember these kids saying like, "You're such a whitey." Like "You're just such a
7   whitey." And I just like, and I couldn't understand like WHAT it was that they were
8   saying. And then eventually like I kind of like, came to that realization it's like, because
9   of the way I talk. Because of the way I dress. You know. And, it was just one of those
10 things where I was like, I don't think that I need to perpetuate like Hispanic
11 stereotypes? And like have to, try and like talk the same way you do? Simply because,

continued

Excerpt 5.5 *continued*

12   you know I don't want to be called a whitey?
13   INTERVIEWER: (laughs)
14   GRACIA: [Um, I was like "Sorry I like school, sorry I'm doing well?" And
15   so like it was like something that was like really SA:D for me at first, because I was
16   just like, you know like "Mom I just don't, understand like why it's such a stigma to
17   like spell out, your WORDS, in a text message," and (laughs) like,
18   INTERVIEWER: (laughs)
19   GRACIA: Um, and you know like put out full sentences, or, do well in CCD
20   I was like "I don't understand it," and she was just like, "Gracia," she was like "You
21   have to understand that like a lot of like, the immigrant population? In like this
22   particular area? Like THEY'RE not, particularly like well-educated, they don't,
23   necessarily like enshrine the values of education. For them it's like, a lot more work-
24   oriented. It's, what are you gonna do to get a good job, kind of deal?"
25   INTERVIEWER: Mmhmm.
26   GRACIA: So education like wasn't necessarily like their main focus.
27   INTERVIEWER: Mmhmm.
28   GRACIA: And so I definitely think that, getting used to, um, my parents'
29   mentality? and like what the mentality of like the majority of Hispanics that I knew was?
30   Was really difficult for me because I was just like well, you know AM I a whitey? And,
31   INTERVIEWER: (laughs)
32   GRACIA: [Uh, (laughs) so I was having like a serious identity crisis, (laughs) thirty-three at like TEN.

Gracia's canonical Labovian narrative highlights raciolinguistic ideologies about Latinx identity, where intersectional discourses of race and social class are embodied by an iconic Latinx figure that is racialized as non-White.[13] As Gracia came of age, she participated in Catholic preparation activities for her first communion, an important cultural activity for many Latinxs. In these classes she met children from different socioeconomic backgrounds than her own. The differences between them—which she describes in terms of language, educational attitudes and achievement, and forms of dress— were perceivable to all. Gracia was forced to question her own Latinx identity as the other children called her "a whitey" (line 6), coming to realize that this is a racialization associated with social privilege. Her realization was aided by her mother's explanation that many Latinxs have fewer opportunities than she has had and have what she describes as a different mentality (i.e., they are less focused on education) (lines 22–23). Gracia understands this characterization as referring to the local population, but elsewhere in her interview she generalizes it to the US Latinx experience more broadly.

In Gracia's story, the local Latinx figure has certain characteristics and is defined in terms of immigration, education, and social class, with more-privileged Latinxs seen as outside of the norm. This image is racialized as non-White, irrespective of the physical appearances of the Latinxs involved (Gracia is mestiza). The way that Gracia speaks is conflated with her racialization as White; when the other children say to her, "You're such a whitey," they de/reracialize her and position her as an inauthentic Latina. Gracia explains that the way she talks is "educated," using the example of formal writing and doing well at school to support this point (lines 14–19), saying that this contrasts with "Hispanic stereotypes," as embodied by the children who reject her (lines 9–12). Indeed, Gracia uses pronunciations typical of middle-class White American English rather than Latinx English or African American features. In this brief excerpt from her interview, she uses the word "like" forty-two times in its discourse marker form, which is indexically associated with middle-class White Americans and particularly White women.[14] The raciolinguistic ideology that Gracia articulates resonates with discourses of language privilege and standardization, where White middle-class English is privileged as the unmarked norm and enjoys status over marked ethnic dialects such as Latino English or African American English.[15] However, in the story world's context, her way of speaking is not prestigious, in keeping with research showing that speech norms and prestige, while operating within broader hegemonic settings (Gracia is aware that Latinx-sounding children experience "stereotypes"), are context dependent.[16] In this Gracia's peers' evaluation of her English aligns with previous research where standard English is seen as White and inauthentic and where "sounding White" is mocked as inauthentic and seen as incompatible with Latinxness, while a more "Latinx" way of speaking enjoys covert prestige.[17]

Centering Salvadorans: Pride and Prejudice

Many participants' comments depicted the "local" social figure as Salvadoran or, by extension, Central American. While DC Latinxs celebrate diversity, they also perceive Salvadorans as locally prominent due to their numbers and visibility.

"Félix," an upper-middle-class Washingtonian Latino of mixed Caribbean and South American heritage who grew up in the affluent Northwest quadrant of the city, shared his perception of the DC Latinx community:

Excerpt 5.6

INTERVIEWER: So like, what do you think like what do you think has been sort of the like, like the Latino community in DC kind of,

FÉLIX: I think there's just a massive El Salvadorian um population here? I think that- I actually did this Learn Serve program where I went there and built houses?

INTERVIEWER: In El Salvador? [Cool.

FÉLIX: Mhm yeah for [um yeah it was a really neat experience. BUT um, I think that a lot of people here speak Spanish. There's just there's a lot of like immigrants in DC? Especially like wor- you see them working a lot in DC. U:m, and yeah I think it's definitely really prevalent.

INTERVIEWER: Is it 'cause that's a CHANGE right in the city? There did- it's a pretty sudden wave of immigration I think?

FÉLIX: Yeah there's definitely um, more like Latino people and like, but I mean they jus:t (.) it's nothing like- extremely noticeable.

INTERVIEWER: It's just sort of another, just kind of another wave of, people coming in?

FÉLIX: Yeah. There's there's just like SO many different people that like, you know there's, ALREADY every culture that, if you add a couple more from one culture I feel like no one's freaking out. (laughs) No no one's freaking out.

Félix characterizes the DC Latinx community as "a massive El Salvadorian population." As in the narratives above, this identity was class-associated ("workers"). While he himself identifies as a Latino Washingtonian, his use of the pronoun "them" rather than "we" shows that he considers the canonical figure to be different from himself. While he views DC Latinxs as working-class Salvadorans—in this case, immigrants—elsewhere in his interview he identifies as "international," which is a term that is both descriptive and often laden with class associations in the DC area.

Emanuel, a proud Salvadoran, centers Salvadorans in his Labovian narrative about their migration to DC.

Excerpt 5.7

EMANUEL: Whe:n, the Salvadorian war and the Nicaraguan- war, and the Guatemalan war and, conflict in Honduras so, Central America basically just exploded. So with THA:T (.) you know, we were like shrapnel you know (makes flying sound), we just flew everywhere. Some people fled to *Mé:xico*, you know, lot of people fled to *Costa Rica* (.) And a LOT of people just headed here headed north, you know. . . . All of a sudden in a matter of, I think between eighty and eight, fou:r? (.) It was just the largest influx of El Salvadorians an:, you know and a lot of us I think- you know (.) I think most of us, thought "Oh well we'll be out for a while and when things calm down we'll come back." I think that was the thinking on everybody's part. I don't think that most people came here with plans to stay. (burps) It was just uh, survival mode.

INTERVIEWER: But then they stayed?

EMANUEL: We HAVE stayed. We're the only- region in. The whole country where we're the majority, when it comes to Latino populations.

INTERVIEWER: Mmhmm. I had heard that from people 'cause they were always saying "Oh yeah El Sal[vadorian people" yeah,

EMANUEL: [Salvadorians. We rule here. Yeah. Yeah we're IT.

INTERVIEWER: Yeah?

EMANUEL: *Pupusa* power. (laughs)

However, he is also very aware that Salvadorans face prejudice.

Excerpt 5.8

EMANUEL: We got a lot of shit, you know from Latinos, for being who we are.

INTERVIEWER: Yeah?

EMANUEL: YEAH, especially our ACCent. 'Cause the majority of Latinxs here? Are um, *e:h*, ↑peasants. You know I come from the countryside. VERY LITTLE education, or some no education at all (.) So we get picked on, because *e:h* we talk like peasants. And we do.

INTERVIEWER: You get picked on by, like, just [all the other Latinxs in the area really?

EMANUEL: [Just- uh huh yeah uh huh.

Emanuel connects the language prejudice that Salvadorans face with social stereotypes related to their class positionality in Latin America, particularly because many DC-area Salvadorans come from rural areas. Emanuel accepts the evaluation of Salvadoran Spanish as sounding rural and uneducated, but he defiantly celebrates it as a symbol of identity and of pride in Salvadorans' accomplishments in DC ("we get made fun of . . . but we don't give a fuck").

Excerpt 5.9

EMANUEL: We get made fun of, being uh, but we don't give a fuck (laughs).

INTERVIEWER: There's more of you (laughs)

EMANUEL: ↑Yeah no but really you know what I mean, we take PRIDE in who- in who we are you know, I mean and then- I'm from the countryside so, ya know, I get teased both ways cause, . . . So, ↑yeah but you know *eh* it is what it is. So we- we are a very THRIVing community you know? Very entrepreneurial. There's shitloads of businesses in this area that belong to, to peasants. People that, started with washing dishes in restaurants and now OWN restaurants.

INTERVIEWER: Good for them. [Good for them.

EMANUEL: [Yeah, and there's a bunch of stories like that. Yeah or grocery store owners? There's a LO:T of them too.

As a proud Salvadoran Washingtonian, Emanuel challenges the deficit positioning imposed on Salvadorans and their language, and he celebrates their local dominance. He deepens this resistant stance through a small story in which he describes Salvadorans as "entrepreneurial" and "a very thriving community." He positions Salvadorans as worthy immigrants who worked their way up, American Dream style: "people that, started with washing dishes . . . and now own restaurants." This description echoes Salvadorans' image as hardworking, working-class "hustlers," as we saw in chapter 3 and will see in the next chapter, and echoes their overall class positionality in the United States.[18] The story articulates a moral discourse of deservingness and authenticity that echoes the "bootstraps" discourse well ingrained in the American national mythology, with the effect of legitimizing Salvadoran's local standing.[19] When he says, "We rule here" (excerpt 5.7) "to rule" means more than numeric presence. "Ruling" refers to identity, pride, and a sense of local prominence, and it stakes a claim of belonging that is directly rooted in the DC Latinx context.

Noemí contrasted Salvadoran's pride and presence with another group's smaller representation: "DC doesn't have a big Ecuadorian community, and like you can have like if you're Salvadoran in DC, you can have like so much pride you know so much fucking pride." Indeed, a Mexican survey respondent commented that Salvadorans say their Spanish is correct and Mexican Spanish is not—an interesting reversal of the usual US pattern. Mexican Spanish is generally dominant in the United States, leading Salvadorans to adopt to it in other areas of the country.[20] In DC, however, Salvadorans' local prominence changes this dynamic.

Voicing "mi gente"

We can see this social figure in discursive action as Héctor voices himself and others in several narratives that showcase his understanding of local Latinx identity. As part of this, he reflects on his own identity and positionality, including his experiences with class mobility as a formerly working-class, now middle-class, Latino; as a light-skinned mestizo; and as an artist and musician. In the process, he grapples with questions of race and class in the local environment and in the broader US and Latin American contexts.

He distinguishes between Latinxs and gringos (White Americans) but also Latinxs "like my family"—working-class, *mestizo*, Salvadoran/Central American, and locally rooted—and "White Latinos" from the Latin American bourgeois and upper classes. As he does so, he reflects on how racialization and diversity among Latinxs affect his personal sociolinguistic identity.

Excerpt 5.10

1 HÉCTOR: When I'm in um, a room full of Latinos, I get tongue-tied. I stutter. I,
2 don't know my TENses. I, preterite, subjunctive, and, blah blah blah blah, I don't- I don't
3 KNOW any of it, like, in my Spanish. My Spanish, you- I speak Spanish,
4 you know, people, down the street can hear me and be like, "his guy's a *gringo*."
5 Like, Latino- *entre Latinos*, I'm a *gringo*. I speak like an American. And it's funny it's like,
6 when I'm WITH people that LOOK like my family? I'm very cool with my Spanish, like it
7 comes out all right. But then, I had a guest here, a *latina*, contemporary, same peer- peer group,
8 and I couldn't talk, I would be- she was sitting on the mic and I was you know, sitting on the
9 mic cause, by the mic talking, and all of a sudden, you know, every time I tried to have a conversation
10 with her in Spanish, I just stuttered, I stopped I- my tongue got tied, like I just couldn't DO it
11 because . . . it's like when I'm with my people my Whiteness or my *gringoness*
12 comes out a lot more, but then when I'm with people that look like my family, like when it
13 comes with like WHITE *latinos, se me traba la lengua*. But when it comes to people who
          I get tongue-tied
14 look more *mestizo*, I'm much more comfortable with them. And so when I, talk to Emanuel,
15 like *"Aha y qué pasó vos?"* You know like that *"y, y qué? Qué pasó?"* He's like *"Sí hombre,"*
       and what's up [with] you?   and, and what['s up]? What's up?   Yeah man
16 blah blah blah, like we can talk like that. But then when I'm talking to like, the DJ crews
17 that I deal with, you know, they're very rich and posh-y and very well-educated and,
18 they're still *latino* but they're like (.) You know that, Lat- yeah, you know they're wearing
19 their indigenous print scarves and being all coo:l and, and hipster Latino'd out, you know, like,
20 long hair, and the five-o-clock shadow thing, and, and being quirky, ETHnic, Afro-neon,
21 hipster thing

Héctor's relationship to Latinx identity shifts depending on the scale he is discussing. He considers himself Latinx yet differentiates between himself as a G2 Latinx and "real" Latinxs. He then recalibrates "my people" to a local, race-, and class-associated schema to explain the language and identity insecurity he experiences and how he negotiates social encounters with other Latinxs.

He begins by noting tensions and insecurity in his own relationship to Spanish and to Latinx identity. In supporting examples, he discusses feeling comfortable or awkward around different types of Latinxs he encounters. Héctor feels uncomfortable around "posh" Latinxs due to their differences from the people he is used to, who "look like [his] family" (line 12). He shares a sequence of small stories as evidence of different Latinx positionings and how they affect him. In these stories he establishes an "us versus them" dynamic in which he, his family, and friends from the community are positioned in opposition to elite Latinxs, whom he presents as rich, "posh," and "well-educated" (line 17) and whom he racializes as White (line 13). He identifies these other Latinxs as part of the privileged "international" Latinxs of DC, whom he sees as different from local Latinxs. His comments on the intersection of race and privilege reflect broader hierarchies in Latin America, replicated among US Latinxs, where (similar to the United States) Whiteness is associated with privilege.[21] Meanwhile, he also confronts the idea of Whiteness in the sense of assimilation or deculturalization and deracialization through needing to prove his own Latinx identity due to his heritage Spanish ("I sound like a gringo") and light skin.

Language directly influences Héctor's identity in both his storyworld identity construction and his reported real-world interactions. He reports that "posh Latinxs" affect his language production, whereas around "his kind" of Latinx, he feels more comfortable and can speak freely. As he describes this, Héctor uses a particular kind of voice in constructed dialogue to voice the local Latinx in-group (as opposed to the "international Latinx Other") and assign them a sociolinguistic identity.[22] This voice is colloquial; Salvadoran, using the pronoun *"vos"* with the rising intonation other participants mentioned;[23] and masculine (*"hombre"*) as he constructs dialogue that is typical of his interactions with a friend (line 15). His use of

Salvadoran language is consistent with other research on US Salvadorans constructing shared identity through marked dialectal features.[24] The voicing also allows him to portray a kind of tough masculinity in line with the image of local Salvadorans as "street," similar to the way other colloquial gendered terms, such as American English "dude" and Mexican Spanish "*güey*," can construct "cool masculinity."[25] Héctor's voicing indexes the local social figure and separates it from the privileged Latinx Other, around whom he literally becomes voiceless. Meanwhile, his pronunciation of the words "posh" and "cool" evoke privileged Whiteness through exaggerated articulation ("posh") and lengthening and fronting of the /u/ vowel in "cool," rendering it something like "kewl" (lines 17 and 19). These stylized pronunciations, which scholars have found can carry associations with Whiteness and related meanings of prissiness and uncoolness, linguistically enrich his portrayal of the Other.[26]

In another example, Héctor shared a Labovian narrative about a reported conflict with an "Othered" Latinx that occurred at his girlfriend's house.

Excerpt 5.11

1   HÉCTOR: Like, this happened actually, over at, at Sarah's house the other night. One of-
2   some friend of- we, Sarah and I walked, into the house, and, one of the roommates was
3   cooking, and then there was this GUY standing there. He looked like Marc Anthony, he
4   ACTED like Marc Anthony you know, and apparently he was Puerto Rican too. He's just a
5   short, shorter version of him. So he says the traditional stuff to me and all this other stuff, and
6   then . . . Um, but no, this dude, he introduced me (*sic*) and then he asked, for my name and I
7   said (subdued tone) "My name is *Héctor*." (clicks tongue) (speaking rapidly)"¡Héctor!
8   ¡Héctor! Where you from, *Héctor*?" You know I'm like, I'm from here. He goes,
9   (clicks tongue) "*No pero* why- where's your accent- where's your name from, where is your
10 family from." So I explain and he gets, he goes "¡↑Ay!" Like he's like "↑Wow! Dude, that's
11 ↑GREAT!" And he's all like (snaps fingers) you know, ch-ch. And I'm like, "THIS
12 motherfucker," like, "You got me in a bad day" (taps table twice for emphasis). And (.) and
13 he started TALKing, and shit and I just went on DEfense at this point. (.) And so I even told,
14 I was being nice, because there was a whole bunch of the housemates in the area. So I just
15 tried to usher my way away, I was like I'm gonna be cool, I'm gonna go away first. And then

16 I told- went towards one uh, of the ROOMmates and I was like "Dude, I don't like this guy."
17 I'm like "I'm just gonna be straight up with you, I don't like this guy." Yeah, so, this guy
18 gave me, gave me grief and I just tried to get away from him as much as possible.

Conflict narratives are well known for highlighting identity construction.[27] Héctor tells this story as an example of how he felt that his identity was questioned and his ethnocultural authenticity challenged by a "posh" Latino. Upon being introduced to the man, he is asked where he is from. He responds, "I'm from here," staking a claim to US Latinx identity (line 8), but is pressed to further identify himself. Héctor resents being questioned about his identity and feels that the man's response is condescending. He distances himself from the other man by portraying him as a foreign, elite Latinx, and cheesily stereotypical through exaggerated voicing and imitation of his body language.

Throughout the narrative, Héctor voices himself with a local Latinx voice—urban, and AAE-influenced through lexicon and intonation. For example, the word "motherfucker" is emphasized with increased volume on the adjective "THIS," and he uses a low-high pitch contour on "you got me in a ↑bad day."[28] In contrast, he uses high pitch, swooping inflection, stereotypical exclamations, and sounds ("ch-ch") to voice the Other and present him as exaggeratedly Latino, a performance that includes body language (fingers snapping, shoulder motions) (lines 6–11). Héctor's use of a "street" voice in English bilingually rebuts the constructed Other—"THIS motherfucker, you got me in a bad day" (lines 11–12). This voicing evokes a tough, masculine persona to distinguish his local, working-class Latinx identity from that of the "posh" Latinx with whom he is in conflict and echoes his earlier construction of the same social figure using Salvadoran Spanish.

Along with Héctor's description of the man as acting like a celebrity (the singer Marc Anthony, lines 3–4), this portrayal ridicules him, undermining his right to judge Héctor's Latinidad and drawing a discursive distance between them, which is reinforced by Héctor's blunt statement, emphasized through repetition: "I don't like this guy" (lines 16–17). This stance allows Héctor to reposition himself based on an understanding of Latinxness that relates to noneliteness (understood along intersecting dimensions of social class and race) and is centered on local norms ("here") rather than Latin America. Ultimately, his telling reifies his own positioning and claim to his identity as a local Latino. Drawing Héctor's examples together, we see that despite his linguistic insecurity, he uses both Spanish and English to bilingually construct a local Latino persona whose legibility depends on the intricacies of local race and class dynamics.

Héctor's examples highlight the importance of the body in raciolinguistic ideologies as he navigates embodied discourses about Latinx identity that he both espouses and does not exactly fit. Language is a nuanced part of his identity construction. For Héctor, Spanish is simultaneously a symbol of Latino identity and a means by which he is Othered. He both internalizes and pushes back against this dynamic, defending a local, working-class mestizo Latinx identity against Othered, international White Latinxs. His own positionality as a light-skinned mestizo Latino heightens the pressure he feels to demonstrate his Latinx identity linguistically. He does not want to be deracialized as a "whitey" or "*gringo/a*," as Gracia was or as Celia was in chapter 3. Nor does he identify as a bourgeois "White Latino" (excerpt 5.10) along lines of Latin American privilege. While he feels that his Latinx authenticity is undermined by his nonnative Spanish fluency, he uses both English and Spanish—and particular kinds of English and Spanish—to construct and authenticate a bilingual, locally grounded self while pushing back against different aspects of class and race hegemony among Latinxs.

We can now sum up several key elements of the social figure that participants described. It is mestizo and nonelite: working class, or a deserving middle class that has worked its way up in an echo of the "bootstraps" moral narrative that immigrants, including Latinxs, have been shown to espouse.[29] This social figure is viewed as non-White in terms of privilege associations within both a US and a Latin American framework. It is associated with Salvadorans, both immigrants and their US-born, or at least US-raised, children. It is bilingual, although its bilingualism is derided. It "sounds Black" and "sounds Salvadoran" (or Central American, more broadly) and is considered to "sound street" or "sound ghetto" in both languages. Finally, while its Salvadoran roots are rural, it is firmly seen as an urban identity in DC through its local associations. While the social figure is regarded with a mixture of respect and disdain, it looms large in the local imagination and is associated with a particular kind of local identity and claim to authenticity and belonging.

This image, manifested through language, also appears in the arts—an important means of how communities understand identity.[30] The local raciomultilingual repertoire and the social circumstances that formed it appear in spoken-word poems and theater by acclaimed local artists such as Quique Avilés, examined by Ana Patricia Rodríguez in her work on transnational Salvadoran identities in the DC area. Performances pointed to an African American–influenced fusion culture in which the voices evoked ranged from Salvadoran Spanish to heritage Spanish and African American English in the younger generation—what Rodríguez calls "Wachintonian"—African Americanized Salvadoran Spanglish, borrowing Avilés's term for Salvadorans who have made DC home.[31]

Naming "Glocal" Class Dynamics

In global cities such as DC, local and global forces can come together to create new "glocal" phenomena.[32] Participants applied a label to class differences that was, as the saying goes in the city, "very DC"—they used the term "international." DC and its metropolitan area, as the seat of US government and international politics and their surrounding ecosystems, are rich in embassies, international organizations, universities, nonprofits, international businesses, and more, as well as the US State Department, Department of Defense, and many other aspects of governance. The international sector tends to be seen as transient, as compared to local Washingtonians, who have put down roots in the area.

This environment gives rise to an international white-collar sector. "International" Latinxs tend to be highly educated and associated with the Latin American bourgeoisie.[33] This figure has race associations, where international Latinxs are imagined as White due to class and race intersections in Latin America, where being of European descent is privileged and tends to correlate with a higher social position, not the idea of "trying to be White" in the sense of "trying to be American." We saw this in Héctor's example, where he clearly sets "White" Latinxs apart from the working-class, mestizo, Central American social figure that he identifies with and that participants saw as proverbially local. On the other hand, Félix distances himself from the local Latinx social figure by describing himself as "international." "Carolina"—an upper-middle-class woman in her early twenties who came to DC from Bolivia as a child—similarly uses the term "international" to distance herself from aspects of "Latinx" identity that she finds unappealing.

Excerpt 5.12

INTERVIEWER: Are your friends like mostly American or international or,

CAROLINA: I have a LOT of like international friends. It's, I (.) It's NOT like I don't like Hispanic people? Because I'm Hispanic, it's, I CAN't say I don't like Hispanic people? (.) But they have, different . . . eduCAtion sometimes (.)in the sense that . . . most of the Hispanic people I know? (.) And unfortunately most of the Hispanic people at [college]A? they enjoy drinki:ng a:nd, I'm not a drinking per↑son, so:, I'm OPen to being friends with, ANy, people but I have certai:n VALues that, it's hard to, have Hispanic friends? Because they don't, share those values? Even if they- (.) I don't mind if they drink? But they PRESsure you to drink, and that's another thing so.

INTERVIEWER: It's with like different values of how you act and like,

CAROLINA: ExACTly.

INTERVIEWER: Like drinking in particular, or like other things too?

CAROLINA: WE:LL (.) mostly drinking.

INTERVIEWER: Oh (laughs), [it's a big one though I mean if you're gonna hang out.

CAROLINA: [Yeah. It's a big one! I mean it's (.) if you DON't drink they, they call you like BORing: a:nd, how they pressure you a lot.

Carolina distinguishes between "international" people, including Latin Americans like herself, and the local Latinxs who are her classmates at a public college. She distances herself from these peers based on attributed behavior, which she frames as conflicting values: her studiousness and avoidance of alcohol as opposed to her perception of Latinxs not taking education seriously and liking to drink and party—a common stereotype.[34]

Deficit Discourses of Deculturalization

Many participant comments centered on later-generation Latinxs raised in the DC area. In addition to the stereotypes we have seen, there was a sense of anxiety about cultural loss and what would replace it. Participants believed that the second generation is "losing their language," by which they mean Spanish, and they viewed this as a personal deficiency, leading to the insecurity and fear of judgment that Héctor described, which I have explored in other work.[35]

Colombian José, from a middle-class background, illustrated these anxieties about cultural loss and what that entails through an example from his own family.

Excerpt 5.13

JOSÉ: My COUsin who is, he was BORN in Colombia, but he pretty much grew up here, because he came here when I was like two, so his Spanish is like very broken:, a:nd his wife is pretty much the same. Oh no, I'm lying! He was born in New Jersey.

INTERVIEWER: Oh, so he's [fully, second generation.

JOSÉ: [He was born in New Jersey, he's fully American, he's fully second-generation American, um, Colombian, sorry. So his Spanish is very broken. His wife is also like that, so that was the first, like, 'cause you know we would have like cheese plate with wine, and they were like "Oh, can we join?" And they would, you know, they'll bring, Velveeta cheese, right, Velveeta cheese with some chips and salsa and we were like eating grapes with, you know, some Roquefort cheese or something like that. So that was funny. But YEAH, it was VERY different in that sense 'cause we, we would get together and play games, lot of, lot of, lot of, um (.) We had a round table? We make sure we bought a dinner table that was round.

continued

Excerpt 5.13 *continued*

INTERVIEWER: That's cool

JOSÉ: Yeah, that was, that was, that kind of the thing. So we always SAT in that table and always played CARDS and things like that and they weren't as: (.) We had to DRAG them there. They weren't as willing, to be, part of that kind of thing.

In this anecdote about social occasions, José describes his cousin as "fully second generation." This description indexes a set of meanings that include but are not limited to Spanish ability. His description of his cousin as "fully American" sets him apart from José and his Latin American friends, with his cousin's "very broken" Spanish—the description repeated twice for emphasis—presented as characteristic of the second generation. José develops the distance between them through two small stories about conflicting social norms. In the first, food choices serve as examples of US-born Latinxs being lower class. While José and his friends eat a "cheese plate and wine," with this food's classy connotations, his cousin and his wife are not aware of the semiotics of an appropriate cheese plate and contribute processed Velveeta cheese—an unsophisticated choice. He also describes how his cousin and his wife have trouble integrating into the communal social ambience of José's group house. In his telling, their reluctance to play cards indicates a lack of shared socialization norms and demonstrates the cultural divide between them and the Latin Americans.

We can see that when participants index class, they mean more than socioeconomic status—they also mean symbolic capital related to higher social status, in which evaluations of different lifestyles and ways of being invoke and legitimize the existing social order.[36] Here I draw on work by Pierre Bourdieu and other well-known sociologists. Narration and discourse, along with other social practices, construct what feminist sociologist Beverly Skeggs calls "classed personhood," which has distinctive characteristics that are embodied by particular kinds of people and their voices. Further, "class formation is . . . fought out at the level of the symbolic."[37] So the question of "good taste"—represented by the cheese plate as an example of sophisticated consumption—also serves as a class index in which, as Skeggs articulates, not having taste is associated with the lower social class.

In the examples we have seen, G1 and G2 immigrants positioned each other as lacking symbolic capital as a way of representing differences between them but along different cultural axes.[38] Thus, some Latin Americans looked down on US-born Latinxs as low class, lacking authentic culture, and troublesomely associated with gangs and other undesirable behavior—a discourse that resonates with the stereotype of the "American-born lower-class Latino" as well as the social and material challenges that many Latinxs face in the United States—problems from which DC is not exempt.[39] Meanwhile, Noemí's comments about her classmates "trying too hard" positioned assimilating immigrants as low class if they oriented to low-prestige US practices. These attitudes speak to the complex dynamics that underlie the "classed nature of social and cultural practices" in a transnational context.[40] There is a flip side, of course, where G2 immigrants admire Latin Americans' cultural knowledge, and G1 immigrants admire later-generation Latinxs' bilingualism—although, as we have seen, their bilingualism is heavily policed and often considered to be lacking.

Jody Agius Vallejo refers to the stereotype of Latinxs as low class as the "immigrant shadow," whereby Latinxs are assumed not to be middle class even if they have worked their way up in the second generations.[41] Noemí alludes to this shadow when she considers "more recent immigrants" to be déclassé; José may be insulated from it by his own social positioning and that of his friends—a reflection of the DC area's class dynamics, where both a sizable middle-class and elite Latinx population and more traditional immigrants are found. Inés's concern that US-raised youth are losing their home cultures also reflects an awareness of this shadow—a fear that they will be decultured but still raced and classed into an undesirable position.[42] She worried that in the absence of a strong sense of their original cultures, Latinx youth—specifically Salvadorans and other Central Americans—were vulnerable to negative self-imagery. Media representation plays a major role in how social figures are understood, and Central Americans tend to be ignored in US media except in stereotypes about gangs, violence, and immigration issues.[43]

Excerpt 5.14

INÉS: The Mexican takes over to the whole entire Latino America because, they promote their culture and they are always, you know they are very: um, *cómo se dice orgulloso?* PROUD of their culture. And then Mexico here Mexico there and then:, you know (.) uh what you hear on the news in El Salvador and Guatemala is all bad ↑news (taps table). All the ↑TIME so there is nothing that is proMOTing their CULture nothing for the kids to feel, you know PROUD of.

INTERVIEWER: Oh because even if there is a Latino month it's all *Cinco de Mayo* and, [like piñatas and stuff (laughs)

INÉS: [Exactly, exactly. You're right. Right, so there's not much of the promotion of our own culture unless in the festival then you SEE it. And but that is not too many kids, you know first they get interested in the *reggaetón* and all that type of music (.) More than, the cultural music the folk music.

Scholars of Central American diaspora note that Central Americans do grapple with cultural *brechas*, gaps or disconnects, due to the region's turmoil. Many have experienced generational trauma, leading to cultural wounds and a rupture in transmission reinforced by official narratives of forgetting that encourage collective silence.[44] Further, Central Americans are invisibilized in the United States, both due to the country's tendency to equate "Latinx" with "Mexican" and as a survival strategy.[45] However, Inés's concerns also shed light into how participants viewed cultural authenticity. She uses a music comparison to contrast the US-raised youth's preference for *reggaetón* (a Caribbean-origin fusion dance genre that has gained international popularity) with the "cultural" or "folk" music that she sees as representative of "our own culture[s]." The contrast positions traditional music as a symbol of the authentic culture that the youth lack, in Kathryn Woolard's sense of authenticity as a perceived "genuine expression of a community or of a person's essential 'Self'. . . . deeply rooted in social and geographic territory."[46] The centering of "culture" in immigrants' countries of origin deauthenticates the fusion culture that Latinxs evolved in DC, even as this culture is celebrated through local outlets as varied as the arts, media, libraries, museums, and community events. However, more recognition is needed. Local musician Cindy Zavala, "La SalvadoReina," commented on this lack in an interview with WAMU 88.5, DC's National Public Radio station, in 2015: "You go to Mt. Pleasant, you go to Columbia Heights, you go to Georgia Avenue—it's predominantly Salvadoran. . . . They're playing their music and they're sharing their culture, but nobody has someone to look up to when it comes to culture in our area."[47] The gap inspired her to start performing a hip-hop-infused *cumbia* (a traditional dance music originally from Colombia but popular throughout Latin America, with many regional variations) to give voice and visibility to this aspect of the local community.

Imagining Local Latinidad

The social figure outlined in this chapter is an image of local Latinidad that has a powerful grip on the local imagination. However, this social figure itself is complex and contested.

Ambiguous Referents

Salvadorans' local importance is highlighted by its central role in how this social figure is imagined. The depictions reveal an ambiguous positionality in which Salvadorans serve as a reference point but are still subject to social and linguistic prejudice. This ambiguous position differs from the positionality of, for example, Cubans in Miami, where they are both the majority group and socially privileged, and from Mexicans in Los Angeles, where they are the unquestioned dominant local group.[48] Salvadorans' contested image in DC is more in line with Puerto Ricans' ambiguous position in New York's Latinx social hierarchy:[49] their presence and sociocultural prominence make them an important local reference point, but they are also stigmatized due to racialized associations and relative poverty. Unlike

Puerto Ricans, DC's Central Americans are not imagined as Afro-Latinx, but they are racialized as non-White and are considered to have proximity to Blackness through peer assimilation. What these comparisons show us is that local hierarchies are complex. They draw on local material circumstances, which themselves often connect to relative privilege in immigrants' countries of origin and the circumstances of their migration. They also reflect broader US and Latin American stereotypes of race, class, education, and more, which privilege Whiteness over Blackness and indigeneity.

The local social figure is considered to "sound Latinx" through a repertoire that encompasses Latinx English, Salvadoran Spanish, and African American–influenced English. In the DC area, Salvadorans and African Americans—both majority groups in their own ways—are seen as local. There is a sense of belonging and pride. Salvadorans are seen, and view themselves, as fundamental parts of the community and the city and are rightfully proud of their accomplishments. Participants also viewed African Americans as a fundamental part of DC—perhaps especially since they are the main point of contact for many Latinxs during the immigration and acculturation experience. Since both groups are viewed as local, the meshing of their language in the Latinx repertoire is seen as normal—an artifact of language and cultural contact in a shared non-White space and a symbol of local identity.

At the same time, broader ideologies of race and class still hold sway. Participants repeatedly described Salvadoran Spanish and Black English with stereotypical pejoratives such as "street" and "ghetto." Crosslinguistic comparisons with Black language—variously described as "not real . . . not what you would find in a dictionary" and "broken down"—furthered the deficit discourse about Salvadoran Spanish. Participants contrasted the local social figure and its associated linguistic repertoire with mainstream American English, which they associated with higher social class and education but also with "sounding White," which brought its own judgments such as not being a "real" Latinx. While Whiteness functions as an index for social and educational privilege and linguistic correctness, in the United States it is often also seen as suburban and inauthentic.[50] Similarly, non-Whiteness can be associated with urban authenticity and "real" culture, particularly in representations of African Americans and Latinxs.[51] These meanings are relevant in the DC context, especially with gentrification, as we will see in the next chapter.

The local voice is also stigmatized in terms of its bilingualism, or perceived lack thereof, in later generations. Héctor noted that "sounding like a gringo" and being "tongue-tied" undermined his claim to Latino identity—a common belief and one that caused him linguistic and social insecurity. José cited language loss as part of cultural loss, which he associated with the second generation—a broader anxiety that many participants shared. Recall, however, that heritage bilingualism and new linguistic practices are often misunderstood. Héctor's internalized sense of being less-than is belied by his sophisticated bilingual voicing in his narratives and by his use of Spanish in real-world contexts to communicate with family and others.

By using a bilingual "DC Latinx" voice in his narratives to distinguish locals from "international" Latinxs, Héctor reclaimed the local voice as a source of pride and used it to navigate race and class differences among DC Latinxs in a way he could not have done in only English or Spanish. The full repertoire was necessary for this identity performance. In Héctor's telling, too, race is made salient along a different class dimension—that of Latin American privilege, where the local figure contrasted with "White Latinos" from the Latin American upper classes. This distinction is local and transnational at the same time: the raciolinguistic discourses that inform it circulate across geographical and political borders but are reified and reinterpreted in light of DC social relations.

The raciomultilingual lens allows us to see dynamic aspects of identity that challenge accepted notions of language and cultural boundaries while at the same time examining how existing ideologies continue to affect social imagination. Participants' attitudes toward Black language and culture encompassed expanded racialization, where "sounding Black" is normalized, but there is also lingering prejudice. While AAE was seen as a normal part of the repertoire, and one that may simply be part of "sounding local" to many, it was not semiotically bleached of its original raciolinguistic indexicalities:[52] participants do not deny Black cultural influence on local Latinxs. The youth they describe, and which we observed in the playground recordings, are not pretending to be Black or crossing into a linguistic identity that does not belong to them. Rather, they acquired Black-influenced English through peer socialization in the local culture, and this language became part of the distinct local Latinx repertoire. At the same time there is still a sense of distinct ethnocultural groupings and boundaries. Noemí referenced this tension around racialized identities to discursively distance herself from her childhood peers, viewing too much assimilation as inauthentic. As she stated, she felt like some of the Latinas around her who oriented to African American culture (indexed by language and hairstyle) were "kind of like trying, to be Black themselves." Participants overall viewed Black influence as an aspect of local Latinidad that emerged naturally from contact rather than an attempt to discard Latinx identity, which—as Noemí's comment makes clear—would be seen as inappropriate. However, raciolinguistic ideologies stigmatizing Black language persisted, despite the deep relational bonds that many participants had with African Americans. Finally, I note that the paradigm may well be different for Afro-Latinxs, who orient to Blackness—as distinct from African Americanness—in different and complex ways, an important direction for future investigation in cities like DC.[53]

While gender has not been the focus of this chapter, it is nevertheless an interesting consideration. Héctor's voicing was gendered as well as classed and raced, constructing an image of "tough masculinity" that resonates with broader US discourses that associate urban areas with minority men through stereotypes of violence but also see these men as sites of authentic ethnoracial authenticity.[54] Meanwhile, Gracia and Noemí did not use these stigmatized repertoire elements and used features such as "like," which are associated with White female speech. This usage is in line with the general sociolinguistic theory that young women are more likely to conform to mainstream linguistic norms and avoid stigmatized features, including ethnic-associated features, that may be more acceptable for men.[55] Similarly, it was women, not men, who attempted to distance themselves from Salvadoran Spanish. These findings should be seen as suggestive rather than representative of a "female Latina" pattern. Rather, their importance lies in revealing raciomultilingual ideologies and their uptake in the local environment.

Discursive Heterogeneity

The social figure we have examined is a central, if contested, referent for local Latinidad. However, this does not mean that it is the only one. Multiple narratives coexist about DC Latinx identity. By providing a multilevel perspective, the scalar raciomultilingual approach allows us to see this heterogeneity as natural and normal while at the same time providing a cohesive framework.

Participants were well aware of diversity among Latinxs, and these differences were a source of identity and pride. Diversity itself is seen as an identifying characteristic of DC Latinxs—as, indeed, it is of the region as a whole. At the same time, divisions are present, particularly in relationship to intersectional discourses of social class and its proxies. These discourses function in terms of US social beliefs but also in terms of Latin American ones. Stereotypes in this paradigm are also reductive. Salvadoran Spanish—conflated with a rural, working-class variety—is seen as a local identity marker, but Salvadorans themselves noted more class and regional diversity than is generally visible to others. Salvadoran Spanish tends to be seen as a proxy for Central American language at higher scalar levels. Other Latinxs were apt to lump them together; Perla, from Peru, commented that unless she hears *"pupusa"* or *"baleada"* (traditional foods of El Salvador and Honduras, respectively), she cannot tell these speakers apart. However, Central Americans were aware of differences. As a young Salvadoran man who worked in construction commented, *"Es que en Centroamérica hablan varios acentos. Nicaragua, Honduras, son diferentes."* (It is that in Central America they speak [with] different accents. Nicaragua, Honduras, are different [than Salvadoran Spanish].)

Research on the ways in which Latinx identity is linguistically constructed in the DC metropolitan region sheds new light into the diversity of experiences contained within broad notions of "Latinidad" and the ways in which cohesion and tension coexist and are perceived with local communities and their understandings of the broader ethnocultural identity. These findings add a linguistic dimension to more general research on how Latinxs understand and negotiate diversity, cohesion, and tension among themselves. Latinidad is internally diverse and contested, incorporating many factors—among them, citizenship, relationship to home country, upbringing, education, race, language[56]—that Latinxs use to negotiate intragroup identities and social positioning. Frances Aparicio notes that increasingly diverse Latin American migration leads to "new forms of interaction, affinities, and power dynamics between and among Latinas/os from various national groups" as well as "different forms of affiliations, solidarity, identifications, desire, and intermarriage among Latinas/os."[57] DC-area Latinxs have a sense of shared identity based on a common language and cultural similarities as well as collective local interests and an awareness of marginalization in the United States. They are also very aware of diversity among themselves, which is a source of both pride and tension. Their negotiated (dis)affiliations, as manifested through language and "talk about language," shine a light on how complex and uniquely local understandings of identity relate to the broader picture of migration and "making a new place home."

Conclusions

The importance of a raciomultilingual perspective is foregrounded in this chapter, where crosslinguistic ideologies affect perceptions of participants' Spanish and English and the ways they are used and understood together. Without examining how racialized language ideologies intersect and relate to the multilingual repertoire as a whole, important aspects of the local Latinx figure and its voicing—as well as its implications for Latinxs' social relations and immigrant and diasporic contexts more generally—could not be understood.

This perspective advances the theoretical conversation, allowing for the coexistence of multiple, sometimes contradictory discourses in coalescing Latinx group identity as well as the evolution of new language norms with their own referential ideological centers of authenticity and the racialization of place-related linguistic identity. Participants constructed their sociolinguistic identities in relationship to multiple local and broader scales: ideologies are transmitted (trans)nationally but recentered locally, as language and ethnicity are reinterpreted and complexified in relation to the DC social landscape. My findings add insight into the heterogeneity and dynamism—rather than homogeneity—inherent among Latinxs and other minoritized groups and the ways in which ethnic identification is constructed and negotiated through language.[58]

A raciomultilingual framework offers a principled means of investigating how new identities are created in later immigrant generations through the interaction of language repertoires and complex, sometimes contradictory ideologies of race, ethnicity, class, culture, and more. These beliefs relate to broader cultural discourses ultimately traceable to colonial thought but also accrue compelling new meanings in the local environment. But shades of gray are present—as participants' comments show, normalization does not mean semiotic bleaching, as new local meanings and local and broader stereotypes can coexist. This nuanced understanding underscores that migrants and their descendants are not tabula rasa, as Devyani Sharma points out: they bring homeland ideologies with them, and these can continue to evolve if the diasporic links remain current.[59] But they are also not tabula rasa in terms of perceptions of the receiving country. For example, my participants reported already having a racialized view of "American" as White upon their arrival in the United States due to media consumption, a perception that lingers in their normalization of Whiteness as "American" and African American language, for example, as existing in relationship to this norm. However, participants' comments show an added element of hybrid identity construction that is specific to DC's local ethnoracial dynamics. Without taking DC's current and historical social situation into account, they could not be understood.

6

"We're Washingtonians"

Constructing Local Identity and Authenticity

I was introduced to Marcos—the subject of this chapter—by mutual friends at a bar where he was celebrating his birthday. After learning about my research, he invited me to interview him at his home, where I also met his wife and son. It was a pleasant day when I interviewed Marcos, and I walked from the Georgia Avenue Metro stop to his home in the Petworth neighborhood in Northwest DC. The neighborhood was still primarily Black, older, and working to middle class—as the *Washington Post* put it the year before, "on the verge of gentrification"—but without the demographic changes and new businesses that have taken place since then.[1] Marcos and I spoke in his kitchen for over two hours as he shared his thoughts on DC and its Latinx community, sometimes in response to my questions about language and identity but often unprompted.

Marcos is a proud Washingtonian, a second-generation man of Salvadoran and Mexican heritage, born and raised in the District of Columbia. Marcos grew up in a working-class, single-parent household during the 1980s, a decade that saw Latinx community growth fueled by Central American migration. The 1980s were also a period of economic struggle in DC, along with social problems such as the crack cocaine epidemic and a high crime rate. However, they are also remembered as years of cultural richness. Go-go bands, the iconic DC music, flourished, as did local clothing brands such as Universal Madness and events such as Halloween block parties with "people walking around with real pumpkins on their heads"—all phenomena mentioned by Marcos during his interview.

Marcos grew up in Latinx and Black neighborhoods. When he was a teenager, his mother attempted to keep him out of trouble by moving across the city line—although the DC/Maryland border suburbs also turned out to be plagued by violence. Later she tried again to keep him out of trouble by sending him to El Salvador to live with family for a year. However, Marcos always viewed DC as home. He returned to the city for good after serving in the military. He now lives in the Petworth neighborhood, a historically Black, low- to middle-income neighborhood, with his wife, who is White; his young son; and an old friend who rents part of the house.

No single experience represents all Latinxs in the DC area. Nevertheless, Marcos sees himself as a representative Washingtonian Latino. My interviews and ethnography make it clear that his perception of a particular kind of "DC Latinidad" is shared by others. His interview is thus an instructive look at how DC Latinxs imagine their collective identity as *Washingtonian* Latinxs while still (as seen in previous chapters) recognizing diversity among themselves.

Throughout his interview Marcos constructs an "authentic Washingtonian" identity, which is mutually exclusive with gentrifier identity. The discourses he draws on about who "real Washingtonians" are related to race, diversity, culture, values, and continuity as part of rootedness in DC as a place with its own unique identity. As Marcos speaks, he constructs Washingtonian and, specifically, Washingtonian Latinx identity, through the languages and dialects he uses to tell his story and through his portrayal of himself and others. Changing social circumstances such as gentrification tend to increase the desire for authenticity, or the notion of what is "real or true."[2] Marcos's argument for belonging is of broader significance, as gentrification displaces DC's poorer minorities in favor of wealthier, often White residents.

Languaging Identity

Language's role in identity construction relies on both style and discourse. As people talk, their speech style adapts to different situations, people, and topics. Deliberately or not, they emphasize or downplay different aspects of their identities through language.[3] Language choice; translanguaging; and differences in pronunciation, grammar, and vocabulary can all signal identity—theories that I present in more depth in chapter 1.[4] This flexible "languaging" simultaneously shapes and reflects attitudes and ideologies so that what it means to "sound Latinx," "sound Washingtonian," or both, are socially grounded but able to evolve. For example, a study of adolescents in a majority-Latinx school in California found that Chicano English's ethnic association became secondary in relation to local meanings of "being normal" and "being cool," even for non-Latinxs, whereas in this context Whiteness was seen as "other."[5]

Marcos's linguistic repertoire is wide. He "languages" fluidly—indeed, he describes himself as a linguistic "chameleon" who uses his full repertoire to "get things done." Marcos is bilingual in English and Spanish and was exposed to both languages from birth. He learned Salvadoran Spanish from his family and his time in El Salvador. He also learned Mexican Spanish through his paternal family and reports being able to shift between the two as needed. His English reflects Latinx and African American speech patterns. This, too, varies. During our interview, he used more ethnic-associated language while speaking about the past and "authentic" DC, and less when talking about the present day or neutral topics such as scheduling a follow-up interview. He considers Black and Latinx English (LE) to be his "original" way of speaking, although he feels he has also acquired a more mainstream way of speaking as he became more "middle class."

People also construct their own identities and project identities onto others through narratives. Stories are an important part of how we construct the world and its inhabitants. Canonical stories—with beginnings, sequences of events in the middle, and ends—are a powerful way to portray ourselves and others as particular kinds of people and to seize—or disrupt—the moral high ground.[6] However, storytelling is not limited to canonical narratives. "Small stories," everyday retellings of events real or imagined, or even about nothing in particular, also play an important role in identity construction.

In addition to the stories we tell and the ways that we tell them, our orientations to different topics help construct the identities that we present to the world. The stances we take project our identities and position us as particular kinds of people.[7] This type of identity work is particularly relevant in situations when there are contested claims to belonging, such as the gentrification debate in DC, where different groups dispute their moral rights to the city.[8] For example, we will see Marcos take positive stances toward Washingtonians and their culture and negative stances toward gentrifiers and the values (or lack thereof) and behavior that they embody. He positions himself, and other native or long-term Washingtonians, as authentic residents and legitimizes their claim to the city while simultaneously delegitimizing gentrifiers—portrayed as wealthy new residents who are displacing "real Washingtonians" and, importantly, do not share their values or make an effort to participate in local culture and community. While talk may seem ephemeral, it ties into broader beliefs about people and places. Like other habitual behavior, it can further or change these beliefs. Identities are talked into being.

In the following sections we will see how Marcos constructs an authentic Washingtonian identity through describing the city and different kinds of residents, seen as opposites: "locals" and "gentrifiers." As he does so, his language itself reflects these divides. Marcos uses Spanish, LE, and African American English (AAE) when discussing topics related to the "real," pregentrification DC. Linguistic features include the low, backed /ae/, trilled r, /ɪ/ raising, and syllable timing typical of LE, as well as Spanish itself, which echoes the well-established association between Spanish and Latinx identity.[9] Marcos's way of speaking also includes the r-lessness, monophthongal /aɪ/, and zero copula typical of AAE.[10] For example, the ten-minute stretch of discourse from which excerpts 6.1–6.9 are extracted have a higher rate of low (15 percent) or backed (17 percent) /ae/ tokens than Marcos's interview averages overall (13 percent and 12 percent, respectively). The same ten-minute stretch of discourse shows a higher rate of /aɪ/ weakening (21 percent) than a random three-minute sample (11 percent). These vowel tokens cluster in identity-relevant places in discourse as Marcos positions himself and others, such as Washingtonians and gentrifiers, as deserving or undeserving residents.[11] When he is reminiscing, he uses more AAE, a pattern that has been observed in other narratives about "old DC" by African American speakers.[12]

Voicing—or imparting words, voice, and sometimes bodily attitudes to a protagonist—is an important strategy by which speakers represent identities through language.[13] In his interview Marcos voices Washingtonians and gentrifiers as part of constructing their identities and positioning them in contrast to each other as opposed to being part of the same group. Finally, Marcos's metalinguistic commentary makes explicit the connection between language and local identity. He describes a "DC accent" that is part of DC's diverse, African American–based culture. This accent contrasts with the exaggerated White voice he uses to imitate gentrifiers.

The idea of authenticity plays an important role in identity construction and legitimation strategies, allowing people to present "[their] own or another's identity as genuine or credible."[14] However, authenticity, like identity, is itself socially constructed through language and other interactional and symbolic practices.[15] Notions of authenticity typically relate to historicity, time depth, and continuity.[16] Indeed, nostalgia is a powerful dimension of authenticity, as is the idea of having "roots" through continuous association with a place or culture.[17] Authenticity is also associated with shared culture and an awareness of cultural value.[18] Language, particularly local language, plays an important role in this cultural commonality.[19] At the same time, it is important to recognize that "authentic" language and identity are themselves ever evolving—a point that carries weight when we think about immigrants arriving in a new country and the languages and cultures they absorb in the new environment.

"We have our own shit here": Washingtonians versus Gentrifiers

> *We do have our own language our own music our own dress, our own dance our own everything. Like, New York and LA (makes farting sound) We have our own shit here. Too.*
> —Marcos

Cities are not simply places where people live but sites of community and imagination. Geographic spaces are lived and imagined into being as social places through human interactions large and small, including language.[20] Thus, DC's moniker as "Chocolate City" reflects not just its Black majority in the second half of the twentieth century but also its Black governance and rich Black history.[21] Like many cities, DC is contested space. Diversity and segregation historically lived side by side, a dynamic that persists in residential distribution to this day. In this context, gentrification is hotly debated. While the intersectional forces at work are acknowledged, gentrification is racialized along White/Black or, more broadly, non-White lines.[22]

Marcos sees DC as a diverse city centered on a Black cultural identity. In addition, it is a city of neighborhoods and neighborliness, of grandmothers keeping watch from porches, of go-go music and Latinxs celebrating their cultural traditions in the streets. This city of his childhood has been overwritten in the present by gentrifiers, portrayed as transient interlopers and racialized as White. He sees these outsiders as taking advantage of the city without sharing its past or participating in its culture.

While he is nostalgic, Marcos does not sugarcoat the past. He candidly discusses the urban neglect that DC suffered in the last decades of the twentieth century, speaking of poverty, drugs, violence, and crime—topics that other long-term residents also acknowledged. But he also describes a rich, diverse local culture that flourished at the same time, along with a sense of community that was intensified by the pressures of daily life and the need to "take care of each other" in order to survive.

Throughout his interview Marcos names specific places in the city. Neighborhoods are an important social orientation for locals. DC is a city of neighborhoods, and "neighborhood" is a means of placing each other in the social landscape and claiming an identity. The neighborhoods he and others refer to in their interviews—Columbia Heights, Adams Morgan, and Mount Pleasant—were initial sites of Latinx settlement and cultural activity and hold an important symbolic role in local Latinidad.[23] However, they are now contested territory, as Gabriella Modan notes in her 2008 ethnography of Mount Pleasant—a process that is even more advanced as I write fifteen years later.[24] People will often establish their roots by stating that they came to Columbia Heights and even naming the streets they lived on. This placemaking is highly relevant as gentrification continues to displace working-class Latinxs and African Americans from city neighborhoods in favor of wealthier White new arrivals. Roots are a protean way of demonstrating authenticity. By naming specific places—neighborhoods, streets, hospitals, and more—Marcos and others symbolically root themselves in the city terrain.

Table 6.1 describes key themes in Marcos's understanding of Washingtonian identity and gentrifier characteristics. The textual examples that follow illustrate how each dimension helps him to construct a "real Washingtonian" identity for himself, and for DC Latinxs and Washingtonians more broadly. This positioning bolsters their claim to the city and, through contrast, delegitimizes that of gentrifiers.

Table 6.1. Characteristics of Washingtonians and Gentrifiers

Dimension	Washingtonian	Gentrifier
Place	District of Columbia;* urban	Elsewhere (Vermont, Iowa); nonurban
Time	Past; native or long-term residency; continuity; roots	Present; transiency; lack of roots
Race	Non-White (Black, other minorities)	White
Culture	Food, music, dance, clothes, values, shared experiences	Food, lack of "culture," lack of values, lack of struggle
Language	AAE	Hyperarticulated White American English

*Marcos considers DC to be the District of Columbia proper, but he states that younger generations see the DMV as more connected to DC than it was in his youth, as the metropolitan area has extended into the surrounding "urban suburbs" of Maryland and Virginia.

"We used to be Chocolate City. . . . It was an infusion of whatever culture you had, with the Black culture"

Marcos lovingly describes "old" DC's rich and diverse culture and mourns its present-day erasure as "lost." His reminiscence paints a picture of a local Latinx community that maintained its own traditions while also assimilating to aspects of local African American culture.

Excerpt 6.1

1 MARCOS: So the childhood is hazy but I, just the Hispanic culture and the pride we had
2 back then that's what I remember. The musics, at night. The go-go music the music
3 blaring from other people was SO awesome. Like those PBS channels about like
4 Voces and stuff? Like, THAT'S what it was but, THAT was in the Bronx or, or New
5 York. Well WE had that HERE, AS vibrant. You know [I] WISH could, like, make it more vivid.
             [monophthongal /aɪ/]
6 Like listening to congos at two in the morning, as you heard them down here
7 (laughs). You know, that was AWEsome to me. The parties that we would have were,
8 LAVISH. [I] mean, uh fifteen-year-olds it was like a wedding with like the [people]
 [monophthongal /aɪ/]   [/l/ vocalization]
9 the bridesmaids and all that, like the gentlemen, and, in the neighborhoods.

Echoing the theme of diversity we have seen throughout the book, Marcos remembers the Latinx community of his childhood as full of cultural pride. There were shared traditions such as the "fifteen-year" quinceañera ceremony celebrating girls' coming of age. As he describes elsewhere in his interview, there was also the original Latino Festival, where different countries paraded their cultures through the barrios' streets.[25] At the same time, he recalls iconic local African American cultural forms such as go-go music (lines 1–3). The juxtaposition portrays DC Latinx culture as blended with local Black culture, a theme that he returns to time and again in his interview.

Marcos takes great pride in DC Latinx culture, comparing it to other Latinx and Black communities such as the Bronx, which were legendary for their culture and creativity (lines 4–5). Elsewhere in the interview he commented, "Breakdancing was coming into play the, go-go was kind of, you know here and there, so my background in music (slaps hands) was listening to *cumbia* from El Salvador *rancheras* from Mexico, go-go from DC, and this new thing called hip-hop." His description of the music he grew up with represents the dynamic cultural medley that surrounded him.

168 Chapter 6

However, culture also encompasses less obvious qualities. Marcos continues his narrative:

Excerpt 6.1 (continued)

10 MARCOS: That was so much fun as where NOW, (sighs) it's all lost
11 nobody KNOWS anyone, you know? It's, it's, it's lost. You know everyone's a
12 [stranger]. People walk around looking at their phones, they don't say hi. As it's odd because
   [/s/ palatalization]
13 that WASN'T, DC. That when, DC when you were, driving around, you ↑say [hi] to people.
                                                                          [monophthongal /aɪ/]
14 ↑Otherwise you get randomly smacked by somebody's grand[mother],
                                                          [rlessness]
15 INTERVIEWER: (laughs)
16 MARCOS: Um, God Miss Jones she lived downstairs on the first floor, like, [I] loved her,
                                                                              [monophthongal /aɪ/]
17 you know. She took care of me a lot and she was Black and, and Dwayne, D.J., I used to
18 hang out with them, and, they took care of me and that's how [I] learned how to
                                                                [monophthongal /aɪ/]
19 (making braiding gestures) braid HAIR and doing this and that, and they would ↑tell you,
20 "You say [hi] to people." You know "Don't be [shy]." She's like "This is still the South,
   [monophthongal /aɪ/]   [monophthongal /aɪ/]
21 we're- we're still south of the Mason Dixon [line]," (laughs) "you need to keep some
                                               [monophthongal /aɪ/]
22 Southern hospitality" and [I] would say [hi] to people. And I still do. You know I'll
                              [monophthongal /aɪ/] [monophthongal /aɪ/]
23 be walking down the- to the Metro and I'll, "Good morning."

DC culture for Marcos also consists of intangible community values that he again associates with Black culture. Cultural norms were collectively conveyed and upheld ("you get randomly smacked by somebody's grandmother," line 14). One important value that is a recurrent theme for him and others I spoke with is the pragmatic (politeness) norm of saying hello. Marcos describes his own education on this by Ms. Jones, the African American neighbor who helped raise him (lines 16–22): "You say hi to people. Don't be shy." He also learned other aspects of Black culture from her such as how to braid hair. Marcos's memories of Ms. Jones illustrate the neighborliness he remembers and underscore the contact between Latinxs and African Americans that many other interviewees described, as exemplified by the playground recordings in chapter 4.

However, this DC is now part of the past (line 11). Marcos uses the word "lost" to describe this, punctuating his feelings with a sigh. The sense of community is gone, and new residents don't greet others—a common complaint among interviewees. Gentrifier's violation of DC politeness norms underscores their lack of belonging and is seen as disrespectful. In Marcos's portrayal, this rudeness undercuts new residents' moral right to the city, supporting the rights of "real" Washingtonians who share in the local culture and know how to behave. These moral claims are part of a broader discursive struggle in what Modan calls "turf wars" over the gentrifying city, as represented by the Adams Morgan neighborhood she studied, and indeed are an important part of how identities are constructed and positioned relative to each other more generally.[26]

The passages above also serve as a good example of Marcos's linguistic identity construction. The language he uses when discussing "real," pre-gentrification DC reflects the Latinx and African American cultural blend of his childhood, which his words describe. As he describes his childhood, he uses Spanish when naming Latinx cultural elements such as the *Voces* program. He also frequently uses AAE phonetic elements such as monophthongal [ai], as highlighted in his voicing of Ms. Jones telling him, "'You say hi [monophthongized] to people. Don't be shy [monophthongized]'" (line 20). In this voicing he also uses gestures to embody her and her son D.J., making braiding gestures as he describes the Black cultural framework of their mutual interactions. Taken together, through this portrayal and others throughout the interview, Marcos paints a picture of "real Washingtonians," whom he racializes as non-White—an important contrast with how he portrays gentrifiers, as we will see.

"New England chowder": Gentrification and Racialized Displacement

Union Market, a fixture since 1871, was once DC's largest market. Also known as the Florida Avenue Market, it sold food, retail and wholesale, and was historically staffed by immigrant and African American vendors. The market area suffered neglect along with much of the city in the later part of the twentieth century. It was renovated as a gourmet food vendor space in 2012 and, as I write, is an upscale shopping and dining area surrounded by luxury condos.[27] This gentrification, with intersectional connections to race and class, has been criticized. Popular-access forums such as Yelp show residents' feelings of displacement under threads such as "Union Market: not for Black people?" (November 2, 2012), which discuss the market's long-standing importance to the Black community and the marginalization of the low-income Black elders who depended on it for decades.

Excerpt 6.2

1   MARCOS: So that- I like going to the farmer's markets, not Eastern (laughs) Market. But I
2   like Union Market- Union Market? That's up and coming- but NOW do you see who's
3   coming IN the, outsiders. Who started Union Market. DC, Washingtonians.
4   INTERVIEWER: Locals.
5   MARCOS: Now who's doing it. "Oh, New England chowder." Eh? This. Wha:t? Ah. WE
6   [always] joke and we want to make soul food and this and this and that, because that's
      [/l/ vocalization]
7   the DC we remember, had, cultural food. You know making, [empanada pupusas]
                                                              [Latinx, Salvadoran foods]
8   but also [having] cauliflower green- and greens on the [side] too. That's DC. A
             [back /ae/]   [monophthongal /aɪ/]
9   fusion. Chocolate City? We used to be Chocolate City. Nobody knows who Chocolate
10 City is. THAT was DC. Chocolate City. It was an infusion of whatever culture you had
11 with, the [Black] culture.
              [low /ae/]

Marcos sees the gentrification of Union Market as an example of Washingtonians' physical and symbolic displacement. He asks rhetorically, "Now who's coming in the, outsiders. Who started Union Market. DC, Washingtonians" (lines 2–3). The time and space deictics in this utterance set up a past–present dynamic and sense of outside versus insiderness. Washingtonians "started" the market, an action located in the past. He contrasts this condition with the present day, which he emphasizes through increased volume: "NOW do you see who's coming IN?" (lines 2–3). Meanwhile, the sense of "outsiders" coming "in" creates an inside/outside dynamic, where Washingtonians are insiders—the real residents—and gentrifiers, coming from elsewhere, literally and figuratively, do not belong. Marcos discursively resists Washingtonians' displacement through expressing disdain for these changes (and for Eastern Market, where gentrification took place earlier).

Food is an important part of culture and often serves as a metaphor for such. Marcos uses food to contrast Washingtonians and gentrifiers. Washingtonians are racialized as Black and, more broadly, non-White through race mentions and cultural blending ("It was an infusion of whatever culture you had with, the Black culture," lines 10–11). Marcos's DC Latinxs eat *"empanadas pupusas* but also having cauliflower, green- and greens on the side." *Pupusas*—thick corn tortillas served with various savory fillings such as beans, cheese, and meat, accompanied by a shredded, pickled cabbage slaw called *curtido*—are the national food of El Salvador. They are iconic in DC, which celebrates an annual Pupusa Festival, due to its large Salvadoran population.[28] Indeed, in his interview, Emanuel—a proud DC Salvadoran—used the term "Pupusa Power" as a symbol of local Salvadoran pride and prominence. Meanwhile, collard greens are a classic "soul food," the Southern Black culinary tradition whose moniker is a symbol of cultural pride.[29]

Marcos's metacommentary articulates the cultural hybridity that his food symbolism evokes: "That's DC. A fusion ... Chocolate City. ... It was an infusion of whatever culture you had with, the Black culture" (lines 8–11). He repeats "Chocolate City" four times, emphasizing DC's identity as a Black city. However, his idea of Washingtonians is not exclusively Black. Rather, Blackness is the primary cultural reference in his understanding of the city's diversity—a diversity that stands in contrast to the Whiteness of gentrifiers.

Marcos views "New England chowder" as symbolic of gentrification's changes. New England clam chowder indexes non-Washingtonianness in two ways. First, since it is associated with a different region, it is inherently nonlocal. Second, it indexes Whiteness. New England is popularly imagined as a White region, and the Whiteness of New England clam chowder is attested in studies of Latinx identity and cultural production.[30]

Marcos also enacts the indexical relationship between New England clam chowder and Whiteness through linguistic performance. He voices gentrifiers by speaking the term "New England chowder" with an exaggeratedly clear pronunciation and intonation. This voicing contrasts with the Latinx and AAE that Marcos uses while voicing Washingtonians and resonates with other studies that show that exaggerated diction evokes Whiteness.[31] He follows this utterance with the interrogative "Eh?" expressing incredulity, and a low, long "What?" in its AAE-related function as "exclamation or challenge," rejecting the clam chowder and what it represents.[32] His use of the demonstrative pronoun "this" as a stand-alone phrase emphasizes its referent—White, encroaching outsiders—and makes them symbolic of a broader pattern.

Marcos's discursive construction of White gentrifier identity stands in contrast to Washingtonian identity. His desire for local food encodes a positive affective stance that he broadens from himself as an individual to the collective level through the plural pronoun "we," emphasized through louder speech: "We always . . . want to make soul food . . . because that's the DC we remember, had, cultural food" (lines 5–7). Washingtonians are aligned in solidarity through the desire to maintain their culture and are positioned in antitheses to the "outsiders," who are overwriting Black-infused local food culture with White-associated New England clam chowder. Marcos is keenly aware of these changes: "We used to be Chocolate City. Nobody knows who Chocolate City is" (lines 9–10). This statement serves as a metaphor for the erasure wrought by gentrification more broadly.

The Whiteness of Gentrifiers

While many new residents are White, the Whiteness of gentrifiers is more broadly symbolic. As much ethnic studies literature makes clear, Whiteness in the United States is a gate-kept form of racial capital closely tied in with historic social hierarchies and economics whose effects continue in the present day.[33] There are certainly White Washingtonians. Marcos spoke about "Big White," his friend and housemate who grew up in the 95 percent Black Southeast quadrant, as a "real" Washingtonian.[34] The city has also always had wealthy White neighborhoods—and it is worth reiterating that there are long-standing wealthy Black neighborhoods too, in the city and in the suburbs, and socioeconomic divides among African Americans are also salient in the gentrification debate.[35]

Nevertheless, Marcos's racialization of gentrifiers as White is a common perception among my participants and in the DC area, one that reflects a steady increase in the White population since the 1970s, particularly since 2000.[36] In 2022 White residents increased the most in almost every area of the city.[37] Beyond the demographics, however, the Whiteness of gentrifiers is symbolic in the DC context and more broadly.

Marcos positions Whiteness as "other"—as somehow different from or even antithetical to local DC identity and culture. Marcos's description of gentrifiers as White also invokes privilege. He portrays them as "rich kids" from White-coded places such as New England, Vermont, and (elsewhere in the interview) Utah and Wyoming. This description resonates with other participants' discussion of race and privilege. Growing up in the 1970s, "Sofía" identified with her Black classmates because, as she expressed it, they were poor together, and their White classmates were rich. This dynamic also connects to the broader US racial hegemony, where Whiteness is socially and materially privileged. Gracia, raised in the 1990s, was called a whitey for her relatively privileged background and level of education, as reflected by the "non-ethnic" way she talks. There is a cross-cultural connection as well. Héctor sees White Latinxs, where Whiteness again indexes higher social class, as distanced from local Latinidad. Whiteness's broader intersectional privilege relates to the

US and Latin American racialized hegemonies, which are both relevant to US Latinxs. Since Whiteness indexes outsiderness and privilege, Marcos, by emphasizing gentrifier's Whiteness, distances them from "authentic" local DC identity, which he views as "non-White" along race and class parameters.

Beyond my interviews, race's relevance in the gentrification debate is attested in media outlets from the *New York Times*, the *Washington Post*, and WAMU 88.5 FM to less-formal outlets such as the *Prince of Petworth* blog and curbed.com. In these characterizations, gentrification, Whiteness, and affluence are related in the displacement of minority Washingtonians. Race and gentrification have been documented in other scholarship on DC African Americans and Latinxs.[38] Indeed, Modan notes that her Whiteness was renegotiated when a Latino neighbor, upon learning that her father was from Israel, commented that he previously "thought she was just White"—a repositioning that perhaps was a sign of her acceptance as a resident in Mount Pleasant, where White gentrifiers were (and are) widely seen as displacing Latinx residents.[39]

"It's still hundreds of ingredients, just different":
Diversity in New DC

Having established this paradigm, Marcos has to engage with the racialization of DC identity and its symbolism in changing times in his own family as he claims a local identity for his young son.

Excerpt 6.3

1   MARCOS: So, even in [my] family I see it. As where, you would have totally thought [I]
                 [monophthongal /aɪ/]   [monophthongal /aɪ/]
2   would be with like a Hispanic or a Black girl, and, [I] ended up, with a, a, White woman.
3   So I'VE changed. And I still [**HOLD**] ON to my DC but, I have changed as [well].
                        [l vocalization]   [l vocalization]
4   You know and, and, and, being able to accept all that is, like the beauty of it too. So,
5   MY kid is mixed, you know he's got- he's, what, like EIGHT different things, you know, and, [and,

6   INTERVIEWER: [(hhhh) He's all-American.
7   MARCOS: he IS the definition of a melting pot. He's all-American. He's all-American.
8   He's, complete- he's a [melting pot].
                              [syllabification]
9   He's Washingtonian. He's, a, [melting of different things all together.]
                                  [l vocalization]

Marcos notes that, given his upbringing and the city he grew up in, "you would have totally thought I would be with like a Hispanic or a Black girl" (lines 1–2). However, his wife is White. He is able to connect his family into the narrative of Washingtonian identity by expanding the "fusion" metaphor to a message of diversity and change. As he says elsewhere in his interview, "The new DC, we're still a melting pot? May no longer be Chocolate City, yet we're a melting pot. It's just uh, the ingredients are different. But that's the beauty though, it's STILL, HUNdreds of ingredients. Just different." In this "melting pot" discourse of local identity with "different ingredients," he finds room for his son, who he is raising to be Washingtonian despite the changing times, as we will see.

Sounding Washingtonian

Identifying and claiming DC language enhances Marcos's discursive construction of an "authentic" Washingtonian identity with legitimate rights to the city for himself, his son, and Washingtonians more broadly. Since language is part of culture, local language is often associated with local identity, particularly in times of change.[40] Throughout Marcos's interview he draws on AAE and LE aspects of his linguistic repertoire with more frequency when speaking nostalgically of "old" DC and his childhood, and in other identity-relevant stretches of talk. He uses less AAE and LE features when discussing present-day DC or tasks such as welcoming me to his home or scheduling a follow-up interview. His use of AAE when discussing past DC resonates with research showing the same pattern when DC-area African Americans talk about the past and about gentrification.[41]

Voicing also plays an important role in Marcos's linguistic construction of Washingtonian identity. He voices Ms. Jones and his neighbors past and present using AAE. His voicing of his son, whom he describes as having the local accent, makes it clear that he views this accent as Black language:

Excerpt 6.4

1   MARCOS: Yeah. You know he's awesome. And, and, HE has a little slang too. You know and, he,
2   yeah. He'll like he'll walk into the room he'll see you and you'll be like "Aw you're so cute."
3   "[I] [already] know."
    [monophthongal /aɪ/] [/l/ vocalization]
4   And, "[I] [already] know." But with that little accent. "[I] [already] know."
    [monophthongal /aɪ/] [/l/ vocalization]   [monophthongal /aɪ/] [/l/ vocalization]
5   You know.
6   INTERVIEWER: Oh yeah he's got it a little the accent, [he's got a little? (laughs)
7   MARCOS: [Yep. He's got a little bit of it.
8   You know, so it, . . . That's the awesome part you know we do have our own language our own music our own
9   dress, our own dance our own everything. Like, New York and LA (makes farting sound) We
10 have our own shit here. Too.

Marcos voices the Washingtonian accent by imitating his son using AAE features such as /aɪ/ weakening and /l/ vocalization in the phrase, "I already know" (line 4). This resonates with other scholarship on the "DC accent," which, while debated, is broadly perceived as African American.[42]

However, Marcos's metalinguistic commentary shows that he associates "Washingtonian language" with a Black-influenced place identity rather than only with Black speakers. In this further meaning—what linguistic anthropologists call "second-level indexicalities"[43]—AAE-influenced English is understood more broadly as a local way of speaking. Marcos cites language as an aspect of DC's intangible culture, which sets it apart from other places, indexing a collective identity and proprietorship by repeating the phrase "we ... have our own": "We do have our own language our own music our own dress, our own dance our own everything. ... We have our own shit here" (lines 8–10). This local identity encompasses Latinx through the "blending" with Black culture that he described through food and other cultural referents. For Marcos, "sounding local" happens through repertoires that encompass AAE, LE, and Spanish—all from the languages that surrounded DC Latinxs as children. These sociolinguistic perceptions are amply attested throughout my data.

A raciolinguistic perspective is also relevant to Marcos's portrayal of the White Other. Marcos uses exaggeratedly precise voicing to mockingly imitate gentrifiers ("Oh, New England chowder"). Hyperarticulation is a common means of expressing "gringo voice" and indexing Whiteness, in general and by Latinxs.[44] Marcos's voicing of gentrifiers adds to the construction of their Whiteness, and he positions them as outsiders. As we saw through his commentary on saying hello, linguistic associations with identity are not limited to pronunciation and vocabulary but also to pragmatic norms—a well-rounded understanding of Black language as local language, which reflects its important role in the city's culture and day-to-day interactions.

While Marcos's description of his son's "DC accent" foregrounded English, elsewhere in the interview he explained that his son is learning Spanish from his grandmother. Through family transmission, this aspect of Latinx identity continues. These repertoire elements are the same ones that Marcos himself uses when he speaks and that he used in identity-related passages. However, he added still another local dimension to his son's language by saying that his son is also learning Ethiopian words from family friends. This detail is unique to the DC area, which is home to the largest Ethiopian community outside of Africa.[45] Marcos views this multilingual learning as a symbol of DC's diversity and cultural mixing portrayed through the openness of a child to the languages that surround him. This discourse of diversity as defining the city resonates with his broader message and with the comments of other participants. As we also saw in chapters 3 and 4, this discourse of diversity as the defining local characteristic coexists with discourses centered on prominent local groups: Central Americans, particularly Salvadorans, among Latinxs, and African Americans in DC more generally.

Clearly, Marcos is aware of AAE's racial associations. Blackness is a primary point of reference in his experience of local culture and his understanding of its language. However, he is not trying to be Black. Rather, he is drawing on an element of his repertoire that was his native variety of English to represent local identity. This identity has ethnoracial associations due to DC's—and DC Latinxs'—social and cultural history.

Through language, Marcos stakes a claim to an expanded racialized local identity that he views as incompatible with the Whiteness of gentrifiers. This racialization is not literal but ideological, where Whiteness indexes nonlocalness and the social privilege that is displacing locals and broadly present in the US hegemony.

While Marcos uses AAE-influenced speech, he does not appear to be mocking or passing, as in other studies of Latinxs and other ethnicities' use of Black-influenced speech.[46] He is also not using Black language without attribution or respect, as is commonly the case in cultural appropriation.[47] His example raises theoretical questions for how we understand immigrant language acquisition and that of their immediate descendants. While Marcos is not African American, it would not be accurate to say that his way of speaking is crossing, or that he is using the language of a group to which he does not belong.[48] He was exposed to AAE throughout his childhood and grew up in the Washingtonian social group that speaks this "local" English. As with the case of the Latina girls in the Smithsonian playground recording that I examine in chapter 4, his way of speaking appears to have been acquired from and accepted by African American peers. His linguistic repertoire is thus more in line with Julie Sweetland's notion of non-co-ethnic authentic speakers, or with Django Paris's theory of language sharing, where Latinxs immersed in African American culture can acquire aspects of AAE and be accepted as legitimate language users.[49]

The raciomultilingual repertoires and associated meanings that I have described so far are more broadly relevant to my participants. The combination of Spanish, LE, and AAE that Marcos uses to project a DC Latinx identity is the same one that Noemí describes—and characterizes as "street"—when asked if there is a DC Latinx way of speaking. It also resonates with Héctor's linguistic construction of local Latinx identity and contrasts with Gracia's peers accusing her of "sounding like a whitey" (chapters 5 and in this chapter, respectively). In all of these cases the "local" voice contrasts with Whiteness and privilege.

Given that Latinxs comprise a diasporic community, however, these meanings exist biculturally and transnationally. For example, Héctor contrasts local Latinxs' intersectional identities with elite, "White" Latinxs whose privilege derives *from Latin America*, not merely from passing as White in the United States. These transnational, intersectional distinctions are relevant to DC Latinxs, for the Latinx population mirrors the extreme diversity and stratification of the region more broadly, where members of the same ethnic group have vastly different socioeconomic backgrounds, levels of education, and experiences of migration as well as racial positionings. In all the cases I have examined, local and more widely circulated raciomultilingual ideologies informed the ways in which participants understood and constructed ethnocultural identity through language. However, their identity construction also relates to uniquely DC social distinctions and concerns.

Putting Down Roots: Moral Positioning and Claims to the City

Roots, which literally anchor plants to their native places, are a classic metaphor for authenticity and belonging. Roots encompass culture via signifiers such as food, which we saw in the example of "*pupusas* and greens on the side," but also via intangible aspects of culture such as shared values and through community involvement, socialization, and continuity. In cities, with their histories of continuous migration, roots are constructed not only through nativity but also through longtime residence and interactions with neighbors and neighborhoods. This rootedness confers a moral right to belonging, which is especially important as cities change.[50]

Previously, I mentioned that the moral positioning of different groups is an important part of their competing claims to DC. People often use claims to moral behavior to construct the self and the other—stances that are particularly relevant in contested claims to belonging.[51] Claiming the moral high ground serves to legitimize a claim. For example, in Modan's study of Mount Pleasant, she found that gentrifiers positioned themselves as adding value to the neighborhood and thus as deserving residents, and portrayed Latinx residents as immoral—dirty, drunk, unruly, and even threatening.[52] In contrast, Marcos presents gentrifiers as the problem and Washingtonians as legitimate residents.

Values often represent deservingness as well as culture. We see this over and over in the public sphere, for example, often weaponized against minorities in debates about who "real Americans" are and their values.[53] In Marcos's interview he describes local values—collectively honed through a shared struggle for survival—as an important aspect of DC culture. He sees as Washingtonian "street values" such as hard work, resilience, ingenuity, and taking care of others, even through unorthodox or illegal channels. Throughout Marcos's interview, he gives examples of these values in action, from street sales of candy and bootleg tapes to drug dealing, prostitution, and helping others through drug withdrawal—all of which he witnessed growing up. While he does not approve of criminal activity, he considers "hustling" part of the local value system that evolved to survive urban neglect, commenting elsewhere in his interview that this environment was "all he knew" as a child.

Excerpt 6.5

1   MARCOS: Ages twenty-ONE instead of getting rims on my car and, getting a stereo system, I
2   BOUGHT, a home. And I bought it in Germantown Maryland. Because there was farmlands up
3   there. [King's] Farmland, this and that, and now there's a Mercedes dealership a SmartCar
     [/ɪ/ **raising**]
4   dealership or a Lamborghini dealership,
5   INTERVIEWER: Oh (laughs) really?
6   MARCOS: I sold it, [I], purchased it for, one thirty-five, [I] sold it for over five hundred?
        [monophthongal /aɪ/]   [monophthongal /aɪ/]

7   INTERVIEWER: Oh my God. Wow.
8   MARCOS: THAT'S where [I] was fortunate.
                    [monophthongal /aɪ/]
9   You know, I- I, I- wasn't STUPID with [my] money, at an early age. Because of what I learned
                                          [monophthongal /aɪ/]
10 in DC. You know I learned morals. I got my VALues from here, and they weren't ↑YEAH they
11 were, somewhat hustler-ish or street-ish, WHATEVER. I just learned to take care of my
12 [FAMILY]. And to take care of OTHers. You know and, and then I moved back into
    [low /ae/]
13 DC and I bought my mom's home, and, she lives out THERE where, I had enough money to
14 put into the condo and I sold that and, I met [my] wife and now I live here in
                                                  [monophthongal /aɪ/]
15 Petworth. It's because I chose [Petworth and- and I didn't choose like Upper Northwest]
                                   [syllable timing]
16 because I believe this is gonna get better and I BELIEVE that my kid can go down the park
17 and be in a soccer team. I don't [have] to BE, off of Sixteenth Street or F, you know,
                                     [low /ae/]
18 up the street on . . . You shouldn't have to do that.

Marcos begins the narrative of his return to DC by describing his financial decisions. Instead of wasting his money on short-term items such as flashy car improvements, he invested in a home outside the city in what was at the time an affordable rural area. Next, he describes the positive financial outcome of this decision. His property value increased, and he was able to sell at a profit, allowing him to purchase another home, this time in the city. Marcos takes a positive stance toward these decisions and, by extension, the values that informed them. While acknowledging that some of his activities as a youth may have been "street" or "hustler," he maintains that they nevertheless reflected the key value of taking "care of family, of others" and the solidarity of surviving difficult times together. Driving the point home, he rejects any potential criticism of local values with the word "whatever," emphasized by louder volume.

Marcos's description of his neighborhood is also meaningful. He contrasts Petworth, a diverse, majority–African American neighborhood that was not yet gentrified when he moved in, with the upper Northwest quadrant, a wealthy, White area of the city.[54] More granularly, 16th Street traditionally separated White neighborhoods from working-class African American and Latinx neighborhoods—a comment made by my participants and shared by long-term African American residents.[55] Living in Petworth creates continuity between the DC Marcos remembers and the one he lives in today, furthering his symbolic roots and commitment to the city. Marcos's avowed DC values bolster his claim to be an authentic Washingtonian and set him apart from interloping gentrifiers despite his current middle-class status.

"You're just here to leech off it and move on":
Washingtonians versus Transients

Marcos began his interview by telling me he was a native Washingtonian, even demonstrating his local roots by naming the hospital where he was born. However, his DC roots also rest on long-term residency and community involvement as well as a sense of shared culture, struggle, and participation.

Excerpt 6.6

1 MARCOS: You know, I did a lot of community service. I've PAINTED Malcom- you know, uh,
2 SEVERAL (.) uh elementary schools? These are MARYLAND, fraternities University of
3 Maryland, sororities that you know would come in and **[I]** would go with THEM.
                                                        [monophthongal /aɪ/]
4 And, my friends were in college I wasn't but I joined them, to go do community
5 things, for here. Where's the community people are helping here? "Well this ain't my
6 community I'm just here for two years." There's a lot of TRANsient people. So they come here
7 to, take advantage of everything that's given to them, but they don't, contribute. Not everyone.
8 But the majority [do. DID that.
9 INTERVIEWER: [But it's like their life isn't part of the community.
10 MARCOS: They're- Yeah. "We're just here." "Oh this place sucks" everybody complains well
11 what have you done, to make this place better? (. . .) And, we want to make it better.
12 You know. So all these things, you know, we're all here, we're not all, just running away from it.

13 We want to make it better but, we have to WORK twenty-four seven, and we don't get to
14 enJOY it? And WE'RE Washingtonians. It DOES hurt.
15 INTERVIEWER: Yeah that sucks.
16 MARCOS: You know? It DOES suck. Yeah. Like, YOU'RE giving it a bad image. YOU'RE just
17 here to kind of leech off of it and move on once you leave, and go [back to Vermont] or
                                   [syllable timing]
18 wherever YOU'RE from, AND, [I'm] stuck here with the trash. [I'm] here with the leftovers.
           [monophthongal /aɪ/]   [monophthongal /aɪ/]

Marcos shared a small story of community service that demonstrates his personal commitment to city and, by extension, that of Washingtonians (lines 1–6). He begins it by explicitly mentioning community, repeating the word four times and tying the community to DC through the deictic pronoun "here." While "community" is a noun, for Marcos being part of the community is a question of actions. These caretaking actions help define the collective Washingtonian identity (lines 11–14). He sees the desire to contribute as a local value that represents investment in the city and community. By painting schools, he and his friends took care of the city as a physical place but also as a social space.[56] Caring for the city and for the community roots Washingtonians and helps authenticate their claim to belonging.

In contrast, Marcos depicts gentrifiers as unrooted and lacking community spirit, using "you" as if to address them directly: "YOU're giving it a bad image" (line 16). This "you" is clearly distanced from the Washingtonian "we" that is socially invested in the city. Marcos's accusation "flips the script" in two ways. First, it defends DC against its "bad image"—a stereotype that positions it as a site that faces urban blight and in which racial stereotyping plays a prominent role.[57] Second, it repositions gentrifiers—whom the city government often lauds for revitalizing urban neighborhoods—as causing harm. The idea of a tight-knit original community and shared survival in the face of adversity is an important part of authenticity.[58] In Marcos's view, gentrifiers are not putting down roots.

Their lack of social involvement makes them "leeches," sucking the city's lifeblood, and they create "trash" rather than caring for the city as he and his friends (locals who were attending college)—and, by extension, other local residents—do (lines 17–18). Their rootlessness is related to both their actions and their transience: gentrifiers will "move on," leaving real Washingtonians to pick up the pieces (lines 17–18). When they leave, they will "go back to Vermont or wherever [they're] from" (lines 17–18). This place association continues the racialization of gentrifiers as White, which we saw in Marcos's comment about "New England chowder," since the popular imagination associates Vermont with Whiteness.[59]

Marcos's portrayal presents Washingtonians as rooted in the area and morally repositions gentrifiers as "leeching" newcomers. This contrast furthers his argument that Washingtonians are authentic and deserving residents with a legitimate claim to space who are being unjustly marginalized. There is also a sense that the city is misunderstood by outsiders and that its rich culture and resiliency is overlooked.

There is a real sense of hurt and exclusion in Marcos's words and for many Washingtonians I spoke with: "And we're Washingtonians. It does hurt" (line 14, emphasized through increased volume). Marcos's feelings resonate with many other interviewees' comments, such as Emanuel, who stated, "We wanted it to get better, we just didn't realize it would get better for everyone else." Relegated to the "leftovers" of gentrification, Washingtonians work hard but can barely scrape by in the increasingly expensive city (line 13).

"That's the community that I remember":
Community and Continuity

However, according to Marcos, DC culture and values, honed through shared struggle, still persist among "real Washingtonians."

Excerpt 6.7

1   MARCOS: You know, [that's] the [last] thing I said you know, if they- if, when, if,
                     [low /ae/] [back /ae/]

2   something [happened] we would, keep it in house. We would take care of it ↑in house.
              [back /ae/]

3   We wouldn't call the police. What GOOD are THEY gonna do.

4   INTERVIEWER: (laughs) It's just stir everything up for everybody else.

5   MARCOS: That's it. When stuff [happens] even in HERE, you- NOW, you'll see NEIGHbors
              [/ɪ/ raising]

6   come out and be like "↑He:y, man, what's wrong." Because, you're concerned for your fellow

7   neighbor. You call the police, they're gonna come in and just arrest them. What GOOD is that

8   gonna do. NO, none. Uh we should have, mental health, we should have more clinics we

9   should have people to help OUT the community. You know [I] would take my friends out like,
              [monophthongal /aɪ/]

10 [and they would be freaked out], "[I] don't know who [I] slept </>
    [syllable timing]   [monophthongal /aɪ/] [monophthongal /aɪ/]

11 with, this and this and that." I'd take them down to the Whitman Walker Clinic.

12 "Let's go get you tested [man]." That's the community that I remember not just, [throwing]
              [back /ae/]   [trilled /r/]

13 them away and, you know running away from other people. You know those were the things

14 that were- I miss from DC. And that's what we [try] to celebrate here in the area you know
              [monophthongal /aɪ/]

15 like the, death with, when Chuck Brown died, you saw the community come toGETHER you

16 know, EVERYbody came together and other [people] just out of curiosity, came
              [/l/ vocalization]

17 together. But that was the beauty of it. THAT would happen, on the DAILY.

Here Marcos shares several small stories about a tight-knit community taking care of itself, trusting interpersonal relationships rather than civic institutions for aid. As with the other "street values" he has described, this attitude was the product of necessity in times of poverty and municipal corruption and mismanagement.[60] Instead, friends and neighbors helped each other. Marcos's protagonist role in the narrative about taking friends to the free clinic (lines 11–12) allows him to both bear first-person witness—strengthening his epistemic claim of knowing DC values—and to position himself as a personification of these values.[61] In his view, taking care of others is a foundational Washingtonian value: "That's the community that I remember not just, throwing them away and, you know running away from other people" (lines 12–13). This sense of active community contrasts with the antisocial habits he attributes to gentrifiers and the lack of connection he sees today.

The survival of community values represents a continuity of Washingtonian identity between the past and the present. However, Washingtonian culture is under threat as the city changes: "Those were the things that were- I miss from DC" (lines 13–14). Mentioning Chuck Brown's funeral also shows a sense of change and loss. Chuck Brown, the "Godfather of go-go," invented DC's iconic music in the 1970s. Go-go was made DC's official music in 2020, and its presence in the streets is a site of symbolic struggle between DC as a Black city and gentrifiers.[62] Chuck Brown's funeral in 2012 was an important and visible event, which Marcos cites as an example of community coming together—something that he remembers as typical in the past but that rarely happens now.

"He's a Washingtonian": The Next Generation

Toward the end of the interview, Marcos spoke about his young son, whom he loves dearly. I have previously discussed his positioning of his son's Washingtonian identity in terms of language and racialization. Let's now take a look at how Marcos constructed his son's Washington identity in terms of cultural continuity as he argues for his right to the city as another Washingtonian.

Excerpt 6.8

1   MARCOS: I mean [my] wife has been pushing to move back out to the Midwest or
                [monophthongal /aɪ/]
2   something where she's from and [I'm] like, "No:."
                            [monophthongal /aɪ/]

Constructing Local Identity, Authenticity 187

3   INTERVIEWER: (hhh)
4   MARCOS: Now, MY son is, BORN here, you know HE was born in SIBLEY Hospital, and, uh,
5   HE'S a [Washingtonian]. I want him to feel what I felt. That, that, the pride. But, the
         [alveolar nasal]
6   connection the root connection to, a town. You know, that this is OUR place. And you know
7   he- he can [decide] [otherwise], but as of right now I still want him to have the
         [monophthongal /aɪ/][rlessness, monophthongal /aɪ/]
8   pride from here. [I] want him to know what it is. That's why [I] BELIEVE that this area's
            [monophthongal /aɪ/]   [monophthongal /aɪ/]
9   gonna get better. You know and- I DO believe. And it's GOTTEN better.
10 INTERVIEWER: Yeah. [That's cool.
11 MARCOS: [A LOT better. But it's uh, we have to FIGHT. The ones in the middle class we
12 need to fight [to keep] our areas. Not to sell 'em to the rich kids. No:, no:. Kins keep it.
          [vowel shortening]
13 You know this is [DOABLE].
              [/l/ vocalization]

Marcos wants his son to have the same pride, roots, and ownership of the city that Marcos feels (lines 4–8). He discursively roots his son to the city by right of birth and further anchors him through specific place references. His loud and emphatic utterance of the first-person plural pronoun "our" underscores that DC belongs to Washingtonians such as him and his son. But this birthright is threatened by gentrification. In order to secure the future for the next generation, Marcos feels that Washingtonians need to "fight" to keep their areas (lines 11–12). This oppositional positioning deepens the distance between Washingtonians and gentrifiers through the metaphor of battle.

Marcos's defense of his son's right to the city positions him as a righteous defender. This discursive positioning enhances his moral authority and, by extension, that of Washingtonians. As a father, he is fighting not just for his own right to the city but for that of his son. The desire to keep his son from being displaced gives Marcos added motivation to "fight" for his right to the city—a fight that he sees as necessary for all low- and, now, middle-income Washingtonians, unified by the slang term "kins," who are being displaced by "rich

188   Chapter 6

kid" gentrifiers. The fecklessness implied by the term "rich kids" contrasts unfavorably with Marcos's and, by extension, Washingtonians' responsibilities and hard work, deepening his claim to the moral high ground.

Marcos's parental role also further develops his own identity as a Washingtonian committed to the city and to cultural continuity. As a parent, Marcos has an active role in nurturing the next generation. Cultural transmission is a form of resistance and of identity survival. His responsibility for helping his son develop his roots positions him as a knowledgeable older community member. Meanwhile, his son represents the future.

"We do say hi": Teaching Washingtonian Values

Transmitting DC culture to the next generation is particularly important to Marcos since his son is growing up in an increasingly unrecognizable city. Elsewhere, he states, "He won't have what I had. That's gone. That's long gone. That that, that cultural pride in, from where you came, that's gone." Marcos laments that his son will not be able to know the vibrant DC of his own childhood, full of neighborhood-based Latinx cultural pride. However, he is still able to teach him how to be Washingtonian by passing on community values.

As we have seen, Marcos views saying hello as an important part of local culture. Now, with the next generation, he is raising his son according to the same values he learned from Ms. Jones as a child. This continuity is part of their rootedness amid a changing city.

Excerpt 6.9

1   MARCOS: And it's gotten that way and now we walk around,
    [people starting] to know us,
    [copula absence]

2   you know people are accustomed to us, "Oh," you know "They're gonna say [hi]."
                                                                    [monophthongal /aɪ/]

3   INTERVIEWER: That's cool.

4   MARCOS: We do say [hi]. You know we're walking by, I have my kid, you know either in
                    [monophthongal /aɪ/]

5   a [stroller] or up in my arms I'm like, "Okay somebody's coming say 'good morning,'
    [/s/ palatalization]
6   we say 'good morning.'" You know, we want people to know that, DC's nice. Even if it's
7   just us two,
8   INTERVIEWER: That must be nice.
9   MARCOS: Hell, people see it's contagious. Good, good manners are contagious.
10 INTERVIEWER: Especially for the older people, that must be really nice. 'Cause people,
11 MARCOS: It is. And they're like "Huh." (mimics turning around to look over his shoulder)
12 They- the people stop and they're like, they're amazed. And- then, (smiles and waves)
13 "Good morning." We might be ten feet away from them at this point but, they acknowledged
14 it but it's such a shock. It SHOULDN'T be. It's a SHAME that's a shock.

Marcos sees greetings as part of DC's identity as a "nice," community-oriented place, even as the habit is disappearing—a frequent complaint by other interviewees and Washingtonians in general. By pointing out older Washingtonians' surprise and positive reactions, he shows that the community—represented by these elders—approves of the friendly behavior but also that it is now unexpected. Their positive stance authenticates the Washingtonian identity he is discursively constructing for himself and his son as representative examples. Meanwhile, by taking a negative stance toward the loss of this custom, evaluating it as "a shame" (line 14), he also judges the cultural erasure wrought by gentrification.

Who Are the Real Washingtonians? Authenticating Identity

Who are the real Washingtonians? The question of authenticity is part of Marcos's larger argument for Washingtonians' rights to the contested cityscape. Authenticity is typically associated with nativity, in the sense of native birth, history, time depth, and continuity, and with language, culture, community, and often ethnicity.[63] All of these points can be seen as Marcos constructs and authenticates a particular Washingtonian identity.

While authentication strategies often rest on notions of origins, "origins" in cities also refers to a "moral right to inhabit a space" by putting down roots. Sociologist Sharon Zukin describes this rootedness as "a continuous process of living and working, a gradual buildup of everyday experience, the expectation that neighbors and buildings that are here today will be here tomorrow."[64] Marcos invokes this moral right by portraying Washingtonians as rooted and invested in the city and their community through their actions and continuity. In contrast, he portrays gentrifiers as unrooted based on their transience and, more important, their lack of engagement. In a broader sense, they do not take care of the city as a physical or social entity. As he puts it, they "take" but "don't contribute" (excerpt 6.6).

Marcos is proud of DC's culture: language, music, food, community, politeness norms, and more. To him, gentrifiers' rejection of this culture symbolizes their lack of belonging and contributes to their negative impact on the city. Take politeness as an example. As Marcos and other participants describe it, gentrifiers do not say hello—a perception that is widespread in DC.[65] Marcos associates this lack of manners with gentrified neighborhoods and, elsewhere in his interview, evaluates it as "sad": "You know uh, it's just sad to see that. But that's- it's, the THRIVING places that you see that." Gentrifiers' lack of greeting is a violation of local cultural norms. The erasure of longtime residents that it represents—making them invisible—also symbolizes their marginalization. Indeed, Emanuel reported being seen as out of place or even suspicious and being questioned about his right to be in his old apartment building when visiting a friend in the now-gentrified barrio. As Marcos expressed elsewhere in his interview, the "real" DC still survives: "If you go to different pockets there's still family. There's still good stuff there's still good food good people good music, FROM here. You just gotta know where to go." However, this culture is now underground and imperiled rather than the norm as it was in the past.

Through contrasts such as these, Marcos legitimizes Washingtonians' claim to the city and positions gentrifiers as undeserving outsiders who are displacing "real Washingtonians." This displacement is symbolically represented by the clam chowder–ization of Union Market and other neighborhood transformations. Marcos also depicts these changes through discussing how Latinx neighborhoods and the Latino Festival that paraded through them has changed.

We would do like little festivals right there in Adams Morgan, because see back THEN when we had the Spanish cultures festival, it was a parade. Like an actual floating parade. It was really cool back then you know so it, I felt like it was much more uh, your cultures and ALL different cultures were celebrated, more. NOT like toDAY, it's, like, you know you're going to Spanish culture and there's like, White people serving tacos. You're- "What?"

Marcos contrasts the authenticity of the past parade, where all "Spanish" cultures were represented, with current celebrations, which he sees as less authentic. His use of "now" contrasts "White people selling tacos" and the commodification of diversity with the city's Latinx past.[66] His rhetorical "What?," with low, drawn-out delivery, shows his disapproval of this change.

Constructing authenticity often includes nostalgia.[67] Marcos is nostalgic for a DC that is being literally and symbolically overwritten by new residents and real estate development. While there were hard times, a sense of community flourished in response. His nostalgia lends authenticity to the Washingtonian identity his words evoke. He sees gentrifiers as antithetical to this local identity since they contribute to its loss and erasure.

Racializing the City

Marcos's understanding of race and gentrification resonates with local perceptions generally, as attested to by my other participants and ethnography as well as other scholars.[68] Gentrification is also a racialized debate in the United States more broadly, where it is seen as Whites displacing working-class Blacks and Latinxs in cities from New York to Detroit to Los Angeles.[69] This discourse in turn resonates with the racialization of urban identity as well as broader perceptions and realities of the racialized US social hegemony.

Urbanness and non-Whiteness—Blackness and Brownness—are linked in the US imaginary. This imagination intersects with class and feeds stereotypes of race, crime, and violence. However, despite the stereotype of cities as dangerous, non-White sites, they are also seen as havens for minority communities.[70] "Because urban areas are home to so many people of color, both literally and figuratively, there is an abundance of images of urban areas as romantic, nurturing, accepting havens from a cold outside (read: suburban) world. . . . Authentic cultural practices [such as language and food] are thought to abound in urban neighborhoods."[71]

The image of cities as bastions of minority communities and cultures resonates with Marcos's description of Washington, DC. He portrays a city with unique, Black-normed cultural practices and a tight-knit local community that "took care of their own" in the face of many challenges. This dynamic creates a discourse in which urbanity legitimizes minority identity, particularly Black and Brown identity, and vice versa. Urban places as minority spaces are also seen as having their own type of authenticity. Urbanness is a way of authenticating ethnoracial identity and conflating race and class.[72] Indeed, urban minority identity is sometimes seen as possessing an intrinsic "realness" and authenticity lacking in Whiteness and suburbs.[73] This paradigm of racialized urban authenticity is perhaps particularly relevant in the local environment due to DC's iconic Black history and culture, Marcos's own experiences, and the history of the Latinx community within this context.

In contrast, Whiteness in the United States more broadly is associated with social privilege but also with homogeneity, lack of culture, and even appropriation.[74] "Cultural foods" and diversity often serve as an object for White consumption.[75] Marcos's description of Adams Morgan Day as "White people selling tacos" speaks to the relationship between cultural appropriation with gentrification, on the one hand, and displacement of the very groups that create and are represented by ethnic foods, on the other—a trend and debate in the country more broadly.[76] Similarly, DC is a diverse place, and diversity in different forms is an important part of its self-identity. However, this diversity has also been commodified as a means of "selling" the city—often literally.[77] Diversity is a selling point mentioned in real estate ads for gentrified neighborhoods like Columbia Heights.[78] But as participants commented, new residents don't interact with longtime residents. I have also observed this. Walking the streets in Mount Pleasant or Columbia Heights today is like watching two worlds that occupy the same physical place but pass each other by.[79]

Conclusions

Racialized debates over class, crime, wealth, gentrification, and even White people selling tacos are not unique to DC. What is unique is the local aspect: the sense of a particular diverse culture that arose in a particular place and time and is being lost. As Marcos notes, New York City—home of rap—is famous for this. DC, however, with its own original local music and traditions, is relatively overlooked in the popular imagination. Similarly, Latinx language in the changing Chocolate City, variously now described as "vanilla swirl" and "cappuccino," has received relatively little sociolinguistic attention.[80] Marcos's words, and those of others in this book, help to tell this story.

Marcos sees himself as representative of a type: Washingtonians, defined through culture, experience, and social signifiers such as race. Of course, one man cannot speak for the entirety of DC Latinx experience—nor, indeed, for the many identities expressed within the city and its surroundings. Nevertheless, his perspective is consistent with that expressed by my other participants and resonates with broadly circulating discourses about DC as a city and about gentrification. This abundant evidence indicates a shared semiosis around the idea of what is authentically Washingtonian and what it means to be Latinx within this social imaginary.

In his interview Marcos constructs a Washingtonian identity through examples of culture, language, race, and continuity to make an argument for Washingtonians as rooted and belonging in the city. As he does so, he positions gentrifiers as diametrically opposed to Washingtonians along the same parameters. This discursive identity construction advanced his argument that real Washingtonians have a legitimate right to the city at a time when they are increasingly displaced by gentrifiers. This argument is salient locally and to Marcos personally as a native Washingtonian who desires to stake a clear claim to his local identity and belonging and to distinguish himself—as a returned, now-middle-class resident—from gentrifying outsiders.

Marcos's discursive identity construction presents Washingtonians as deserving, ethnically diverse residents who contribute to the community and share a culture and history of struggle. In contrast, he portrays White gentrifiers as undeserving outsiders who do not participate in the community and lack culture and values.

The gentrification debate is affected by current and historic race relations in the city and more broadly. Marcos describes DC as an African American–dominant Chocolate City whose culture influenced Latinxs, particularly those born there or who migrated at an early age. This perspective agrees with my participants' general memories of life in pre-gentrification DC. It makes sense, then, that Blackness holds a special role in Marcos's understanding of DC's culture and identity as a city. More broadly, he envisions DC as defined by diversity rather than the homogeneity attributed to Whiteness, expressed through the metaphor of Whites as lacking culture.

Identity and ideology function on multiple levels, all of which affect language and identity. Marcos's local understandings of authenticity as seen in this interview resonate with broader discourses of race and class, where Whiteness is associated with privilege and where Brownness and Blackness are stigmatized but imbued with urban authenticity and "covert" prestige. However, the nuanced identity that he constructs and the legitimacy claim that it supports are only legible and relevant in the local Washington, DC, social context.

Marcos constructed and authenticated a Washingtonian identity through language and "talk about language" as well as other aspects of culture and identity. He drew on different aspects of his multilingual repertoire (Spanish, LE, AAE) as he constructed a local Latinx identity that drew on both Latinx and African American language and culture. This linguistic identity construction both draws on and expands preexisting notions of identity. Marcos is not attempting to co-opt Black identity. Rather, he is constructing a hybrid local identity that is racialized as non-White and that contrasts with Whiteness, and vice versa. Blackness is a key referent, due to DC's historic Black majority and culture and its history of close contact between

Latinxs and African Americans in working-class city neighborhoods. For Marcos, the DC accent indexes localness and Washingtonian identity rather than race per se. However, its original ethnoracial associations are not forgotten, and its expanded indexicality is still racialized. Both stand in contrast to Whiteness.

The 1980s were not a utopia. Marcos, as well as my participants more broadly, remembered tensions as well as friendship between African Americans and Latinxs. Marcos recalled certain areas of the city where, according to him, he could not go, both because of violence and because he was the "wrong color." He referred to these areas as "no ground." Other participants, such as Emanuel and Alonso, were candid about conflict—sometimes physical or even fatal—between Black and Latinx youth. In my broader experience in the community, this is a memory shared by many of that generation. It was the motivation for Quique Avilés and Michelle Banks to found LatiNegro, a youth theater group that strove to build understanding between the two groups. At the same time, many formed lasting friendships. Overall, contact and socialization made Black language and culture important linguistic input and cultural reference points for many local Latinxs as they integrated into the DC environment.

Marcos's example, as with others in this book, draws attention to problematic aspects of ethnic-associated language labels. Despite years of research challenging essentialism across the sciences and humanities, fundamental notions of authentic language use remain in the assumptions that underly multilingual repertoires. What language are immigrants and their children assumed to speak, and who decides? Marcos's example, like that of the children in the 1980s playground recording with their Black peers, challenges the assumption that any ethnic language other than that of one's "own" group is necessarily inauthentic. These and more questions are encompassed by what I call the "raciomultilingual repertoire," a concept developed throughout this book, which examines how racialized groups' language is perceived across the full range of their repertoires and centers their multilingualism and its social-semiotic associations.

At the same time, it must be reiterated that although Marcos did not demonstrate any negativity toward Black language in my time with him, other participants had more ambivalent stances toward the "DC way of talking" and "sounding Black." Overall, Blackness was an "ambiguous referent" for my participants, to apply the term that Rosalyn Negrón developed in her research on New York Puerto Ricans—centered due to the local environment but uneasily, due to lingering US and Latin American race perceptions.[81] Again, this parallels participants' perception of Salvadorans and, more broadly, Central Americans as an ambiguous referent in local Latinidad—centered but also disparaged due to race and class associations.

It is worth reiterating that Marcos and my participants overall do not identify as Afro-Latinx or report being perceived as Black. In this respect, my work differs from the bulk of previous research on Latinx/African American contact, which has largely been conducted on Puerto Rican and Dominican populations, who have more prominent Afro-descent and their own complicated racial hierarchies. However, there is an important Afro-Latinx history in the DC area that is receiving more and more attention due to the Afro-Latinx community's own activism. Given the DC areas' racial dynamics, local Afro-Latinx linguistic repertoires and their roles in identity should certainly receive attention in the future.

Marcos's language raises questions of what is considered to be "authentic" language use even by scholars, versus the lived experience of many immigrants, particularly immigrants of color. As Mary Bucholtz notes, the notion of authenticity in sociolinguistics must "face the problem of essentialism."[82] Part of this task is that, as Bucholtz further observes, bilingualism is still considered to be marked or unusual. The question of *what* English immigrants and their children are authentically "allowed" to speak perhaps says more about mainstream assumptions of what is "normal"—White, middle-class English—and the subject gaze that generates it than it does about the actual lived experiences and language acquisition of many immigrants. The diverse contexts that surround immigrants' linguistic and cultural socialization warrant further exploration.

The ways in which Marcos constructs local identity deepen our understanding of DC Latinx identity in relationship to discourses about who belongs in DC and what they, and the city itself, are like.

These insights shed light into the complex ways in which racialized identities function for multilingual immigrants and their children in majority-minority urban spaces. They have implications for their orientation to race as something relevant nationally and across national borders but whose particular meanings depend on the local context even as they draw on more widely circulating ideologies. They thus also have implications for how immigrants understand local social semiosis as they "make a new place home," in the words of the 1988 Smithsonian Folklife Festival that focused on DC-area immigration.

Marcos is the product of a particular cultural blend at a particular moment in time—one that is not identical for all DC-area Latinxs. I have given examples of other participants' conflicting attitudes toward Blackness elsewhere, such as in chapter 5. Taken as a whole, these examples highlight the complexity and diversity that exist between Latinxs. They also show that Latinxs draw on US and bicultural ideologies grounded in historicity, colorism, and colonialism to make sense of their social world. However, the manifestations of these social discourses are locally understood. Ultimately, identity (including ethnocultural identity), rather than being static or simplistic, is intersectional, multilayered, contextual, and dynamic.

Conclusion

"We're so rich with different types of culture"

The book's introduction begins with a memory—a moment in time that served as a point of reflection on the DC Latinx experience. But like all snapshots, it captures only one moment; memory is selective, and communities change.

Multiple stories, voices, and discourses cohabitate in Washington, DC, and its surroundings. As Marcos said, "We're so rich with different types of culture and different little things here and there and pockets of this and that—it's awesome." The story told in this book is one of many, and many more remain to be told. The story about life in the nation's capital and for the Latinx diaspora in the United States is nevertheless an important one.

Although Latinxs as a whole are racialized as non-White in the United States, ideologies of race, class, and colorism are present among Latin Americans and their descendants, as they are in other immigrant and diasporic groups.[1] Traditional racialized hierarchies and discourses privileging Whiteness are present in Washington, DC, but are complicated by the city's demographics, where Salvadorans are the largest Latinx group; African Americans, historically the majority group; and Whites, a minority until recently. These dynamics lend prominence to the symbolic role of Salvadoran and African American languages in local understandings of Latinx language and identity while still being dogged by sociolinguistic stereotypes.

Salvadorans are seen as representative of local Latinidad due to their demographic prominence and contributions to the region. They are also seen as working class, and many Salvadorans originate in rural areas of El Salvador. The combination, as well as their intersectional race and class positioning as non-White, create an ambiguous situation where their prominence and pride coexists with stigmatization. My participants of all Latin American backgrounds frequently commented on Salvadoran Spanish, which was commonly described as "badly spoken," "humble," "rural," "vulgar," "street," "bad words," "not formal," and "ghetto." These attitudes are in line with what Lucinda Hart-González found in 1985 in the only other Spanish dialect study of DC.[2] The stability of these attitudes reflects enduring colonially descended cultural narratives in both the United States and Latin America as well as Salvadorans' local positioning.

Stigmatization of Salvadoran Spanish has to do with a conjunction of class, race, and urban/rural associations along with general prestige ideologies that stigmatize features such as /s/ weakening and *voseo*.[3] The same features, however, are not widely stigmatized when it comes to the speech of White-associated Latinxs such as Argentinians. Since Salvadorans are the largest Latinx group in the DC area, their Spanish, while disparaged, is also normalized and seen as representative of DC Spanish even while the diversity of dialects present is acknowledged. Many participants also commented on Salvadoran pride. Salvadorans themselves often described their Spanish as "normal." They also pushed back against deficit discourses, and their language served as a source of solidarity.

African American English (AAE) was also ambiguously positioned: both normalized and stigmatized as part of the local Latinx contact-infused repertoire. Participants described DC Latinxs' English as AAE-influenced as well as Spanish-influenced. They often referred to AAE as "slang," "ghetto," or "street"—descriptions that indicate its deficit positioning and echo descriptions of Salvadoran Spanish. AAE was also seen as a symbol of DC identity—among other cultural markers such as music, clothing, food, values, and pragmatic norms—and thus as part of DC Latinx identity. For example, Marcos made frequent reference to blended Latinx and African American culture, mentioning foods such as "*empanadas* and *pupusas*"—a traditional Salvadoran dish—served with soul food, and to traditional Latin American music and DC's local go-go music playing in the streets. His narratives are part of a broader telling of "old" and "new" DC in which he constructs an authentic local identity that includes hybrid Latinidad and contrasts with that of White gentrifiers. Current in local and broader media, this is a racialized debate that I have also noted in ethnographic observation and that resonates with research on African American language and identity around gentrification in Washington, DC.[4]

AAE's racial associations therefore operate on multiple levels, with meanings that relate to but are not limited to Blackness. They comprise an expanded racialization in Latinx ethnic identity formation within a local and broader framework where Latinxs and African Americans tend to be in contact due to material circumstances and the legacy of racial segregation. The racial associations of AAE are not bleached for DC Latinxs. However, neither are they attempting to perform an African American identity. Rather, the local contact situation and DC's demographics and place identity seem to make AAE an index of a local identity disaligned with Whiteness and its associations of power and privilege, as seen in discourses of gentrification and of "Washington" (the seat of national power) versus "DC" (the local city). At the same time, AAE's negative status associations persisted.

Advantages of a Raciomultilingual Framework

A raciomultilingual perspective advances the theoretical conversation, allowing for the coexistence of multiple, sometimes contradictory discourses about ethnocultural identity that draw both on existing discourses and on the evolution of new sociolinguistic norms with their own ideological centers. Ideologies cross language boundaries and traverse space and time to cohere around social figures that are racialized along multiple linguistic and cultural dimensions. These social figures in turn are associated with further indexical meanings such as authenticity and belonging that draw on and continue the racialization of place-related linguistic identity. The framework goes beyond associating the ethnolinguistic repertoire with a singular ethnocultural group; it examines the raciolinguistic ideologies that attach to its various components and to multilingualism itself or its perceived absence, as well as the less-examined ways these elements influence identity construction. It accepts the coexistence of multiple discourses: diversity and cohesion, acceptance and discrimination, solidarity and tension. Rather than a single story, community identity is an ongoing conversation. A raciomultilingual approach allows us to embrace this complexity while identifying both continuities and new beliefs and practices.

Not everyone who identifies as Latinx in the District of Columbia and its surrounding Maryland and Virginia suburbs, known as the DMV, talks the same way, of course. Not everyone shares the ethnolinguistic repertoire, and those who do may have some but not all of its elements. Nevertheless, it is a recognized way of speaking in the area, making it available as a resource for identity construction and for social meanings that go beyond their original indexicalities, as we have seen.

Centering Racialized Multilingualism

Centering multilingual repertoires, and the identity work that coheres around them in racial and ethnic identity construction, moves away from taking monolingualism and associated discourses as the norm. As multilinguals do not experience their languages in isolation, they do not think about them in strict separation either.[5] While particular ideologies and indexicalities may attach to particular features, speakers hold systemic beliefs that also operate on multiple levels but are broadly influenced by normative logics. Groupings of features and their indexical meanings do not necessarily operate in isolation within language and varietal boundaries but rather in constellations across boundaries, even while these boundaries retain symbolic meaning for speakers. This perspective helps the investigator examine the social motivations for named languages' importance to speakers while their languaging challenges the adequacy of these constructs in understanding fluid language practices.[6] Without a holistic view, perspectives on the languages of multilinguals will necessarily be fragmented and viewed through a partial lens to the impoverishment of interpretation.

Sociolinguistic ideologies are not limited to particular aspects of the repertoire but are underlain by systematic beliefs that affect all aspects of minoritized linguistic repertoires. A raciomultilingual lens illuminates unifying systemic beliefs that can explain sociolinguistic ideology on "both sides" of the linguistic repertoire. In my data, similar ideological processes affected the positioning of Salvadoran Spanish and AAE. The use of some but not all features of AAE were enough to position speakers as "sounding Black," which was both stigmatized and locally normalized—and even prestigious, as a marker of local identity. Salvadoran Spanish was similarly stigmatized, normalized, and seen as local. These associations were mobilized in identity construction, which positions constructed selves and others in terms of race and related discourses of class, authenticity, and belonging. In contrast, White American English and Peninsular Spanish were seen as the most correct. Without looking at the repertoire holistically, commonalities in this racialization of English and Spanish and their sociohistorical as well as local motivations could be overlooked.

More broadly, a holistic approach provides a lens through which to understand the continued impact of beliefs about language proficiency and linguistic correctness that persist in communities and individuals as well as in schools and society. It reveals how concepts such as "proficiency" and "prescriptivism," which are often considered separate, in fact interact and reinforce each other. Both concepts are manifestations of a belief in language correctness that—in its privileging and marginalization of different ways of speaking—ultimately reflects postcolonial racialized hierarchies.

Comparisons that my participants drew between heritage Salvadoran Spanish as "broken" and uneducated and AAE and Jamaican English as "broken" and "improper . . . not what you would find in the dictionary" show that both perceived lack of proficiency and lack of adherence to prescriptivist rules fall under the concept of "bad language" for speakers. In another crosslinguistic example of deficit positioning, second-generation Latinxs, mainly Salvadorans, were described as sounding "just like a Black kid, and if you hear their Spanish it's worse, broken." As this shows, later-generation Latinxs bore the double burden of their Spanish being seen as inadequate in terms of both dialect and fluency, an observation also made by scholars such as Jennifer Leeman.[7] The conflation of these language judgments in participants' attitudes demonstrates that prescriptivism and notions of proficiency or fully developed language are not as separate for speakers as they are for analysts but rather can merge into generalized beliefs about incorrectness that adhere to marginalized speakers, echoing calls by Dennis Preston and by Nathan Albury for the importance of folk attitudes in critical linguistic analysis.[8] The concepts are ideologically connected, since beliefs about correctness, normed on the speech of dominant sectors of society, were historically privileged and codified through nation building and imposed on other regions through colonialism.[9]

Ideological Continuity and Change

Participants' comments showed that their understandings of language, race, and multilingualism simultaneously reified and challenged traditional notions that assign one language or variety per identity. This finding suggests that language and social boundaries are more porous than is often assumed. However, culturally and historically rooted raciolinguistic discourses also continued to hold sway.

Established raciomultilingual ideologies lingered even as community language changed. Essentialist beliefs that stigmatized heritage Spanish practices and viewed them as a sign of Americanization persisted, causing cultural and linguistic insecurity in later generations despite their general bilingualism and desire to maintain the language.[10]

African American influence on Latinx language was normalized and seen as a natural outcome of local culture, pointing to the porosity of ethnoracial boundaries. At the same time, AAE influence was marked enough to be commented on, and its cultural heritage was recognized. Indeed, while most participants viewed this fusion culture to be a normal part of local life, for some at least there was also a sense that it was possible to take it too far. The discourse of "trying too hard" that Noemí invoked is another way of maintaining boundaries. Deep-rooted racialized prestige discourses from the United States and Latin America that privilege Whiteness over Blackness and Indigeneity also continued to hold sway.

Scalar Semiotics and Recentering

A raciomultilingual view offers a framework in which racialized linguistic identity can be interpreted in relationship to the multiple levels and centers of semiotic reference at which social beliefs proliferate and are understood. Participants racialized Salvadoran language in ways that related to Latin American and US prestige hierarchies but also to the Washington, DC, context. The intersection of "DC Latinidad" with local African American language and culture—seen as an index of place identity—also relies on DC as a semiotic center. This scalar perspective accommodates a simultaneity of discourses that encompass diversity and contradiction. Other meanings coexisted at multiple scalar levels and were constantly being reified and contested. Stereotypes about Salvadorans, for example, drew on local and broader discourses but could be scaled up or down to represent "DC Salvadorans," "DC Latinidad" in general, or Central Americans more broadly. And the same semiotic center could serve as a reference point for multiple discourses. For example, diversity itself is symbolic of DC Latinx identity, while the Salvadoran figure also occupies a central role.

Scalar discourses also informed participants' understandings of ethnolinguistic authenticity. "Real Latinxs" were perceived to speak Spanish and, in general, to not "sound White" (meaning code-switching and ethnic-associated linguistic features in English) and to have cultural knowledge. Cultural knowledge also operated at different levels in relationship to different semiotic centers, whether normed on Latin America (e.g., music such as *marimba, merengue,* and *ranchera*), oriented to newer forms popular with youth in the United States (e.g., reggaeton, hip-hop), or based on DC culture itself (go-go). "Real Latinxs" were also physically assumed to look mestizo or at least not "gringo" (blond and blue-eyed) despite much diversity in Latin Americans and among DC Latinxs themselves. This perception may link to local demographics in which working-class Central Americans predominate as well as to a broader US racialization of Latinxs and the prominence of discourses of *mestizaje* in Latin America.[11] And this perception also intersects with an idea of "real Washingtonians" as non-White based on DC's history, the circumstances of Latinx assimilation, and a general nonelite image. "Real Washingtonians" were depicted as long-term residents and working people rather than transient elites, echoing the local tradition of seeing "DC," the working city that keeps the lights on, as separate from the "Washington" of wealth and power. These discourses came together in one influential social figure of "DC Latinxs" as mestizo, working-class Salvadorans, with locally raised generations speaking a bilingual, African American–influenced repertoire.

Migration and Global Cities

Examining the discourses that coalesce around minoritized people and their language in migratory contexts is an essential means of tracing connections between sociohistorically grounded beliefs and their continued resilience and reconfiguration. In my data, similarities and differences among Latinxs that were indexed by language drew on broader Latin American discourses but were grounded in local solidarity and tensions. Further, stances toward Spanish as part of ethnic identity differed between initial immigrants and their descendants but retained a moral weight, in common with other findings that later US generations do not necessarily consider Spanish essential to Latinx identity.[12] Nevertheless, second-generation participants were still affected by deficit discourses that potentially reduce community sociability due to language shame.

Globalization is inherently an influence on Latinx migration to DC: neoliberalism and its social and political consequences for Latin America were and remain a major motivation for migration, and the DC Latinx community's embassy roots speak to globalization's direct influence on its origins. "Glocal" discourses where the global and local intersect, such as the salient division between "local" and "international" Latinxs, are historically founded in this dynamic. They also are inherent in continuing differences of material resources and social capital linked to DC's global-city dynamics as well as in different histories of migration and social positionings.[13] The global-city environment creates a particular elite group of "international" Latinxs who are conceived of as White but within a Latinx framework and dual-colonial transnational class/whitening hierarchy rather than conceived of as "White" being seen as Anglo-American, as it is within the US framework. This "local" versus "international" distinction takes on a particular significance that is "glocal" in the sense of being simultaneously globally and locally derived, within DC's diverse and stratified Latinx social context. As this observation suggests, there is room for more research on the nuances of how class is imagined within "panethnic" identities in diaspora, particularly as global cities and mobility under late capitalism increase social stratification.[14]

Indeed, globalization is changing intraethnic dynamics, hierarchies, and ideologies at multiple scalar levels. Within this, there is a continued role for diaspora studies since dynamics and memories of migration influence language and ideology, a perspective that Lars Hinrichs and I have argued is important for interpreting current sociolinguistic understandings of contact repertoires.[15] In my data, I show that notions of authenticity are linked to understandings origins and rootedness that orient to different centers in diaspora and are transmitted by individuals but also hold broader sway at a collective ideological level.

Changing Metropolises

Change is a constant, and DC like all places is constantly changing. Gentrification has advanced apace—indeed, participants I have remained in touch with remark that they don't recognize the city and that the displacement of "people like them" from their old neighborhoods is nearly complete. The discourses articulated by Marcos and Emanuel, among others, are still heard today, but with more resignation. As such, it remains to be seen what will change or remain the same in DC Latinidad's sociolinguistic story moving forward.

The DC region is in a moment of change and reflection. It will be very interesting to see what the future holds socially, discursively, and linguistically. Gentrification's effects on racialized discourses about language are clearly demonstrated in my research and that of others.[16] The study of language, race, and gentrification is growing, particularly in linguistic landscape and education research, but more work is necessary in general and in terms of intergroup dynamics and immigration.[17]

City and suburban dynamics are also changing. US suburbs have traditionally been perceived as White due to their growth during middle-class "White flight" from cities, in contrast with, for example, Europe and Latin America, where suburban areas are often inhabited by working-class residents and migrants.[18] However, US suburbs are increasingly diverse and are the largest area of immigrant settlement and population growth.[19] The DC metropolitan area's suburbs are highly diverse with respect to race, immigration, and socioeconomic status, and there are nonetheless White-dominated and Black-dominated areas as well as Latinx enclaves in the suburbs.[20] Suburbs thus offer a rich and relatively underexplored area for the study of race and immigrant language.[21] Anecdotally, parents have told me that "kids of all backgrounds sound Black" and that "kids of all backgrounds sound White" in the suburbs. These contrasting opinions suggest that suburban raciolinguistic patterns are likely nuanced in their localization but that broader raciolinguistic perceptions also continue to hold sway—an intriguing direction for future investigation. More broadly, the DC metropolitan area offers rich potential for linguistic research on the many diverse communities that inhabit it.

I, Too, Speak America

In his poem "I, Too," the famous African American poet Langston Hughes reflects on the "darker brother's" marginalization and looks forward to a more inclusive future.[22] He uses the metaphor of song; I substitute the more prosaic "speak," which, as I have shown, is fundamental to issues of representation. Much has changed since Hughes wrote his poem in 1926, and much remains to be done. A fundamental point I am making is that we still have much to learn about how immigrants and other minority groups interact and imagine themselves in relationship to each other.

While immigration is often pictured in terms of assimilation into mainstream White America, immigrants frequently settle in areas where they primarily come into contact with other US minorities.[23] How these groups imagine each other is essential to understanding the United States and, as I have shown, may well not be exactly the same as the way the White mainstream understands racialized identities and race relations. As sociologist and race scholar George Lipsitz notes, members of different groups can come to perceive similarities and hence solidarity or "families of resemblance" between themselves, often due to shared alienation.[24] We need more research on dynamics between groups, how they imagine themselves and others, and how they maintain and blend their social boundaries.

Sociolinguistic contact in diasporic communities in "majority-minority" contexts provides a lens for decentering the dominant lens. White-normed "standard American English" is not the only or primary input variety for many immigrants, as Django Paris and Awad Ibrahim have noted in their concepts of Learners of American Englishes and Black English as a Second Language.[25] As Paris's African American participants commented about Latinx youth, "They're in my culture, they speak the same way."[26] The United States is an increasingly majority-minority country. As such, the dynamics between different groups, on the one hand, and how we imagine these contexts and encounters, on the other, warrants further investigation.[27]

Participants' words add nuances to contact between African Americans and Latinxs. We saw, for example, how anti-Black stereotypes from Latin America and the United States are perpetuated and reinterpreted by immigrants through a diasporic lens. Participants were also aware of nuances that monolithic framings of "Blackness" do not recognize. The DC area's Black population is diverse. For one thing, it encompasses both historic and new diaspora; participants viewed African immigrants as different from African Americans. Participants were aware of class differences among African Americans, although they still expressed prestige in terms of Whiteness ("the educated ones sound White"), which, in DC's dialectal setting, with its long-established middle-class and elite Black groups, is not necessarily true. They were also aware of experiences of privilege and prejudice with African Americans. And they reported experiencing linguistic prejudice from African Americans in the workplace, drawing attention to nativism among African Americans as a dimension of their interactions with Latinxs.[28] These observations indicate directions for fruitful collaboration between linguistics, African American studies, and Latinx studies as well as other avenues for cross-pollination and theory. And this is laying aside for the moment the question of Afro-Latinidad, whether from areas of Latin America with many *afrodescendientes* or from mixed families in the United States, which I return to shortly.

> *What color is this Latinhood of mine? What language does it speak?*
> —Quique Avilés, *Latinhood*, 2003

The stories shared in this book increase our understanding of different dimensions of diversity within "Latinidad," with implications for other panethnic identities and theorizing processes of ethnoracial category construction more broadly. Language is a powerful aspect of how identity is constructed and imagined. Research in significant Latinx population centers such as New York City and Miami shows that sociolinguistic perception relates to complex local hierarchies that draw on colorism, material conditions, and circumstances of migration, among other factors, although Jonathan Rosa's work in Chicago notes that social relations can be more nuanced and entwined than these divisions might imply.[29] My research on Washington, DC, reveals similar complex hierarchies and processes of ideological cohesion and tension around how Latinx identity is imagined in the local environment—a dynamic encapsulated by the epigraph above from Salvadoran DC poet Quique Avilés. Sociolinguistic attitudes showed both a Salvadoran-normed narrative that enjoyed a central yet ambiguous symbolic role in local Latinx language and identity and a robust coexisting discourse of dialect diversity. Both discourses inform sociolinguistic understandings of "local Latinidad"; they have coexisted since at least the 1980s and appear to be holding steady.[30] This polyphony is characteristic of diverse DC Latinxs and speaks to the dynamic complexity of language and beliefs within groups often assumed to be more homogenous. Contributing to our understanding of Latinidad more broadly, DC Latinidad is not a question of diversity or cohesion but of both at the same time, as expressed by Latinxs themselves.[31] At the same time, participants' perceptions of Salvadorans contribute to the growing area of Central American studies in the United States.

A raciomultilingual lens sharpens our understanding of diversity among Latinxs and of the ways it affects community language use and other social practices. It offers a productive look at racialization among Latinxs via processes that draw on long-standing associations of race with social hierarchy and (dis)privilege in different regions of the Americas that nevertheless share White-centered colonial history yet are also fundamentally connected to local social meanings. Numerous semiotic centers exist in diaspora, and these centers are neither static nor uncontested but are in constant processes of reification and reimagination.

While Blackness in general was the focus of a good deal of overt or covert discussion among my participants, most of this revolved around African Americans. Participants said little about Latinxs of African descent. This contrasts with research in New York, Miami, and Chicago, where Black associations with Caribbean Latinxs were influential.[32] Only three participants, to my knowledge, identified as Afro-Latinx. One, a community activist, perceived an erasure of Black Latinxs in current understandings of the DC community despite the Afro-Latinx roots of many founding members, such as Dominican organizer Casilda Luna.

Many of the participants I talked to were from Central American regions where African-descent populations historically have been expelled and erased from the national narrative. Several of these participants mentioned being surprised upon first meeting Black Americans, a comment echoed by artist and poet Quique Avilés, who prefaced his poetry reading at the memorial service for legendary local Afro-Cuban musician Francisco Rigores with comments on Central American migration to DC as a learning experience: "Ignorance ... we didn't know what it meant to be Black, we didn't know what it meant to be Latino, a lot of us, never ever heard that word before." This lack of awareness related to the erasure of Blackness in Central American national consciousnesses might have contributed to the infrequent mentions of Afro-Latinxs in my study.[33]

Since this data was collected, awareness of Afro-Latinidad has increased locally thanks to activists such as Roland Roebuck and the DC Afro Latino Caucus, and public conversation about Afro-Latinidad has increased in the United States and Latin America as a whole. However, much linguistic research remains to be done in this area. Given the important contributions that Afro-Latinx studies can make to sociolinguistics and vice versa, research in this vein in DC as a historically Black city undergoing rapid change presents an important future direction.[34] And there are many other aspects of racial and ethnic diversity ready for exploration in the diverse panoply of Latinxs of different Indigenous and immigrant backgrounds. The language and identity of Asian Latinxs, for example—how they are viewed by others and dynamics among themselves—remains to be fully investigated.[35]

Mixed cultural heritage was another theme that arose in my data. Several of my participants had parents of different Latinx backgrounds, and a few had one Latinx and another non-Latinx parent. I found most part-Salvadorans identified with the Salvadoran aspect of their heritage, but for those who were part–South American, their South American heritage took precedence. This indicates that the intra-Latinx hierarchical ideology and clear patterns of prestige and stigma evinced throughout the data are also active among those of mixed heritage. However, this finding could also be related to maternal influence, since in most cases participants of mixed heritage identified most strongly with their mother's Latinx or national heritage. In Chicago, Kim Potowski found that speakers of mixed Mexican and Puerto Rican heritage tended to use more Mexican Spanish, likely due to its greater local prestige, unless they were raised by Puerto Rican women, in which case the mother or stepmother's influence lent itself to greater Puerto Rican linguistic influence.[36] She also found that these speakers claimed dual identities, but their families considered the identities and the language they used to index their identities mutually exclusive (i.e., looking and sounding like or unlike a "real Puerto Rican or Mexican"). Further study of raciomultilingual patterns and imaginings among speakers of mixed heritage in the DC region, where mixed families are common, would be interesting, and this aspect of diversity is growing in the United States as a whole.[37]

Decentering the Hegemonic Gaze

A raciomultilingual lens reminds us that while there are many subject gazes, certain ones tend to be centered. A White-normed gaze informed by the history of colonization and race relations—including the concept of race itself—remains normalized in Western societies. This hegemonic framework marks non-White groups as "other," imposes essentialized notions of homogeneity onto their actual diversity, and affects assumptions about how different groups speak and behave, with implications for concepts such as authenticity.[38] Questions such as how distinctiveness is determined and how language is assigned to a group, and vice versa, continue to be debated.[39] Scholars have drawn attention to the ideological basis of the idea of authenticity and fundamental constructs such as that of the native speaker.[40] "Surprising" language—language use that deviates from established norms—may not be surprising to speakers themselves and to their peers, particularly in situations of hybridity, underscoring the question of whose gaze is centered in research and how this paradigm can further the very dynamics that it often seeks to question.[41] Perennial theoretical questions such as the ongoing tension between boundaries and fluidity in linguistics cannot be understood without taking the linguistic repertoire as a whole into account.

Migration and contact situations highlight these questions. For example, Ben Rampton's early attempts to explain crossing—or language use by "people who are not accepted members of the group associated with the second language that they are using (code-switching into varieties that are not generally thought to belong to them)"—by youth in a multilingual, multiracial environment does not unpack how language is assigned or assumed in these contexts.[42] In the case of language acquisition, which non–heritage language would "belong" to immigrants and their descendants other than that of the people surrounding them? Without taking the local context into account, my participants' use of AAE-influenced English could be seen as "crossing" rather than the emergence of a local ethnic way of speaking.

Turning a raciomultilingual lens on our own practices as researchers can help us subvert paradigmatic assumptions and decenter Whiteness while still recognizing its ideological power. Sociolinguistic ideologies gain their continued relevance through regular reification, including through research paradigms. Scholars who desire to change hegemonic dynamics must acknowledge them in order to disrupt them. On a philosophical level, we can question how our work and social engagement challenge or perpetuate the systems that we inherit and inhabit. A focus on illuminating and challenging hegemonic paradigms is in line with sociolinguistics' foundational interest in social justice. By carefully theorizing relationships between racial and linguistic structures and understanding the context through which they come into being, we can further imagine how our work contributes to society and how to improve research and application. Directions such as these continue to grow, but much remains to be done.

A Methodological Note

Multipronged approaches are essential in order to unpack the ways in which linguistic identities are constructed and understood in relationship to the myriad factors that affect minoritization. It is always necessary to take the local and broader social context into account—what Ana Celia Zentella calls an "anthropolitical linguistic" perspective[43]—in keeping with critical approaches in sociolinguistics and heritage languages studies and with the "social turn" in applied linguistics.[44] Fine-grained and individual factors and the broader systemic context are mutually influential. Without in-depth analysis of linguistic features, it would not be possible to observe the linguistic repertoire and to describe language in the community and how it is influenced by broad social dynamics. But without qualitative analysis, its interpretation would necessarily be limited. As our technical methods become more sophisticated, we must not lose sight of the human element in our research questions and approaches. Pioneering sociolinguist William Labov stressed that while increasingly sophisticated technology provides valuable insights, sociolinguistics necessarily involves human interaction:

> All of this technology could easily carry us away from the human issues involved in the use of language ... that might win the game but lose the match.... The work that I really want to do, the excitement and adventure of the field, comes in meeting the speakers of the language face to face, entering their homes, hanging out on corners, porches, taverns, pubs and bars.[45]

In-depth field observation and other qualitative methods are as necessary now as ever to understand fundamentally *socio*linguistic questions.

The More Things Change, the More They Stay the Same?

DC is a fitting site for the examination of complex raciomultilingual identity construction. In many ways Washington, DC, is a non-White city not only in the demographic sense but in the sense of a gap between White-associated structures of power ("Washington," the seat of government and of entrenched power and privilege) and the local community. DC, "Chocolate City," was majority Black for most of the twentieth century and is still majority non-White—with people of color, immigrants, and a generally diverse populace living in close contact throughout the metropolitan area—although race and class distinctions are pertinent, and gentrification is rapidly changing settlement patterns. This composition produces fruitful directions for future research. DC is also historically an activist city, such as the Black civil rights activism that later served as a model for local Latinx organization. This antiestablishment stance of resistance to hegemonic power structures also positions it as non-White to a certain degree, as can be seen in political rationales for denying DC statehood as "not White enough" and "too liberal"—a discourse that resonates with similar opposition to Puerto Rican statehood.[46] This racialized place identity informed some of the discourses that my participants shared about being Washingtonian: not trying to be Black but laying claim to a broader non-White local identity, even as they were also influenced by Black language and culture—an influence that they recognized and gave attribution.

While conflicts of course exist, participants generally reported getting along with those of other backgrounds. Part of this harmony is due to simple familiarity with difference.[47] It is also due to a discourse of diversity and multicultural celebration as part of the city's identity, although as Modan notes, this discourse can paper over social divides and become part of the neoliberal commodification of diversity in gentrification.[48] A great deal of contact between Latinxs of different backgrounds has taken place since the community's beginning, and this contact continues to this day. There is genuine interest in different cultures and where people are from; at the same time, joking and rivalry occur. While this jostling is often part of friendly discourse, an edge can also be present due to the different hierarchies and positionalities we saw in the preceding chapters.

I have shown how a raciomultilingual perspective advances the study of sociolinguistic meaning. The insights provided extend beyond sociolinguistics to topics of interest to the social sciences and humanities more broadly. Ultimately, they raise questions about the impact of hegemonic gazes in fundamental understandings of language and race. By so doing, they reflect on foundational questions about language itself and as part of society and social change.

Questions of language, identity, power, and representation are arguably more important now than ever. Benedict Anderson wrote about imagined communities at a time when the world order was changing.[49] Arguments about race, ethnicity, and belonging have intensified in recent years and continue to draw in language as a proxy for more overt discrimination in schools and society.[50] Populism is on the rise, and migrant and refugee rights are under threat.[51] In the United States, the perennial debate over Latinx immigration was inflamed by the presidential elections of 2016 and 2024.[52] Meanwhile, diversity, mobility, and multilingualism continue; understandings of identity are challenged and reinscribed; and new beliefs emerge even as traditional ideologies remain. In these times, it is essential that we understand processes of language and identity in order to develop more just societies.

Notes

Introduction

1. Cadaval, *Creating a Latino Identity*.
2. Modan, *Turf Wars*.
3. Cadaval, *Creating a Latino Identity*.
4. Jessica Weiss, "Meridian Hill Park Drum Circle: Still Going Strong," *Washingtonian*, May 10, 2011, https://www.washingtonian.com/2011/05/10/meridian-hill-park-drum-circle-still-going-strong/.
5. Ron Elving, "Trump Is Still Running against the City and Idea of Washington, DC," NPR, June 27, 2020, https://www.npr.org/2020/06/27/883759400/trump-is-still-running-against-the-city-and-idea-of-washington-d-c.
6. Rosa and Flores, "Unsettling Race and Language."
7. García and Li, "Translanguaging."
8. Erker, "The Limits of Named Language Varieties."
9. Bucholtz, "Sociolinguistic Nostalgia."
10. Rampton, "Language Crossing."
11. Cheng, "1.5 Generation Korean Americans"; and Dolberg and Amit, "On a Fast-Track to Adulthood."
12. Faez, "Linguistic Identities and Experiences," 125.
13. Eckert, *Meaning and Linguistic Variation*; and Martínez and Train, *Tension and Contention in Language Education*.
14. Sabrina Tavernise, "A Population Changes, Uneasily," *New York Times*, July 17, 2011, https://www.nytimes.com/2011/07/18/us/18dc.html.
15. National Science Foundation Doctoral Dissertation Research Improvement Grant 1324387.
16. Many thanks to Noemí and our student research assistants for collaboration with data collection and to the American University Center for Latin American and Latino Studies and Metropolitan Research Center for research support.
17. Coupland, *Style*; Schilling-Estes, "Constructing Ethnicity in Interaction"; and Tseng, "Vowel Variation, Style, and Identity Construction."
18. Davies and Harré, "Positioning"; Du Bois, "The Stance Triangle"; Harré, "Positioning Theory"; Jaffe, *Stance*; and Kiesling, "Style as Stance."
19. García and Li, "Translanguaging"; Johnstone, "A New Role for Narrative"; and Kiesling, "Style as Stance."

20. De Fina, *Identity in Narrative*; De Fina, "Positioning Level 3"; De Fina, "Discourse and Identity"; Mushin, *Evidentiality and Epistemological Stance*; and Ochs, "Constructing Social Identity."

21. Blommaert, *The Sociolinguistics of Globalization*; and Tseng, "Advancing a Sociolinguistics of Complexity."

22. While these are also features of other dialects, such as Argentinian Spanish, their use is not always stigmatized. The different prestige assigned to different Spanishes is based on a complex range of ideological factors grounded in current and historical-colonial social hierarchies, which I explore in following chapters.

23. Tseng, "Vowel Variation, Style, and Identity Construction."

24. Slomanson and Newman, "Peer Group Identification."

25. Fought, *Chicano English in Context*.

26. However, on "ethnic dialect," see Eckert's critique of the term "ethnolect" as unequally applied to White and racioethnically marked varieties. Eckert, *Meaning and Linguistic Variation*.

27. The capitalization of "Whiteness," as with other race/ethnic terminology, continues to be debated. Pérez Huber, for example, does not capitalize "white," in order to symbolically undermine White supremacy. However, others capitalize "White" to underscore that rather than being a neutral identity, Whiteness itself is a racialized category (Lopes and Thomas). There is no single convention: style guides such as the American Psychological Association *Publication Manual* and the *Chicago Manual of Style* allow for the capitalization of both, while the Associated Press does not capitalize "white." John Daniszewski, "Why We Will Lowercase White," July 20, 2020, "https://blog.ap.org/announcements/why-we-will-lowercase-white." In this book I capitalize "White" to emphasize that racialization does not only affect minority groups and to interrupt Whiteness's privilege of normative nonmarkedness—a point that is salient in my DC research, where Whiteness is marked and its privileges are often contested.

28. Tseng, "Nativized Exoticism."

29. Blommaert, *The Sociolinguistics of Globalization*.

Chapter 1

1. Braiding hair is a distinctive aspect of African, African American, and diaspora culture.

2. Sassen, "The Global City." The DMV is a hip-hop coinage for "DC-Maryland-Virginia" now widely used in the metropolitan area. Opinions on the exact boundaries of the DMV vary, but locals generally understand it to mean DC proper and the surrounding urbanized suburbs served by the Washington Metropolitan Area Transit Authority (WMATA) metro. This is a narrower definition than the Census definition of the greater DC metropolitan

area, which encompasses more of Virginia and Maryland and part of West Virginia. See MCS staff, "What Is Considered Part of the DMV?," *The MOCOSHOW*, December 19, 2020, https://mocoshow.com/2020/12/19/a-deeper-look-at-what-is-considered-part-of-the-dmv/; MCS staff, "The Story behind 'The DMV,'" *The MOCOSHOW*, November 17, 2020, https://mocoshow.com/2020/11/17/the-story-behind-the-dmv/; and US Bureau of Labor Statistics, "Washington-Arlington-Alexandria."

3. Richardson, Mitchell, and Edlebi, *Gentrification and Disinvestment 2020*; and Richardson, Mitchell, and Franco, *Shifting Neighborhoods*.

4. On raciolinguistic theory, see Rosa and Flores, "Unsettling Race and Language." On language ideology, linguistic embodiment, and authenticity, see Bucholtz and Hall, "Embodied Sociolinguistics"; Heller, "Bilingualism as Ideology and Practice"; Woolard, *Singular and Plural*; and Woolard and Schieffelin, "Language Ideology." On bilingualism, heritage languages, and the sociolinguistics of globalization, see Blommaert, *The Sociolinguistics of Globalization*; de Houwer, "Bilingual Language Acquisition"; Li, *The Bilingualism Reader*; Potowski, *The Routledge Handbook of Spanish as a Heritage Language*; and Schalley and Eisenchlas, *Handbook of Home Language Maintenance and Development*.

5. Flores and Rosa, "Undoing Appropriateness"; Rosa and Flores, "Unsettling Race and Language."

6. Martínez and Train, *Tension and Contention in Language Education*.

7. Bucholtz and Hall, "Embodied Sociolinguistics," 175.

8. Alim, "Who's Afraid of the Transracial Subject?"

9. García and Li, "Translanguaging."

10. Irvine and Gal, "Language Ideology"; and Woolard, *Singular and Plural*.

11. Benor, "Ethnolinguistic Repertoire."

12. Blommaert, *The Sociolinguistics of Globalization*.

13. Blommaert, *The Sociolinguistics of Globalization*.

14. Blommaert and Rampton, "Language and Superdiversity," 3.

15. On storytelling, see De Fina, "Positioning Level 3." On stylistic language use, see Schilling, "Investigating Stylistic Variation." On taking stances toward different conversational topics, see Du Bois, "The Stance Triangle." On positioning themselves in alignment or opposition to others, see Harré, "Positioning Theory."

16. Eckert, *Meaning and Linguistic Variation*; and Irvine and Gal, "Language Ideology."

17. Bamberg, De Fina, and Schiffrin, "Discourse and Identity Construction."

18. Anderson, *Imagined Communities*.

19. Eckert, *Meaning and Linguistic Variation*; and Silverstein, "Indexical Order."

20. Correa, "Advocating for Critical Pedagogical Approaches."

21. Duff, "Transnationalism, Multilingualism, and Identity"; Kerswill,

"Identity, Ethnicity and Place"; and Lytra and Jørgensen, *Multilingualism and Identities*.

22. García and Li, "Translanguaging." The implications of the translanguaging versus code-switching paradigm for theoretical linguistics continue to be debated. MacSwan, "A Multilingual Perspective on Translanguaging"; Otheguy, García, and Reid, "A Translanguaging View"; Li, "Translanguaging as a Practical Theory"; and Lewis, Jones, and Baker, "Translanguaging."

23. Zentella, "TWB (Talking while Bilingual)."

24. Pennycook, *Global Englishes*.

25. Woolard, *Singular and Plural*.

26. Bucholtz and Hall, "Language and Identity."

27. Bucholtz and Hall, "Embodied Sociolinguistics."

28. Irvine and Gal, "Language Ideology."

29. Inequality based on race and ethnicity was historically ingrained across all dimensions of US society, most notably through the enslavement of African and Indigenous peoples, segregation, and other legal, institutional, and daily practices that separated groups based on phenotype, discriminated against non-Whites, and were upheld through violence.

30. On accent discrimination, see Baugh, "Linguistic Profiling and Discrimination"; and Lippi-Green, *English with an Accent*. On English-only legislation, see Zentella, "The Hispanophobia of the Official English Movement."

31. Gee, *Social Linguistics and Literacies*, 142.

32. The notion of "speaking a language" is itself ideological. Tseng, "'Qué barbaridad.'"

33. Irvine and Gal, "Language Ideology."

34. Leonardo and Hunter, "Imagining the Urban."

35. Carris, "La Voz Gringa."

36. Britain, "Countering the Urbanist Agenda"; Eckert, "The Future of Variation Studies"; and Kerswill, "Migration and Language."

37. On the neighborhood-grounded social studies tradition, see Labov, *Language in the Inner City*. On the relationship between physical places, lived social spaces, and language, see Johnstone, "Place, Globalization, and Linguistic Variation"; and Auer and Schmidt, *Language and Space*.

38. On traditional and emergent immigrant gateways and diverse global neighborhoods, see Singer, "Twenty-First Century Gateways"; and Zhang and Logan, "Global Neighborhoods." On more homogenous ethnic enclaves, see Lacayo, "Latinos Need to Stay in Their Place."

39. S. Martin, "Climate Change, Migration, and Governance"; and Sassen, "The Global City."

40. For "global cities," see Sassen, "The Global City." For "superdiversity," see Vertovec, "Super-Diversity and Its Implications."

41. Lynch, *The Routledge Handbook of Spanish in the Global City*; cf. Caravedo,

"Las ciudades como espacios mentales y lingüísticos." For "organized heterogeneity," see Eriksen, *Globalization*.

42. Blommaert, *The Sociolinguistics of Globalization*; and Blommaert and Rampton, "Language and Superdiversity."

43. Critiques of the term as Eurocentric are provided by Makoni, "A Critique of Language, Languaging, and Supervernacular"; Ndhlovu, "A Decolonial Critique"; and Pavlenko, "Superdiversity and Why It Isn't."

44. Lynch, *The Routledge Handbook of Spanish in the Global City*; and Márquez-Reiter and Rojo, *A Sociolinguistics of Diaspora*.

45. Aparicio, *Negotiating Latinidad*; and Potowski, *IntraLatino Language and Identity*.

46. Okamoto and Mora, "Panethnicity."

47. On Latinxs as a single category, see Rumbaut, "Pigments of Our Imagination." On Latinx activism and media creating solidarity, see Gutiérrez, "What's in a Name?"; and Mora, *Making Hispanics*.

48. Aparicio, *Negotiating Latinidad*; Aparicio, "(Re)constructing Latinidad"; and Rumbaut, "Pigments of Our Imagination."

49. Negrón, "Ethnic Identification," 189. See also Negrón, "Spanish as a Heritage Language."

50. Negrón, "Spanish as a Heritage Language."

51. Aparicio, "(Re)constructing Latinidad"; and Muñoz, "Feeling Brown."

52. Aparicio, "(Re)constructing Latinidad," 42–43.

53. Aparicio, *Negotiating Latinidad*; see also Flores-González, "Puerto Rican High Achievers"; García and Rúa, "Processing Latinidad"; and Sándoval-Sánchez, "José, can you see?"

54. Mora, *Making Hispanics*.

55. Rosa, *Looking like a Language*.

56. Rosa, 2–4.

57. Negrón, "Ethnic Identification," 208.

58. Rosa, *Looking like a Language*, 2–4; and Rumbaut, "Pigments of Our Imagination," 19–20.

59. Swain, "Languaging, Agency and Collaboration," 96.

60. On habits and beliefs, see Bourdieu, "Habitus."

61. Lee and Dovchin, *Translinguistics*.

62. Erker, "The Limits of Named Language Varieties."

63. Walsh and High, "Rethinking the Concept of Community."

64. Tallentire, "Strategies of Memory."

65. Tallentire.

66. Morgan, "Speech Community"; and Wenger, *Communities of Practice*.

67. Gumperz, "Linguistic and Social Interaction."

68. Gumperz, *Language and Social Identity*, 155. While "dialect" is common in popular usage, linguists often use "language varieties" as a more neutral and

precise term that avoids ingrained assumptions of superiority or subordination. For example, subordinated Indigenous languages in Latin America and nonofficial languages in China are often referred to as "dialects" rather than languages, a designation that reflects their social positioning rather than their linguistic characteristics. Moreover, one dialect of a language can be elevated over others due to social reasons such as political dominance. This positioning is famously the case with the Iberian Peninsula's Castilian Romance dialect. Via the Reconquista, this dialect became the dominant language variety in the emergent nation-state of Spain and was transferred to Latin America through conquest and colonization. The idea of Castilian Peninsular Spanish retains prestige to this day, despite the strong historical influence of southern (Andalucían) Spanish in Latin America and the evolution of diverse regional Spanishes throughout the Americas.

69. Blommaert and Backus, "Superdiverse Repertoires and the Individual"; and Busch, "The Linguistic Repertoire Revisited."

70. Benor, "Ethnolinguistic Repertoire," 159.

71. Tseng, "'Qué barbaridad.'"

72. Leeman, "Critical Language Awareness"; Rosa and Flores, "Unsettling Race and Language"; and Zentella, "TWB (Talking while Bilingual)."

73. García and Li, "Translanguaging." The notion of "languages" and their varieties is well documented as an abstraction, and their definition is necessarily imprecise (for a thorough discussion focusing on Spanish, see Erker, "The Limits of Named Language Varieties"). The theoretical implications of this debate for language description and ideology lies beyond the scope of this book. However, given the importance of named languages to speakers and the long tradition in the field, I use terms such as "English" "Spanish," "Salvadoran Spanish," and "Latinx English" for ease of communication while recognizing their limitations.

74. On those who consider themselves learners of their languages and cultures, see Hornberger and Wang, "Who Are Our Heritage Language Learners?" On those who have some proficiency in the language, see Valdés, "Heritage Language Students."

75. Schalley and Eisenchlas provide a succinct comparison of terms such as "heritage language," "home language," and so on used in different contexts; see Schalley and Eisenchlas, *Handbook of Home Language Maintenance and Development*.

76. Bloomfield, *Language*.

77. Kupisch and Rothman, "Terminology Matters!"

78. Holliday, "Native-Speakerism"; and Tseng et al., *Research in Heritage Speaker Bilingualism*, 2025.

79. Wiley, "Accessing Language Rights in Education."

80. Fishman, *Language Loyalty in the United States*.

81. Rumbaut, Massey, and Bean, "Linguistic Life Expectancies"; and Carreira, "The Vitality of Spanish in the United States."
82. Carreira, "The Vitality of Spanish in the United States."
83. Flores, Tseng, and Subtirelu, *Bilingualism for All?*
84. Smith, "Changing Racial Labels."
85. Gutiérrez, "What's in a Name?"; and Mora, *Making Hispanics*.
86. Mora.
87. D'Vera Cohn, "Census History"; and Gutiérrez, "What's in a Name?"
88. Aparicio, "Latinidad/es"; Calderón, "'Hispanic' and 'Latino'"; Martínez and Gonzalez, "Panethnicity as a Reactive Identity"; and Oboler, *Ethnic Labels, Latino Lives*.
89. Gorman, "Connecting US Latina/o Cultural Identities and Language."
90. Jones-Correa and Leal, "Becoming 'Hispanic'"; and Lopez, Gonzalez-Barrera, and López, *Hispanic Identity Fades*.
91. José A. Del Real, "'Latinx' Hasn't Even Caught on among Latinos. It Never Will," *Washington Post*, December 18, 2020, https://www.washing-gtonpost.com/outlook/latinx-latinos-unpopular-gender-term/2020/12/18/bf177c5c-3b41-11eb-9276-ae0ca72729be_story.html; Vidal-Ortiz and Martínez, "Latinx Thoughts"; and Zentella, "'Limpia, fija y da esplendor.'"
92. Morales, *Latinx*; Noe-Bustamante, Mora, and Lopez, "About One-in-Four US Hispanics"; Salinas, "The Complexity of the 'x; in Latinx"; and Salinas and Lozano, "Mapping and Recontextualizing the Evolution of the Term Latinx." The terminological debate is ongoing; its full scale lies outside the scope of this book.
93. Vidal-Ortiz and Martínez, "Latinx Thoughts."
94. B. Martin, "From Negro to Black."
95. B. Martin.
96. Burns, Granz, and Williams, "Support for Native-Themed Mascots."
97. Barreto and Napolio, "Bifurcating American Identity"; Morales, "Opinion: What Sarah Huckabee Sanders Gets Wrong."
98. Cultural debates about gender-neutral language are taking place in many countries, such as France, Germany, and Brazil. Karina Piser, "Aux Armes, Citoyen·nes!," *Foreign Policy*, July 4, 2021, https://foreignpolicy.com/2021/07/04/france-gender-language-ecriture-inclusive-aux-armes-citoyennes/.
99. Also documented in Roth, *Race Migrations*.

Chapter 2

1. Matthew Schwartz, "Why Is There Such a Large Ethiopian Population in the Washington Region?," WAMU 88.5, April 21, 2016, https://wamu.org/story/16/04/21/how_did_the_dc_region_become_home_to_the_largest_population_of_ethiopians_in_the_us/.

2. Hopkinson, *Go-Go Live*.

3. Natalie Hopkinson, "Farewell to Chocolate City," *New York Times*, June 23, 2012, https://www.nytimes.com/2012/06/24/opinion/sunday/farewell-to-chocolate-city.html; Executive Office of the Mayor, Government of the District of Columbia, "Mayor Bowser Signs Bill to Designate Go-Go Music as the Official Music of DC; Molette Green, "DC Has Big Plans for the Go-Go Museum Coming Soon to Anacostia," *NBC4 Washington*, November 15, 2023, https://www.nbcwashington.com/news/local/dc-has-big-plans-for-the-go-go-museum-coming-soon-to-anacostia/3471485/; and Mike Maguire, "Photos: DC Celebrates New Marion Berry Avenue SE with Anacostia Block Party," *DCist*, November 20, 2023, https://dcist.com/story/23/11/20/dc-renames-marion-barry-avenue-se-from-good-hope-road/; and Grieser, *The Black Side of the River*.

4. Wennersten, *Anacostia*.

5. M. Jackson, "Washington, DC."

6. Abbott, *Political Terrain*; and C. Green, *Washington*.

7. Abbott, *Political Terrain*.

8. Washingtonian Staff, "Is Washington Too Southern? Too Northern?," March 18, 2017, https://www.washingtonian.com/2016/03/18/is-washington-dc-too-southern-or-too-northern/.

9. In the United States system of presidential voting, the vote in the Electoral College determines the winning candidate. Each state is allocated a certain number of votes in the Electoral College, and the popular vote determines the winner of each state's Electoral College votes, with the exception of Maine and Nebraska, which split their votes between the overall popular vote and the popular vote in each congressional district.

10. Asch and Musgrove, *Chocolate City*; and Kyla Summers, "The Battle against DC Statehood Is Rooted in Anti-Black Racism," *Washington Post*, March 22, 2021, https://www.washingtonpost.com/outlook/2021/03/22/battle-against-dc-statehood-is-rooted-anti-black-racism/.

11. Kijakazi et al., *The Color of Wealth*; and Lewis, *Washington*.

12. Holland, *Black Men Built the Capitol*.

13. Abbott, *Political Terrain*; Gastner, "Valuing 'Others'"; and Lewis, *Washington*.

14. M. Jackson, "Washington, DC."

15. Schoenfeld, "The History and Evolution of Anacostia's Barry Farm."

16. Price-Spratlen, "Urban Destination Selection."

17. Borchert, "Alley Life in Washington"; and Moore, *Leading the Race*.

18. Jim Crow laws were "a collection of state and local statutes" named after a minstrel show; they "legalized racial segregation" and discrimination against African Americans. They date to immediately after the Thirteenth Amendment abolished slavery and were upheld by the Supreme Court in *Plessy v. Ferguson* (1896), which established that racial segregation was legal if "separate but equal" facilities, such as schools, were provided for African Americans. In practice, these facilities were not "equal." *Brown v. the Board of Education* overturned

Jim Crow laws in 1954. Tischauser, *Jim Crow Laws*. See also Murphy, *Jim Crow Capital*; Pritchett, "A National Issue"; and Yellin, *Racism in the Nation's Service*.

19. Kijakazi et al., *The Color of Wealth*. DC and its environs are also home to much socioeconomic diversity among African Americans, from some of the nation's wealthiest African American suburbs to impoverished neighborhoods, which are both isolated from the city's growing prosperity and increasingly affected by gentrification. Turner and Hayes, *Poor People and Poor Neighborhoods*; and Rusk, *The Great Sort*.

20. On local activism, see C. Green, *Secret City*.

21. On Black DC's involvement with Martin Luther King Jr., see Freeman-Woolpert, "Community Museum Showcases Washington, DC's Long History of Activism"; and Pearlman, *Democracy's Capital*.

22. Williams, *In Search of the Talented Tenth*.

23. Jackson and Ruble, *DC Jazz*; and Ruble, *Washington's U Street*.

24. Summers, *Black in Place*.

25. Hannah et al., *Civil Rights U.S.A.*

26. Grieser, *The Black Side of the River*.

27. Jaffe and Sherwood, *Dream City*.

28. Walker, *Most of 14th Street Is Gone*.

29. Savage, "Homicide and Inequality"; and Summers, *Black in Place*.

30. Farrington and Schilling, "Contextualizing the Corpus."

31. Schwartz, "Why Is There Such a Large Ethiopian Population?"; and Frances Stead Sellers, "Is There a DC Accent? It's a Topic Locals Are Pretty 'Cised' to Discuss," *Washington Post*, July 9, 2014, https://www.washingtonpost.com/lifestyle/style/is-there-a-dc-dialect-its-a-topic-locals-are-pretty-cised-to-discuss/2014/07/09/84a3771c-c418-11e3-bcec-b71ee10e9bc3_story.html.

32. Richardson, Mitchell, and Franco, *Shifting Neighborhoods*.

33. Asch and Musgrove, *Chocolate City*; and Kijakazi et al., *The Color of Wealth*. DC has one of the highest costs of living nationally. Perry Stein, "You Need to Make $108,092 a Year to Live Comfortably in DC, Report Says," *Washington Post*, January 29, 2015, www.washingtonpost.com/news/local/wp/2015/01/29/you-need-to-make-108092-a-year-to-live-comfortably-in-d-c-report-says/. See also Cashin, *The Failures of Integration*; Hyra, *Race, Class, and Politics*; Jaffe and Sherwood, *Dream City*; Modan, *Turf Wars*; and Prince, *African Americans and Gentrification*.

34. Kirkland, "What's Race Got to Do with It?"; and Lees, "Gentrification, Race, and Ethnicity."

35. Grieser, *The Black Side of the River*; Jackson, "The Consequences of Gentrification"; and Prince, *African Americans and Gentrification*. On gentrification as a White phenomenon, see Modan, *Turf Wars*.

36. That is, with White residents as an overall minority in terms of population numbers.

37. Grieser, *The Black Side of the River*.

38. Redfern, "What Makes Gentrification 'Gentrification'?"; and Modan, *Turf Wars*.

39. Hopkinson, "Farewell to Chocolate City."

40. Micha Green, "Washingtonian Magazine Ad Campaign about DC Manages to Include Zero Black People," *Baltimore Afro-American*, May 15, 2018, https://www.afro.com/washingtonian-magazine-ad-campaign-about-dc-manages-to-include-zero-black-people/.

41. Rachel Kurzius, "Shaw's Metro PCS Store Has Been Forced to Turn Off Its Go-Go Music, Owner Says," *DCist*, April 8, 2019, https://dcist.com/story/19/04/08/shaws-metro-pcs-store-has-been-forced-to-turn-off-its-go-go-music-owner-says/.

42. Parliament, *Chocolate City*. Some of the information in this section can also be found in Tseng, "Advancing a Sociolinguistics of Complexity."

43. Singer, "Metropolitan Washington."

44. Abbott, "The Internationalization of Washington, DC"; and Manning, "Multicultural Washington, DC."

45. McDearman, Clark, and Parilla, "The 10 Traits of Globally Fluent Metro Areas," 1–2.

46. Price and Benton-Short, "Immigrants and World Cities," 112.

47. US Census Bureau, Quick Facts District of Columbia, "Population Estimates, July 1, 2022"; US Census Bureau, "American Community Survey 1-Year Estimates"; and US Census Bureau, "American Community Survey 5-Year Estimates."

48. Vertovec, *Transnationalism*.

49. On tension between social groups, see Asch and Musgrove, *Chocolate City*; and Mike DeBonis, "DC's Marion Barry Widely Rebuked for Comments about Asian Business Owners," *Washington Post*, April 5, 2012, https://www.washingtonpost.com/local/dc-politics/dcs-marion-barry-widely-rebuked-for-comments-about-asian-business-owners/2012/04/05/gIQA27SVyS_story.html. On increased tolerance for diversity, see Bader, "Diversity in the D.C. Area."

50. Levey et al., "Roads to Diversity: Adams Morgan Heritage Trail"; Maher, "The Capital of Diversity"; Modan, *Turf Wars*; and Modan, "Mango Fufu Kimchi Yucca."

51. Eckert, "The Future of Variation Studies."

52. Block, *Multilingual Identities in a Global City*; and Sassen, "The Global City."

53. Lynch, *The Routledge Handbook of Spanish in the Global City*.

54. Lynch; see also Caravedo, "Las ciudades como espacios mentales y lingüísticos."

55. By transnationalism, I refer to sustained contact between "home" and "host" cultures and practices, often via new means of communication and transportation rather than the disconnections that often characterized historical

migrations. Vertovec, *Transnationalism*; and De Fina and Perrino, "Transnational Identities."

56. Alim, "Translocal Style Communities"; and Robertson, "Globalisation or Glocalisation?"

57. Shrider et al., *Income and Poverty in the United States*.

58. US Census Bureau, Quick Facts District of Columbia, "Population Estimates, July 1, 2022."

59. Naveed, "Income Inequality in DC Highest in the Country."

60. Shontrice Barnes, "A Glimpse of the Economic Divide in Our Nation's Capital," *Prosperity Now*, February 21, 2023, https://prosperitynow.org/blog/glimpse-economic-divide-our-nations-capital.

61. "Economic Mobility Trends in the DMV."

62. "Economic Mobility Trends in the DMV"; and US Census Bureau, "Census Bureau Releases New Educational Attainment Data."

63. Moslimani and Noe-Bustamante, *Facts on Latinos in the US*; and "Selected Social Characteristics, 2019 American Community Survey 1-Year Estimates, Washington-Arlington-Alexandria, DC-VA-MD-WV Metro Area."

64. Salmerón et al., "Latinos in the District of Columbia."

65. Asch and Musgrove, *Chocolate City*; Cadaval, *Creating a Latino Identity*; and Repak, *Waiting on Washington*.

66. Cadaval, *Creating a Latino Identity*; Molina, *Cruzar fronteras en tiempos de globalización*; Galvez et al., *Three Decades of Mary's Center's Social Change Model*; and Ramirez, "Were You Here?"

67. Cadaval, *Creating a Latino Identity*.

68. The event was referred to at the time as the Mount Pleasant riots, and now often as the Mount Pleasant uprising, as community members and activists interrogate the incident's history and legacy.

69. Cadaval, *Creating a Latino Identity*; Modan, *Turf Wars*; Singer, *Latin American Immigrants*; Sprehn-Malagón, Hernández-Fujigaki, and Robinson, *Latinos in the Washington Metro Area*; and Carmen Torruella-Quander, "Conversation with an Old-School DC Latina," event presented at Historical Society of Washington, DC, 2015.

70. Asch and Musgrove, *Chocolate City*; Cadaval, *Creating a Latino Identity*; and Modan, *Turf Wars*.

71. Menjívar, *Fragmented Ties*; Rodríguez, "'Departamento 15'"; and Scallen, "'The Bombs That Drop in El Salvador.'"

72. Singer, *Latin American Immigrants*; and Singer, "Metropolitan Washington."

73. *American Baptist Churches v. Thornburgh*, 760 F. Supp. 796 (N.D. Cal. 1991); Daniella Cheslow and Hannah Schuster, "Federal Court Ruling Sends Panic through the DC Region's Salvadoran Community," NPR, September 16, 2020, https://www.npr.org/local/305/2020/09/16/913521829/federal-court-ruling-sends-panic-through-the-d-c-region-s-salvadoran-community; Gzesh,

"Central Americans and Asylum Policy"; and Nelson D. Schwartz, "Salvadorans, Washington's Builders, Face Expulsion under Trump," *New York Times*, September 13, 2019, https://www.nytimes.com/2019/09/13/business/economy/salvadoran-immigrant-workers.html.

74. US Commission of Civil Rights, *Racial and Ethnic Tensions in American Communities*.

75. Morrison and Donnelly, "Attracting New Americans."

76. Luna, "Transforming Espacios Culturales."

77. Tseng, "The Ordinariness of Dialect Translinguistics."

78. Prince, *African Americans and Gentrification*.

79. "A Tale of Three Cities"; and Tseng, "Advancing a Sociolinguistics of Complexity."

80. Steven Overly, Delece Smith-Barrow, Katy O'Donnell, and Ming Li, "Washington Was an Icon of Black Political Power. Then Came Gentrification," *Politico*, April 15, 2022, https://www.politico.com/news/magazine/2022/04/15/washington-dc-gentrification-black-political-power-00024515.

81. Modan, "Mango Fufu Kimchi Yucca."

82. I contributed to this project as a panel discussant at the Latina/o Studies Association Conference 2018 and DC History Conference 2018.

83. Modan, "Mango Fufu Kimchi Yucca."

84. Benítez, "Communication and Collective Identity"; and Rodríguez, "¿Dónde estás vos/z?"

85. Tseng, "Playground Learning." See also Fought, *Chicano English in Context*; Mendoza-Denton, *Homegirls*; Negrón, "Ethnic Identification"; Newman, "Focusing, Implicational Scaling"; and Wolfram, *Sociolinguistic Aspects of Assimilation*.

86. Zentella, *Growing Up Bilingual*; and Carter, "Shared Spaces, Shared Structures."

87. Candelario, *Black behind the Ears*; see also Wolford and Evanini, "Features of AAVE."

88. Candelario, *Black behind the Ears*; and Curtis, *Bridging the Americas*.

89. De Fina and King, "Language Problem or Language Conflict?"

90. "Hispanic Population in Select US Metropolitan Areas, 2014"; and "DC-Metro Latino Research Initiative."

91. Brown and López, "Mapping the Latino Population"; Pessar, "The Elusive Enclave"; John Gonzalez, "Hispanic Heritage Month Kicks Off as Latino Impact on DC Continues to Grow," *ABC News 7*, September 15, 2021, https://wjla.com/news/local/hispanic-heritage-month-kicks-off-as-latino-impact-on-dc-continues-to-grow; and Por Bernd Debusmann, "Is Washington DC's Latino Population a 'Sleeping Giant'?," *La Política Online*, July 20, 2021, https://www.lapoliticaonline.com/nota/135458-is-washington-dcs-latino-population-a-sleeping-giant/.

92. Arias, "Central American-Americans"; Parodi, "Contacto de dialectos"; and Rodríguez, "Becoming 'Wachintonians.'"
93. Loughran, "Community Powered Resistance." Mariachi is a Mexican tradition of strolling musical ensembles.
94. Pamela Constable, "DC Area Salvadorans, Once Stuck in Menial Jobs, Now Becoming Business Owners," *Washington Post*, September 22, 2014, https://www.washingtonpost.com/local/dc-area-salvadorans-once-stuck-in-menial-jobs-now-becoming-business-owners/2014/09/22/9e7e611e-3f48-11e4-b0ea-8141703bbf6f_story.html; Rodríguez, "Becoming 'Wachintonians'"; Repak, *Waiting on Washington*; and Patrick Welsh, "Lure of the Latino Gang," *Washington Post*, March 26, 1995.
95. Emily Wax, "National Pride Leaves DC United Fans Divided," *Washington Post*, October 31, 1999, https://www.washingtonpost.com/wp-srv/WPcap/1999-10/31/038r-103199-idx.html.
96. McGuire, "Central American Youth Gangs."
97. Arias, "Central American-Americans."
98. Arias, "Central American-Americans"; and Menjívar, "Liminal Legality."
99. Benítez, "Communication and Collective Identity"; Tseng, "Advancing a Sociolinguistics of Complexity"; and Cindy Zavala, "Five Reasons I Am Proud of Being Salvadoran in Washington, DC," *Latino Rebels*, July 25, 2015, https://www.latinorebels.com/2015/07/25/five-reasons-i-am-proud-of-being-salvadoran-in-washington-d-c/.
100. Benítez, "Communication and Collective Identity."
101. Blommaert and Rampton, "Language and Superdiversity"; and Vertovec, "Super-Diversity and Its Implications." See also Ndhlovu, "A Decolonial Critique"; and Pavlenko, "Superdiversity and Why It Isn't."
102. De Genova and Ramos-Zayas, *Latino Crossings*; Potowski, *IntraLatino Language and Identity*; and Rosa, *Looking like a Language*.
103. Aparicio, "(Re)constructing Latinidad"; and Potowski, *IntraLatino Language and Identity*.
104. Rosado, "Puerto Ricans, Dominicans."
105. Hart-González, "Pan Hispanism and Sub-Community."
106. Lopez, Gonzalez-Barrera, and Cuddington, *Diverse Origins*; and Joel Kotkin and Cox, "The US Cities Where Hispanics Are Doing the Best Economically," Forbes, January 30, 2015, https://www.forbes.com/sites/joelkotkin/2015/01/30/the-u-s-cities-where-hispanics-are-doing-the-best-economically/.
107. Salmerón et al., "Latinos in the District of Columbia."
108. Cai, "Hispanic Immigrants and Citizens in Virginia."
109. Sassen, "The Global City."
110. Hart-González, "Pan Hispanism and Sub-Community."
111. Beals, "Social Stratification in Latin America"; Quijano, "Coloniality of Power"; and Telles and Bailey, "Understanding Latin American Beliefs."

112. On differences in economic opportunities, see Morrison, "Behind the Numbers"; and on differences in education, see Cortina, *Indigenous Education Policy*. On urban versus rural divisions, see Dufour and Piperata, "Rural-to-Urban Migration"; Kay, "Reflections on Rural Poverty"; and Pineo and Baer, *Cities of Hope*.

113. Hunter, "The Persistent Problem of Colorism."

114. Prado Robledo, "Colorism."

115. Lavariega Monforti and Sanchez, "The Politics of Perception."

116. Negrón, "Ethnic Identification."

117. Aranda, Hughes, and Sabogal, *Making a Life in Multiethnic Miami*.

118. Negrón, "New York City's Latino Ethnolinguistic Repertoire"; and Negrón, "Ethnic Identification."

119. Negrón, "Ethnic Identification"; and Zentella, "Lexical Leveling."

120. Duany, "Reconstructing Racial Identity"; Araujo-Dawson, "Understanding the Complexities of Skin Color."

121. Roth, *Race Migrations*.

122. Zentella, "Lexical Leveling."

123. Carter and Callesano, "The Social Meaning of Spanish."

124. Alfaraz, "Miami Cuban Perceptions of Varieties of Spanish."

125. Mallet and Pinto-Coelho, "Investigating Intra-Ethnic Divisions"; and Alfaraz, "Miami Cuban Perceptions of Varieties of Spanish."

126. On the Latino community in Chicago, see De Genova and Ramos-Zayas, *Latino Crossings*; on the Latino community in New Jersey, see Bailey, "Language and Negotiation of Ethnic/Racial Identity."

127. Benítez, "Communication and Collective Identity."

128. On South Americans' higher socioeconomic status in the United States, see Benítez, "Communication and Collective Identity"; and Rodriguez, *The Emerging Latino Middle Class*. On Salvadorans' legal residency, see Menjívar, "Liminal Legality"; and Rodríguez, "Refugees of the South."

129. On race and class stereotypes, see Aranda, Hughes, and Sabogal, *Making a Life in Multiethnic Miami*. On South Americans, particularly Colombians, being seen as more White than other Latinxs, such as Mexicans and Dominicans, who are associated with Indigeneity and Blackness, see Negrón, "Ethnic Identification."

130. De Fina, "Orientation in Immigrant Narratives."

Chapter 3

1. Instituto Cervantes, *El español*.

2. Krogstad and Lopez, "Use of Spanish Declines among Latinos."

3. State Immigration Data Profiles, "District of Columbia, Language & Education"; and "Selected Social Characteristics, 2019 American Community

Survey 1-Year Estimates, Washington-Arlington-Alexandria, DC-VA-MD-WV Metro Area."

4. Krogstad and Lopez, "Use of Spanish Declines among Latinos."

5. James Barragán, "Long the Subject of Rhetoric, Migrants Have Now Become Props in Political Theater," *Texas Tribune*, September 22, 2022, https://www.texastribune.org/2022/09/22/migrant-busing-abbott-desantis/; A. Martínez, Jeevika Verma, Simone Popperl, and Amanda Michelle Gomez. "GOP Governors Sent Buses of Migrants to DC and NYC—with No Plan for What's Next," NPR, August 6, 2022, https://www.npr.org/2022/08/05/1115479280/migration-border-greg-abbott-texas-bus-dc-nyc-mayors; and Patrick Strickland, "Rights Groups Decry Gov. Greg Abbott's 'Political Stunts' as Texas Sends More Migrant Buses to DC," *Dallas Observer*, September 16, 2022, https://www.dallasobserver.com/news/rights-groups-decry-gov-greg-abbotts-political-stunts-as-texas-sends-more-buses-to-dc-14835120.

6. Code of Virginia § 1–511, 1996, 2005, English designated the official language of the Commonwealth, https://law.lis.virginia.gov/vacode/title1/chapter5/section1-511/; "Maryland County Looks to Repeal 'English-Only' Ordinance," Associated Press, NBC4 Washington, January 10, 2020, https://www.nbcwashington.com/news/local/maryland-county-looks-to-repeal-english-only-ordinance/2198483/; and Macedo, "The Colonialism of the English Only Movement."

7. Fishman, "Language Maintenance"; and Tseng et al., *Research in Heritage Speaker Bilingualism*.

8. One G2 survey was missing this response, making the G2 pattern "Mostly Latinx friends: 6," "mostly non-Latinx friends: 3," and "1 N/A."

9. Tseng, "The Ordinariness of Dialect Translinguistics."

10. See, for example, Gonzalez-Barrera, "The Ways Hispanics Describe Their Identity"; and Taylor et al., *When Labels Don't Fit*.

11. Cadaval, *Creating a Latino Identity*.

12. Rodríguez, "¿Dónde estás vos/z?"

13. Tseng, "'Qué barbaridad.'"

14. Tseng, "'Qué barbaridad.'"

15. Beaudrie, Ducar, and Relaño-Pastor, "Curricular Perspectives"; and Bost and Aparicio, Introduction to *The Routledge Companion*.

16. By "first-generation born-here," Ángel is referring to the second generation.

17. Díaz-Campos, *Introducción*; Lipski, *Latin American Spanish*; and Zentella, "TWB (Talking while Bilingual)."

18. *Voseo* is also found in Argentina and in parts of South America; verb conjugations and pragmatic usage vary. Lipski, *Varieties of Spanish in the United States*.

19. Raymond, "Reallocation of Pronouns"; Sorenson, "Voseo to Tuteo Accommodation"; and Rodríguez, "¿Dónde estás vos/z?"

20. Parodi, "Contacto de dialectos"; Raymond, "Generational Divisions"; Raymond, "Reallocation of Pronouns"; Rivera-Mills, "Use of Voseo and Latino Identity"; and Woods and Rivera-Mills, "El tú como un 'mask.'"
21. Sorenson, "Voseo to Tuteo Accommodation."
22. Sorenson; and Parodi, "Contacto de dialectos."
23. Lipski, *Latin American Spanish*.
24. Landolt, Autler, and Baires, "From Hermano Lejano."
25. Canfield, "Andalucismos en la pronunciación salvadoreña"; Canfield, "Observaciones sobre el español salvadoreño"; and Iraheta, "Interdental /s/ in Salvadoran Spanish." I also noted interdental realizations [θ] or voiced sibilants [z] but, as they were minimal (between 0 and 2 percent of any recording), do not include them in the analysis.
26. Lipski, "On the Weakening of /s/"; and Lipski, "/s/ in Central American Spanish."
27. Short or single-word responses such as "*sí*" or "*quizás diferente*" were excluded, as were tokens preceding and following /s/ (e.g., in "*las sillas*," the final "s" in "*las*," and the first "s" in "*sillas*").
28. Aaron and Hernández, "Quantitative Evidence"; Parodi, "Contacto de dialectos"; and Raymond, "Generational Divisions."
29. Lipski, *Latin American Spanish*.
30. Labov, *Sociolinguistic Patterns*; and Iraheta, "Interdental /s/ in Salvadoran Spanish."
31. Lipski, "/s/ in Central American Spanish."
32. Iraheta, "Interdental /s/ in Salvadoran Spanish," 146.
33. Brogan, "Sociophonetically-Based Phonology."
34. Lipski, *Latin American Spanish*.
35. Klee and Caravedo have documented elision and aspiration among Limeños. However, since they found that middle- and upper-middle-class Limeños favored aspiration over elision, the pattern I observed is more consistent with their lower-middle-class findings, which favored elision, although the 12 percent elision rate is much less than the 55 percent that Klee and Caravedo observed. Klee and Caravedo, "Andean Spanish and the Spanish of Lima."
36. Aaron and Hernández, "Quantitative Evidence"; Negrón, "Ethnic Identification"; and Osuna, "Intra-Latina/Latino Encounters."
37. Parodi, "Contacto de dialectos."
38. Negrón, "Ethnic Identification"; and Zentella, "Lexical Leveling."
39. Cadaval, *Creating a Latino Identity*.
40. Modan, *Turf Wars*; and Modan, "Mango Fufu Kimchi Yucca."
41. Sassen, "The Global City."
42. Bernal-Chávez et al., "Linguistic Attitudes"; Hidalgo, "The Emergence of Standard Spanish"; and Negrón, "Ethnic Identification."

43. Carter and Callesano, "The Social Meaning of Spanish"; and Lipski, *Latin American Spanish*.

44. Lynch and Potowski, "La valoración del habla bilingüe"; and Zentella, "'Limpia, fija y da esplendor.'"

45. Rojas Gallardo, "Actitudes lingüísticas en Santiago de Chile"; Rojas Gallardo, "Estatus, solidaridad y representación social"; and Pozo, "Percepción sociolingüística."

46. Moslimani and Noe-Bustamante, *Facts on Latinos in the US*.

47. Institute for Immigration Research, "Colombia: Colombian Population in the Washington, DC and Baltimore, MD Metropolitan Areas"; and Institute for Immigration Research, "El Salvador: Salvadoran Population in the Washington, DC and Baltimore, MD Metro Areas."

48. On Colombian Spanish's reputation for correctness in Latin America, see Bernal-Chávez et al., "Linguistic Attitudes." On Colombian Spanish's high prestige, see Carter and Callesano, "The Social Meaning of Spanish"; Negrón, "Ethnic Identification"; and Zentella, "Lexical Leveling."

49. Zentella, "TWB (Talking while Bilingual)."

50. Hart-González, "Pan Hispanism and Sub-Community."

51. Benítez, "Communication and Collective Identity."

52. Carter and Callesano, "The Social Meaning of Spanish," 85.

53. Negrón, "Ethnic Identification."

54. Negrón, "Ethnic Identification."

55. Carter and Callesano, "The Social Meaning of Spanish"; Joseph, "Taking Race Seriously"; Lorenzi and Batalova, "South American Immigrants"; Negrón, "Spanish as a Heritage Language"; and Veronica Smink, "¿Por qué los latinoamericanos hacen tantos chistes sobre los argentinos?," BBC Mundo, Argentina, October 20, 2015, https://www.bbc.com/mundo/noticias/2015/10/151015_hay_festival_chistes_sobre_argentinos_vs. I note that stereotypes of named national varieties erase the rich linguistic diversity present in each country and are simply a shorthand for perceived shared features attached to a national label for a geographic region. In other words, the existence of the nation as a singular entity creates an assumption of homogeneity within "Salvadoran Spanish," "Argentinean Spanish," and so on despite much sociolinguistic diversity within countries. Moreover, regional linguistic features, such as Andean Spanish, frequently cross national lines, underscoring how named language boundaries are expressions of ideology rather than clearly delineated groupings of unique linguistic features.

56. Hart-González, "Pan Hispanism and Sub-Community."

57. Suárez Büdenbender, "Puerto Ricans' Evaluations."

58. Office of the Mayor, "Mayor Bowser Calls on Congress to Pass a Clean Dream Act, Proclaims Today 'DREAMers Day,'" press release, December 6,

2017, Washington, DC, https://dc.gov/release/mayor-bowser-calls-congress-pass-clean-dream-act-proclaims-today-dreamers-day.
  59. Negrón, "Ethnic Identification."
  60. Negrón, "Ethnic Identification."
  61. Hart-González, "Pan Hispanism and Sub-Community."
  62. Benítez, "Communication and Collective Identity."
  63. Negrón, "Ethnic Identification."
  64. Cadaval, *Creating a Latino Identity*.
  65. Zentella, "'Dime con quién hablas.'"
  66. Aparicio, *Negotiating Latinidad*.
  67. Alim, "Who's Afraid of the Transracial Subject?"
  68. Rosa, *Looking like a Language*.

Chapter 4

  1. Krogstad and Gonzalez-Barrera, "A Majority of English-Speaking Hispanics in the US Are Bilingual."
  2. State Immigration Data Profiles, "District of Columbia, Language & Education"; and "Selected Social Characteristics, 2019 American Community Survey 1-Year Estimates."
  3. Tseng, "Advancing a Sociolinguistics of Complexity."
  4. Bernstein et al., "Ten Years of Language Access."
  5. Bender, "Old Hate in New Bottles"; Lippi-Green, *English with an Accent*; Rosa and Flores, "Unsettling Race and Language"; and Zentella, "The 'Chiquitafication' of US Latinos."
  6. Bernstein et al., "Ten Years of Language Access"; and American University Washington College of Law Immigrant Justice Clinic, *Access Denied*, report based on information and data collected by the DC Language Access Coalition (2012).
  7. Carter, López Valdez, and Sims, "New Dialect Formation"; Mendoza-Denton, "Sociolinguistics and Linguistic Anthropology of US Latinos"; Peñalosa, *Chicano Sociolinguistics*; Rogers and Alvord, "Miami-Cuban Spanish and English /l/"; Slomanson and Newman, "Peer Group Identification"; Wolfram, *Sociolinguistic Aspects of Assimilation*; and Zentella, *Growing Up Bilingual*.
  8. Bayley, "Demographic Categories in Sociolinguistic Studies"; Potowski, *IntraLatino Language and Identity*; and Rosa, *Looking like a Language*.
  9. Tseng, "Vowel Variation, Style, and Identity Construction."
  10. Fought, *Chicano English in Context*; and Santa Ana, "Chicano English."
  11. See Fought, *Chicano English in Context*; Santa Ana and Bayley, "Chicano English: Phonology"; and Poplack, "Dialect Acquisition."
  12. Benor, "Ethnolinguistic Repertoire," 160.
  13. Fought, *Chicano English in Context*; Labov, *A Study of the Non-Standard English*; and Wolfram, *Sociolinguistic Aspects of Assimilation*.

14. Negrón, "Ethnic Identification," 203. See also Wolfram, *Sociolinguistic Aspects of Assimilation*; and Zentella, *Growing Up Bilingual*.

15. Wolford and Evanini, "Features of AAVE."

16. Farrington and Schilling, "Contextualizing the Corpus"; Kendall and Farrington, The Corpus of Regional African American Language, ver. 2020.05; King, "From African American Vernacular English"; Weldon, *Middle-Class African American English*; and Wolfram and Kohn, "Regionality in the Development of African American English."

17. Rickford, *African American Vernacular English*.

18. Fought, *Chicano English in Context*; and Wolfram, *Sociolinguistic Aspects of Assimilation*.

19. Fought, *Chicano English in Context*; and Labov and Harris, "De Facto Segregation."

20. Wolfram, *Sociolinguistic Aspects of Assimilation*.

21. Grieser, *The Black Side of the River*.

22. Grieser, *The Black Side of the River*; and Matthew S. Schwartz, "Is There a Washington, DC Accent?," WAMU 88.5, July 7, 2016, https://wamu.org/story/16/07/07/is_there_a_washington_dc_accent/.

23. Grieser, *The Black Side of the River*; Lee, "High and Mid Back Vowel Fronting"; and Farrington and Schilling, "Contextualizing the Corpus."

24. Tseng, "Playground Learning."

25. Fought, *Chicano English in Context*.

26. Ibrahim, *The Rhizome of Blackness*; although see Mendoza-Denton, *Homegirls*.

27. Carter, "Shared Spaces, Shared Structures."

28. On light intervocalic /l/, see Newman, *New York City English*.

29. On the /ae/ interpretation, see Tseng, "Vowel Variation, Style, and Identity Construction."

30. On the African American English features of /aɪ/ weakening in prevoiced and final phonetic contexts, see Thomas, "Gender and /aɪ/ Monophthongization." On the postvocalic /r/ deletion or vocalization and /l/ vocalization, see L. Green, *African American English*.

31. L. Green, *African American English*.

32. Eckert, *Meaning and Linguistic Variation*; Jonsson, Årman, and Milani, "Youth Language"; and Trudgill, "Sex, Covert Prestige and Linguistic Change."

33. Nevalainen, "Social Variation in Intensifier Use."

34. Cutler, "White Hip-Hoppers."

35. Wolfram, *Sociolinguistic Aspects of Assimilation*.

36. Eckert, *Meaning and Linguistic Variation*; Flores and Rosa, "Undoing Appropriateness"; and Lippi-Green, *English with an Accent*.

37. Orloff, et al., "Racial and Ethnic Tensions."

38. Rahman, "The N Word."

39. Bailey, "The Language of Multiple Identities"; and Solis, Portillos, and Brunson, "Latino Youths' Experiences."

40. Lane, "Rethinking the Brand–Community Relationship"; Alarcón, *War by Candlelight*; "Load My Gun"; Ester Park, "Criminal Minded," *Miami New Times*, April 26, 2007, https://www.miaminewtimes.com/music/criminal-minded-6334285; Sryon, "Fat Joe Defends Joell Ortiz's 'Big Pun Back,'" *HipHop DX*, July 18, 2011, https://hiphopdx.com/news/id.16028/title.fat-joe-defends-joell-ortizs-big-pun-back; East, "My Nigga Dead (In-terlude)"; and Marie, *Grimey 2*.

41. King et al., "Who Has the 'Right' to Use the N-Word?"; Harkness, "Hip Hop Culture"; and Low, "Hip-Hop, Language, and Difference."

42. "Mayors of the District of Columbia since Home Rule"; and "DC Home Rule."

43. Lippi-Green, *English with an Accent*; and Zentella, "TWB (Talking while Bilingual)."

44. Bucholtz, "Sociolinguistic Nostalgia."

45. Ibrahim, *The Rhizome of Blackness*.

46. Blommaert, *The Sociolinguistics of Globalization*.

Chapter 5

1. Siegel, "Creoles and Minority Dialects in Education."
2. Lippi-Green, *English with an Accent*; and Zentella, "'Dime con quién hablas.'"
3. Agha, "Large and Small Scale Forms of Personhood."
4. Agha, "Voice, Footing, Enregisterment."
5. De Fina, *Identity in Narrative*; and De Fina, "Positioning Level 3."
6. De Fina and Georgakopoulou, *Analyzing Narrative*, 381–82.
7. Ochs and Capps, *Living Narrative*, 20.
8. Labov and Waletzky, "Narrative Analysis."
9. Georgakopoulou, *Small Stories*, 1.
10. Agha, "Voice, Footing, Enregisterment"; and Irvine and Gal, "Language Ideology."
11. Fries-Britt and Griffin, "The Black Box"; and Vallejo, "Latina Spaces."
12. D'Arcy, "Like and Language Ideology"; and Carris, "La Voz Gringa."
13. MacDonald and Carrillo, "The United Status of Latinos"; Rosa, *Looking like a Language*; and Rosa and Flores, "Unsettling Race and Language."
14. D'Arcy, "Like and Language Ideology"; and Carris, "La Voz Gringa."
15. Lippi-Green, *English with an Accent*; Rosa and Flores, "Unsettling Race and Language"; and Wolfram and Schilling-Estes, *American English*.
16. Trudgill, "Sex, Covert Prestige and Linguistic Change."

17. On standard and hyperstandard English as White and inauthentic, see Bucholtz, *White Kids*; on "sounding White" being mocked as inauthentic and incompatible with Latinxness, see Carris, "La Voz Gringa."

18. Baker-Cristales, "Salvadoran Transformations."

19. Clark and Araiza, *Margins in Movement*; De Genova and Ramos-Zayas, *Latino Crossings*; and Vandevoordt and Verschraegen, "Demonstrating Deservingness and Dignity."

20. Parodi, "Contacto de dialectos"; Raymond, "Generational Divisions"; Raymond, "Reallocation of Pronouns"; Rivera-Mills, "Use of Voseo and Latino Identity"; and Woods and Rivera-Mills, "El tú como un 'mask.'"

21. Almaguer, "At the Crossroads of Race"; Song, "Who's at the Bottom?"; Telles and Flores, "Not Just Color"; and Zentella, "'Dime con quién hablas.'"

22. On constructed dialogue, see Tannen, "Introducing Constructed Dialogue."

23. Rivera-Mills notes that later-generation Salvadoran males use "vos" as a masculine address term, a finding that resonates with research on masculine solidarity with "dude" and "güey." Rivera-Mills, "Use of Voseo and Latino Identity"; Bucholtz, "From Stance to Style"; and Kiesling, "Dude."

24. Raymond, "Reallocation of Pronouns."

25. Bucholtz, "From Stance to Style"; and Kiesling, "Dude."

26. Bucholtz, *White Kids*; Podesva, "Three Sources of Stylistic Meaning"; and Slobe, "Style, Stance, and Social Meaning."

27. De Fina and King, "Language Problem or Language Conflict?"

28. Holliday, "Perception in Black and White." On the word "motherfucker," see Smitherman, *Black Talk*.

29. House-Niamke and Sato, "Resistance to Systemic Oppression."

30. Lowe, "Creating Community."

31. Rodríguez, "¿Dónde estás vos/z?," 213.

32. Robertson, *Globalization*.

33. See also chapter 2.

34. Valencia, "'Mexican Americans don't value education!'"; and Stewart, Pitts, and Osborne, "Mediated Intergroup Conflict."

35. Tseng, "'Qué barbaridad.'"

36. Bourdieu, "The Economics of Linguistic Exchanges."

37. Skeggs, *Class, Self, Culture*, 5.

38. Bourdieu, "The Forms of Capital."

39. MacDonald and Carrillo, "The United Status of Latinos," 19.

40. Bottero, "Class Identities," 990.

41. Vallejo, "Latina Spaces."

42. Rosa, *Looking like a Language*.

43. Agha, "Large and Small Scale Forms of Personhood"; and Abrego, "On Silences."

44. Alvarado, "Cultural Memory and Making"; and Rodríguez, "Diasporic Reparations."

45. Arias, "Central American-Americans"; Coronado and Paredes, "From Invisible to Visible"; and Lavadenz, "Como hablar en silencio."

46. Woolard, *Singular and Plural*, 22.

47. Courtney Sexton, "La SalvadoReina Wants to Jumpstart Salvadoran Music in D.C., One Cumbia at a Time," *Bandwidth.fm*, WAMU, September 10, 2015. http://bandwidth.wamu.org/index.html%3Fp=56239.html.

48. On Miami, see Carter and Callesano, "The Social Meaning of Spanish"; and on Los Angeles, see Parodi, "Contacto de dialectos."

49. Negrón, "Ethnic Identification."

50. Cutler, "'Keepin' it real'"; and Twine, "Brown Skinned White Girls."

51. Leonardo and Hunter, "Imagining the Urban"; and Reyes, *Language, Identity, and Stereotype*.

52. Squires, "Indexical Bleaching."

53. Bailey, "The Language of Multiple Identities."

54. Leonardo and Hunter, "Imagining the Urban."

55. Eckert, "The Whole Woman"; and Trudgill, "Sex, Covert Prestige and Linguistic Change."

56. Aparicio, *Negotiating Latinidad*.

57. Aparicio, "(Re)constructing Latinidad," 59.

58. Irvine and Gal, "Language Ideology"; Jones-Correa and Leal, "Becoming 'Hispanic'"; and Nagel, "Constructing Ethnicity."

59. Sharma, "Social Class across Borders," 686.

Chapter 6

1. Paul Abowd, "Petworth's Changing Demographics Lead to Challenges, but Also New Ideas," *Washington Post*, July 2, 2012, https://www.washingtonpost.com/local/petworths-changing-demographics-lead-to-challenges-but-also-new-ideas/2012/06/26/gJQA1GHcIW_story.html.

2. Bennet, "Narrating Family Histories," 461; and Milligan, "Displacement and Identity Discontinuity."

3. Coupland, *Style*.

4. Wolfram and Schilling-Estes, *American English*; and Tseng and Cashman, "Code-Switching Pragmatics."

5. Eckert, *Meaning and Linguistic Variation*.

6. Labov and Waletzky, "Narrative Analysis"; and De Fina, "Discourse and Identity."

7. Jaffe, *Stance*; Davies and Harré, "Positioning"; Du Bois, "The Stance Triangle"; and De Fina "Positioning Level 3."

8. Modan, *Turf Wars*.

9. On backed /ae/, see Tseng, "Vowel Variation, Style, and Identity Construction"; and on the association between Spanish and Latinx identity, see Bedolla, "The Identity Paradox."

10. Fought, *Chicano English in Context*; Mendoza-Denton, *Homegirls*; and Thomas, *An Acoustic Analysis of Vowel Variation*. I provide a more in-depth discussion of Latino English and African American English in chapter 4.

11. Podesva, "Phonation Type as a Stylistic Variable."

12. Grieser, *Locating Style*.

13. Agha, "Voice, Footing, Enregisterment"; Bell and Gibson, "Staging Language"; and Keane, "Voice."

14. Bucholtz, "Sociolinguistic Nostalgia," 408–9; see also Bucholtz and Hall, "Identity and Interaction."

15. Bucholtz, "Sociolinguistic Nostalgia"; and Bucholtz and Hall, "Identity and Interaction."

16. Bennet, "Narrating Family Histories"; and Milligan, "Displacement and Identity Discontinuity."

17. Bennet, "Narrating Family Histories."

18. Coupland, "Sociolinguistic Authenticities."

19. Johnstone, "Ideology and Discourse."

20. Johnstone, "Ideology and Discourse"; and Tuan, *Space and Place*.

21. Washington, DC, elected the first Black mayor of any major American city in 1973, and every DC mayor since then has been African American, up to the present day.

22. Grieser, *The Black Side of the River*; and Modan, *Turf Wars*.

23. Cadaval, *Creating a Latino Identity*.

24. Modan, *Turf Wars*.

25. Cadaval, *Creating a Latino Identity*.

26. Modan, *Turf Wars*; see also Relaño Pastor and De Fina, "Contesting Social Place."

27. Union Market's transformation as part of citywide gentrification is nicely encapsulated by the *Washington Post*'s description of the area as a "once-scruffy ... foodie mecca" and "centerpiece for a revitalized neighborhood." Michelle Lerner, "Food-Oriented Apartment Complex to Open Near DC's Union Market," *Washington Post*, May 11, 2017, https://www.washingtonpost.com/news/where-we-live/wp/2017/05/11/food-oriented-apartment-complex-to-open-near-d-c-s-union-market/.

28. In 2019 NBC Washington ran a special called *Pupusas in Washington DC: How the Salvadoran Dish Became Unique to the District*: NBC4 Washington, *Pupusas*.

29. Witt, *Black Hunger*.

30. Vanderbeck, "Vermont and the Imaginative Geographies"; Barrera, "Of 'Chicharrones' and Clam Chowder"; and Saucier, "'We eat cachupa, not clam chowder.'"

31. Bucholtz, *White Kids*.
32. Westbrook, *Hip Hoptionary*, 151.
33. Relaño Pastor and De Fina, "Contesting Social Place."
34. Rusk, *Goodbye to Chocolate City*.
35. Grieser, *The Black Side of the River*.
36. Fichter, "DC's Population Is Exploding"; and *Population Change in the Washington DC Metropolitan Area*.
37. Elizabeth Burton, "DC's Population Growth Has Affected the Racial and Ethnic Composition of Wards 6, 7, and 8," *Urban Institute* (blog), October 7, 2022, https://greaterdc.urban.org/blog/dcs-population-growth-has-affected-racial-and-ethnic-composition-wards-6-7-and-8.
38. On DC African Americans, see Grieser, *The Black Side of the River*; and Prince, *African Americans and Gentrification*. On DC Latinxs, see Modan, *Turf Wars*.
39. Modan, *Turf Wars*.
40. Johnstone, "Ideology and Discourse."
41. Grieser, *The Black Side of the River*; and Podesva, "Stance as a Window."
42. Fasold, *Tense Marking in Black English*; Matthew S. Schwartz, "Is There a Washington, DC Accent?," WAMU 88.5, July 7, 2016, https://wamu.org/story/16/07/07/is_there_a_washington_dc_accent/; and Frances Stead Sellers, "Is There a DC Accent? It's a Topic Locals Are Pretty 'Cised' to Discuss," *Washington Post*, July 9, 2014, https://www.washingtonpost.com/lifestyle/style/is-there-a-dc-dialect-its-a-topic-locals-are-pretty-cised-to-discuss/2014/07/09/84a3771c-c418-11e3-bcec-b71ee10e9bc3_story.html.
43. Silverstein, "Indexical Order."
44. On "gringo voice" and indexing Whiteness, see Carris, "La Voz Gringa." For more on indexing Whiteness, see Bucholtz, *White Kids*.
45. Matthew Schwartz, "Why Is There Such a Large Ethiopian Population in the Washington Region?," WAMU 88.5, April 21, 2016, https://wamu.org/story/16/04/21/how_did_the_dc_region_become_home_to_the_largest_population_of_ethiopians_in_the_us/.
46. Chun, "The Construction of White, Black, and Korean American Identities"; and Negrón, "New York City's Latino Ethnolinguistic Repertoire."
47. Arya, "Cultural Appropriation."
48. Rampton, *Crossing*; and Rampton, "Language Crossing."
49. Sweetland, "Unexpected but Authentic Use"; and Paris, "'They're in My Culture.'"
50. Zukin, *The Naked City*.
51. De Fina, "Discourse and Identity."
52. Modan, *Turf Wars*.
53. Brooker, "3 Real Americans."
54. Petworth has been heavily gentrified since our interview.

55. Grieser, *The Black Side of the River*.
56. Johnstone, "Ideology and Discourse."
57. Summers, *Black in Place*.
58. Bennet, "Narrating Family Histories"; and Milligan, "Displacement and Identity Discontinuity."
59. Vanderbeck, "Vermont and the Imaginative Geographies." *Saturday Night Live*'s "Neo-Confederate Meeting" skit (September 29, 2018) is a light-hearted example of Vermont's popular perception as White. https://www.youtube.com/watch?v=nKcUOUYzDXA.
60. Collins, *Shielded from Justice*.
61. Marcos mentions the Whitman Walker Clinic, a healthcare nonprofit organization now known as Whitman Walker Health. It was founded in 1978 to serve the LGBTQ community but serves DC more broadly—particularly impoverished and vulnerable residents—in sexual healthcare and many other health and community services. The clinic was on the front lines of free healthcare during the AIDS epidemic, which devastated DC in the 1980s.
62. Natalie Hopkinson, "Farewell to Chocolate City," *New York Times*, June 23, 2012, https://www.nytimes.com/2012/06/24/opinion/sunday/farewell-to-chocolate-city.html; and Elliot Williams, "DC Unveils Go-Go Mural at the Apartment Building Where #DontMuteDC Began," NPR, September 15, 2021, https://www.npr.org/local/305/2021/09/15/1037418966/d-c-unveils-go-go-mural-at-the-apartment-building-where-dont-mute-d-c-began.
63. Bennet, "Narrating Family Histories"; Coupland, "Sociolinguistic Authenticities"; Jamal and Hill, "Developing a Framework"; and Woolard, *Singular and Plural*.
64. Zukin, *The Naked City*, 6.
65. Larry Janezich, "The Gentrification of Hill East: Perspective: Jim Myers, Hill East Activist," *Capitol Hill Corner* (blog), August 25, 2014, https://capitolhillcorner.org/2014/08/25/the-gentrification-of-hill-east-perspective-jim-myers-hill-east-activist/.
66. Modan, "Mango Fufu Kimchi Yucca."
67. Bennet, "Narrating Family Histories"; and Milligan, "Displacement and Identity Discontinuity."
68. Grieser, *The Black Side of the River*; Modan, *Turf Wars*; and Prince, *African Americans and Gentrification*.
69. Huante, "A Lighter Shade of Brown?"; Lees, "Gentrification, Race, and Ethnicity"; and Zukin, *The Naked City*.
70. Pain, "Gender, Race, Age and Fear."
71. Leonardo and Hunter, "Imagining the Urban," 785–86.
72. Leonardo and Hunter, 787.
73. Bucholtz, *White Kids*. There are other discourses of authenticity, of course, and conflicts between them can be seen in cultural and political debates

over "the real America," which pit the imagined White heartland against cities, associated with elitism as well as minorities and crime. Ellis, "At Home with 'Real Americans'"; and David Masciotra, "'Real Americans' vs. 'Coastal Elites': What Right-Wing Sneers at City Dwellers Really Mean," *Salon*, November 20, 2016, https://www.salon.com/2016/11/20/real-americans-vs-coastal-elites-what-right-wing-sneers-at-city-dwellers-really-mean/.

74. Ramos-Zayas, "Racializing the 'Invisible' Race."
75. Heldke, *Exotic Appetites*.
76. Joassart-Marcelli, *The $16 Taco*.
77. Modan, "Mango Fufu Kimchi Yucca."
78. Tate Fox, "Why Columbia Heights Is the Perfect Neighborhood for New DC Residents," *Common*, March 8, 2021, https://www.common.com/blog/2021/01/why-columbia-heights-is-the-perfect-neighborhood-for-new-d-c-residents/.
79. Amanda Abrams, "Columbia Heights: DC's Most Diverse Neighborhood, but for How Long?," *Urban Turf*, March 31, 2011, https://dc.urbanturf.com/articles/blog/columbia_heights_dcs_most_diverse_neighborhood_but_for_how_long/3235.
80. Green et al., "Chocolate City, Vanilla Swirl, or Something Else?"; and Hyra, *Race, Class, and Politics*.
81. Negrón, "New York City's Latino Ethnolinguistic Repertoire."
82. Bucholtz, "Sociolinguistic Nostalgia," 400.

Conclusion

1. On Latinxs racialized as non-White in the United States, see MacDonald and Carrillo, "The United Status of Latinos."
2. Hart-González, "Pan Hispanism and Sub-Community." Also see Tseng, "Advancing a Sociolinguistics of Complexity"; and Tseng, "The Ordinariness of Dialect Translinguistics."
3. Lipski, *Latin American Spanish*.
4. Grieser, *The Black Side of the River*.
5. García and Li, "Translanguaging."
6. Erker, "The Limits of Named Language Varieties."
7. Leeman, "Investigating Language Ideologies."
8. Preston, "The Uses of Folk Linguistics"; and Albury, "How Folk Linguistic Methods."
9. Bartal, "From Traditional Bilingualism"; Chimbutane, "Multilingualism in Education"; Del Valle, *A Political History of Spanish*; and Flores, "Silencing the Subaltern."
10. See Achugar and Pessoa, "Power and Place"; Goble, "Linguistic Insecurity"; Oh and Au, "Learning Spanish"; and Tseng, "Advancing a Sociolinguistics of Complexity."

11. Cobas, Duany, and Feagin, "Introduction: Racializing Latinos"; Repak, *Waiting on Washington*; and Rosa, *Looking like a Language*.
12. Lopez, Gonzalez-Barrera, and López, *Hispanic Identity Fades*.
13. On glocal discourses, see Robertson, "Globalisation or Glocalisation?"
14. Márquez-Reiter and Patiño-Santos, "The Politics of Conviviality."
15. Tseng and Hinrichs, "Introduction: Mobility, Polylingualism, and Change."
16. Grieser, *The Black Side of the River*; and Modan, *Turf Wars*.
17. Järlehed, Nielsen, and Rosendal, "Language, Food and Gentrification"; Leeman and Modan, "Commodified Language in Chinatown"; and Valdez, Freire, and Delavan, "The Gentrification of Dual Language Education."
18. On White flight from cities, see Frey, *Diversity Explosion*.
19. Frey.
20. On the DC suburbs' diversity, see Lung-Amam, "An Equitable Future." On racially divided areas, see Bader, "Diversity in the D.C. Area"; Price and Benton-Short, "Immigrants and World Cities"; and Singer, Hardwick, and Brettel, *Twenty-First Century Gateways*.
21. Torres, *Puerto Rican Discourse*.
22. Hughes, *The Collected Poems*, 46.
23. Labov, *A Study of the Non-Standard English*; Portes and Zhou, "Should Immigrants Assimilate?"; and Wolfram, *Sociolinguistic Aspects of Assimilation*. Also see Cheshire et al., "Contact, the Feature Pool."
24. Lipsitz, "Cruising around the Historical Bloc."
25. Paris, "'They're in My Culture'"; Paris, "It Was a Black City"; and Ibrahim, *The Rhizome of Blackness*.
26. Paris, "'They're in My Culture.'"
27. Frey, *Diversity Explosion*.
28. Carter, *American while Black*; and Smitherman, "African Americans and 'English Only.'"
29. On New York, see Negrón, "Ethnic Identification"; and Zentella, "TWB (Talking while Bilingual)." On Miami, see Carter and Callesano, "The Social Meaning of Spanish." On Chicago, see Rosa, *Looking like a Language*.
30. Hart-González, "Pan Hispanism and Sub-Community"; Tseng, "Advancing a Sociolinguistics of Complexity"; and Tseng, "The Ordinariness of Dialect Translinguistics."
31. Aparicio, "(Re)constructing Latinidad."
32. Negrón, "Ethnic Identification"; Potowski, *IntraLatino Language and Identity*; Zentella, "Lexical Leveling"; and Rosado, "Puerto Ricans, Dominicans."
33. On the erasure of Blackness in Central American national consciousnesses, see Gudmunson and Wolfe, *Blacks and Blackness in Central America*.
34. Rosado, "Puerto Ricans, Dominicans."
35. Tseng, "Raciolinguistic Reindexicalization."

36. Potowski, *IntraLatino Language and Identity*.

37. Alba, "The Surge of Young Americans"; and Jones et al., "2020 Census Illuminates Racial and Ethnic Composition."

38. Bucholtz, "Sociolinguistic Nostalgia"; Eckert, *Meaning and Linguistic Variation*; and Lo and Chun, "Language, Race, and Reflexivity."

39. Eckert, *Meaning and Linguistic Variation*; Chun and Lo, "Language and Racialization"; and Sugiharto, "The Multilingual Turn."

40. Bucholtz, "Sociolinguistic Nostalgia"; and Holliday, "Native-Speakerism."

41. Lee and Dovchin, *Translinguistics*.

42. Rampton, "Language Crossing," 485; and see also Rampton, *Crossing*.

43. Zentella, "The 'Chiquitafication' of US Latinos."

44. Block, *The Social Turn in Applied Linguistics*; Canagarajah, "Multilingual Writers"; Carter, "Poststructuralist Theory and Sociolinguistics"; Leeman, "Critical Language Awareness"; Pennycook, *Critical Applied Linguistics*; and Singh, *Towards a Critical Sociolinguistics*.

45. Labov, "How I Got into Linguistics," 459.

46. Asch and Musgrove, *Chocolate City*; Caban, "Puerto Ricans as Contingent Citizens"; and Olivia Reingold, "Is Puerto Rico the Next Senate Battleground?," *Politico*, September 9, 2020, https://www.politico.com/news/magazine/2020/09/09/puerto-rico-statehood-politics-democrats-republicans-senate-409191.

47. Bader, "Diversity in the D.C. Area."

48. Modan, *Turf Wars*; and Modan, "The Semiotics of Urbanness."

49. Anderson, "The New World Disorder."

50. Blackledge, "'As a Country We Do Expect'"; Campbell, "A Dry Hate"; and Macedo, "The Colonialism of the English Only Movement."

51. Wodak, "The Trajectory of Far-Right Populism."

52. Campani et al., "The Rise of Donald Trump Right-Wing Populism."

Bibliography

Aaron, Jessi Elana, and José Esteban Hernández. "Quantitative Evidence for Contact-Induced Accommodation." In *Spanish in Contact: Policy, Social and Linguistic Inquiries*, edited by Kim Potowski and Richard Cameron, 327–41. Amsterdam: John Benjamins, 2007.

Abbott, Carl. "The Internationalization of Washington, DC." *Urban Affairs Review* 31, no. 5 (1996): 571–94.

———. *Political Terrain: Washington, DC, from Tidewater Town to Global Metropolis*. Chapel Hill: University of North Carolina Press, 1999.

Abrego, Leisy J. "On Silences: Salvadoran Refugees Then and Now." *Latino Studies* 15 (2017): 73–85.

Achugar, Mariana, and Silvia Pessoa. "Power and Place: Language Attitudes towards Spanish in a Bilingual Academic Community in Southwest Texas." *Spanish in Context* 6, no. 2 (2009): 199–223.

Agha, Asif. "Large and Small Scale Forms of Personhood." *Language and Communication* 31, no. 3 (July 2011): 171–80.

———. "Voice, Footing, Enregisterment." *Journal of Linguistic Anthropology* 15, no. 1 (2005): 38–59.

Alarcón, Daniel. *War by Candlelight: Stories*. New York: HarperCollins, 2005.

Alba, Richard. "The Surge of Young Americans from Minority-White Mixed Families and Its Significance for the Future." *Daedalus* 150, no. 2 (2021): 199–214.

Albury, Nathan John. "How Folk Linguistic Methods Can Support Critical Sociolinguistics." *Lingua* 199 (2017): 36–49.

Alfaraz, Gabriela G. "Miami Cuban Perceptions of Varieties of Spanish." *Handbook of Perceptual Dialectology* 2 (2002): 1–11.

Alim, H. Samy. "Translocal Style Communities: Hip Hop Youth as Cultural Theorists of Style, Language, and Globalization." *Pragmatics* 19, no. 1 (2009): 103–27.

———. "Who's Afraid of the Transracial Subject?" In *Raciolinguistics: How Language Shapes Our Ideas about Race*, edited by H. Samy Alim, John R. Rickford, and Arnetha F. Ball, 33–50. New York: Oxford University Press, 2016.

Almaguer, Tomás. "At the Crossroads of Race: Latino/a Studies and Race Making in the United States." In *Critical Latin American and Latino Studies*, edited by Juan Poblete, 206–22. Minneapolis: University of Minnesota Press, 2003.

Alvarado, Karina Oliva. "Cultural Memory and Making by US Central Americans." *Latino Studies* 15 (2017): 476–97.
American University Washington College of Law Immigrant Justice Clinic. *Access Denied: The Unfulfilled Promise of the DC Language Access Act.* Report. 2012.
Anderson, Benedict. *Imagined Communities: Reflections on the Origin and Spread of Nationalism.* London: Verso, 2006.
———. "The New World Disorder." *New Left Review* 1, no. 193 (May–June 1992).
Aparicio, Frances R. "Latinidad/es." In *Keywords for Latina/o Studies*, edited by Deborah R. Vargas, Nancy Raquel Mirabel, and Lawrence La Fountain-Stokes, 113–17. New York: New York University Press, 2017.
———. *Negotiating Latinidad: Intralatina/o Lives in Chicago.* Champaign: University of Illinois Press, 2019.
———. "(Re)constructing Latinidad: The Challenge of Latina/o Studies." In *The New Latino Studies Reader: A Twenty-First-Century Perspective*, edited by Rámon A. Gutiérrez and Tomás Almaguer, 39–48. Oakland: University of California Press, 2016.
American Psychological Association. *Publication Manual.* 7th ed. Kindle.
Aranda, Elizabeth M., Sallie Hughes, and Elena Sabogal. *Making a Life in Multiethnic Miami: Immigration and the Rise of a Global City.* Boulder, CO: Lynne Rienner, 2014.
Araujo-Dawson, Beverly. "Understanding the Complexities of Skin Color, Perceptions of Race, and Discrimination among Cubans, Dominicans, and Puerto Ricans." *Hispanic Journal of Behavioral Sciences* 37, no. 2 (2015): 243–56.
Arias, Arturo. "Central American-Americans: Invisibility, Power and Representation in the US Latino World." *Latino Studies* 1, no. 1 (2003): 168–87.
Arya, Rina. "Cultural Appropriation: What It Is and Why It Matters?" *Sociology Compass* 15, no. 10 (2021): e12923.
Asch, Chris Myers, and George Derek Musgrove. *Chocolate City: A History of Race and Democracy in the Nation's Capital.* Chapel Hill: University of North Carolina Press, 2019.
Auer, Peter, and Jürgen Erich Schmidt. *Language and Space: An International Handbook of Linguistic Variation.* Vol. 1, *Theories and Methods.* Berlin: De Gruyter Mouton, 2010.
Avilés, Quique. *Latinhood.* Mexico: Raíces de Papel, the Immigrant Museum, 2003.
Bader, Michael. "Diversity in the D.C. Area: Findings from the 2016 D.C. Area Survey." CLALS Working Papers Series No. 14. Washington, DC: American University, 2016.
Bailey, Benjamin. "Language and Negotiation of Ethnic/Racial Identity among Dominican Americans." *Language in Society* 29, no. 4 (December 2000): 555–82.

———. "The Language of Multiple Identities among Dominican Americans." *Journal of Linguistic Anthropology* 10, no. 2 (December 2000): 190–223.
Baker-Cristales, Beth. "Salvadoran Transformations: Class Consciousness and Ethnic Identity in a Transnational Milieu." *Latin American Perspectives* 31, no. 5 (2004): 15–33.
Bamberg, Michael, Anna De Fina, and Deborah Schiffrin. "Discourse and Identity Construction." In *Handbook of Identity Theory and Research*, edited by Seth J. Schwartz, Koen Luyckx, and Vivian L. Vignoles, 177–99. New York: Springer, 2011.
Barrera, Magdalena. "Of 'Chicharrones' and Clam Chowder: Gender and Consumption in Jorge Ulica's Crónicas Diabólicas." *Bilingual Review/La Revista Bilingüe* 29, no. 1 (2008): 49–65.
Barreto, Amilcar Antonio, and Nicholas G. Napolio. "Bifurcating American Identity: Partisanship, Sexual Orientation, and the 2016 Presidential Election." *Politics, Groups, and Identities* 8, no. 1 (2020): 143–59.
Bartal, Israel. "From Traditional Bilingualism to National Monolingualism." In *Hebrew in Ashkenaz: A Language in Exile*, edited by Lewis Glinert, 141–50. New York: Oxford University Press, 1993.
Baugh, John. "Linguistic Profiling and Discrimination." In *The Oxford Handbook of Language and Society*, edited by Ofelia García, Nelson Flores, and Massimiliano Spotti, 349–68. Oxford: Oxford University Press, 2016.
Bayley, Robert. "Demographic Categories in Sociolinguistic Studies of US Latino Communities." *Language and Linguistics Compass* 8, no. 11 (2014): 536–47.
Beals, Ralph L. "Social Stratification in Latin America." *American Journal of Sociology* 58, no. 4 (1953): 327–39.
Beaudrie, Sara, Cynthia Ducar, and Ana María Relaño-Pastor. "Curricular Perspectives in the Heritage Language Context: Assessing Culture and Identity." *Language, Culture and Curriculum* 22 (2009): 157–74.
Bedolla, Lisa Garcia. "The Identity Paradox: Latino Language, Politics and Selective Dissociation." *Latino Studies* 1, no. 2 (2003): 264–83.
Bell, Allan, and Andy Gibson. "Staging Language: An Introduction to the Sociolinguistics of Performance." *Journal of Sociolinguistics* 15, no. 5 (2011): 555–72.
Bender, Steven W. "Introduction: Old Hate in New Bottles: Privatizing, Localizing, and Bundling Anti-Spanish and Anti-Immigrant Sentiment in the 21st Century." *Nevada Law Journal* 7 (2006): 883–94.
Benítez, José Luis. "Communication and Collective Identity in the Transnational Social Space: A Media Ethnography of the Salvadoran Immigrant Community in the Washington, D.C. Metropolitan Area." PhD diss., Ohio University, 2005.
Bennett, Julia. "Narrating Family Histories: Negotiating Identity and Belonging through Tropes of Nostalgia and Authenticity." *Current Sociology* 66, no. 3 (2018): 449–65.

Benor, Sarah Bunin. "Ethnolinguistic Repertoire: Shifting the Analytic Focus in Language and Ethnicity." *Journal of Sociolinguistics* 14, no. 2 (2010): 159–83.

Bernal-Chávez, Julio Alexander, Camilo Enrique Díaz Romero, and Alejandro Munévar Salazar. "Linguistic Attitudes of the Spanish Speakers from Latin American Countries and Spain Respect to the Spanish Spoken in Colombia." In *LILA '18. III. International Linguistics and Language Studies*, edited by Özgür Öztürk, 109–27. Istanbul: Dakam Yayinlari, March 2018.

Bernstein, Hamutal, Julia Gelatt, Devlin Hanson, and William Monson. "Ten Years of Language Access in Washington." Washington, DC: Urban Institute, April 2014. https://www.urban.org/sites/default/files/alfresco/publication-pdfs/413097-Ten-Years-of-Language-Access-in-Washington-DC.PDF.

Bernstein, Judy B. "Demonstrative Surprises!" In *A Schrift to Fest Kyle Johnson*, edited by Nicholas LaCara, Keir Moulton, and Anne-Michelle Tessier, 55–64. Linguistics Open Access Publications, 2017. https://scholarworks.umass.edu/linguist_oapubs/1/.

Blackledge, Adrian. "'As a Country We Do Expect': The Further Extension of Language Testing Regimes in the United Kingdom." *Language Assessment Quarterly* 6, no. 1 (2009): 6–16.

Block, David. *Multilingual Identities in a Global City: London Stories*. Houndmills, UK: Palgrave Macmillan, 2006.

———. *The Social Turn in Applied Linguistics*. Edinburgh: Edinburgh University Press, 2003.

Blommaert, Jan. *The Sociolinguistics of Globalization*. Cambridge: Cambridge University Press, 2010.

Blommaert, Jan, and Ad Backus. "Superdiverse Repertoires and the Individual." In *Multilingualism and Multimodality: Current Challenges for Educational Studies*, edited by Ingrid de Saint-Georges and Jean-Jacques Weber, 9–32. Leiden, Netherlands: Brill Sense, 2013.

Blommaert, Jan, and Ben Rampton. "Language and Superdiversity." *Diversities* 13, no. 2 (2011): 1–21.

Bloomfield, Leonard. *Language*. New York: Holt, Rhinehart and Winston, 1933.

Borchert, James. "Alley Life in Washington: An Analysis of 600 Photographs." *Records of the Columbia Historical Society, Washington, DC* 49 (1973): 244–59.

Bost, Suzanne, and Frances R. Aparicio. Introduction to *The Routledge Companion to Latino/a Literature*, edited by Suzanne Bost and Frances R. Aparicio, 17–26. London: Routledge, 2012.

Bottero, Wendy. "Class Identities and the Identity of Class." *Sociology* 38, no. 5 (2004): 985–1003.

Bourdieu, Pierre. "The Economics of Linguistic Exchanges." *Social Science Information* 16, no. 6 (1977): 645–68.

———. "The Forms of Capital." In *Handbook of Theory and Research for the*

Sociology of Education, edited by John G. Richardson, 241–58. Westport, CT: Greenwood, 1986.

———. "Habitus." In *Habitus: A Sense of Place*, 2nd ed., edited by Jean Hillier and Emma Rooksby, 59–66. Abingdon, UK: Routledge, 2017.

Britain, David. "Countering the Urbanist Agenda in Variationist Sociolinguistics: Dialect Contact, Demographic Change and the Rural-Urban Dichotomy." In *Dialectological and Folk Dialectological Concepts of Space*, edited by Sandra Hansen, Christian Schwarz, Philipp Stoeckle, and Tobias Streck, 12–30. Berlin: De Gruyter, 2012.

Brogan, Franny D. "Sociophonetically-Based Phonology: An Optimality Theoretic Account of /s/ Lenition in Salvadoran Spanish." PhD diss., University of California, Los Angeles, 2018.

Brooker, Russell. "3 Real Americans: White Identity and the Election of Donald Trump." In *The Unorthodox Presidency of Donald J. Trump*, edited by Paul E. Rutledge and Chapman Rackaway 62–85. Lawrence: University Press of Kansas, 2021.

Brown, Anna, and Mark Hugo López. "Mapping the Latino Population, by State, County and City." Pew Research Center, August 29, 2013. https://www.pewresearch.org/hispanic/2013/08/29/mapping-the-latino-population-by-state-county-and-city/.

Bucholtz, Mary. "From Stance to Style: Gender, Interaction, and Indexicality in Mexican Immigrant Youth Slang." In *Stance: Sociolinguistic Perspectives*, edited by Alexandra M. Jaffe, 146–70. Oxford University Press, 2009.

———. "Sociolinguistic Nostalgia and the Authentication of Identity." *Journal of Sociolinguistics* 7 (2003): 398–416.

———. *White Kids: Language, Race, and Styles of Youth Identity*. Cambridge: Cambridge University Press, 2011.

Bucholtz, Mary, and Kira Hall. "Embodied Sociolinguistics." In *Sociolinguistics: Theoretical Debates*, edited by Nikolas Coupland, 173–97. Cambridge: Cambridge University Press, 2016.

———. "Identity and Interaction: A Sociocultural Linguistics Approach." *Discourse Studies* 7 (2005): 585–614.

———. "Language and Identity." In *A Companion to Linguistic Anthropology*, edited by Alessandro Duranti, 369–94. Malden, MA: Blackwell, 2004.

Burns, Mason D., Erica L. Granz, and Kipling D. Williams. "Support for Native-Themed Mascots and Opposition to Political Correctness." *Group Processes and Intergroup Relations* 26, no. 7 (2022). https://doi.org/10.1177/136843 02221106924.

Busch, Brigitta. "The Linguistic Repertoire Revisited." *Applied Linguistics* 33, no. 5 (2012): 503–23.

Caban, Pedro. "Puerto Ricans as Contingent Citizens: Shifting Mandated Identities and Imperial Disjunctures." Latin American, Caribbean, and U.S.

Latino Studies Faculty Scholarship 1, 2017. https://scholarsarchive.library.albany.edu/lacs_fac_scholar/1.

Cadaval, Olivia. *Creating a Latino Identity in the Nation's Capital: The Latino Festival.* New York: Garland, 1998.

Cai, Qian. "Hispanic Immigrants and Citizens in Virginia." (PDF). Weldon Cooper Center, University of Virginia, Richmond, 2008. www.lgava.org/sites/default/files/publications/2008hispanics.pdf.

Calderón, José. "'Hispanic' and 'Latino': The Viability of Categories for Panethnic Unity." *Latin American Perspectives* 19, no. 4 (1992): 37–44.

Campani, Giovanna, Sunamis Fabelo Concepción, Angel Rodriguez Soler, and Claudia Sánchez Savín. "The Rise of Donald Trump Right-Wing Populism in the United States: Middle American Radicalism and Anti-Immigration Discourse." *Societies* 12, no. 6 (2022): 154. https://doi.org/10.3390/soc12060154.

Campbell, Kristina M. "A Dry Hate: White Supremacy and Anti-Immigrant Rhetoric in the Humanitarian Crisis on the US–Mexico Border." *West Virginia Law Review* 117, no. 3 (2014): 1081.

Canagarajah, Suresh. "Multilingual Writers and the Struggle for Voice in Academic Discourse." In *Negotiation of Identities in Multilingual Contexts*, edited by Aneta Pavlenko and Adrian Blackledge, 266–89. Clevedon, UK: Multilingual Matters, 2004.

Candelario, Ginetta E. *Black behind the Ears: Dominican Racial Identity from Museums to Beauty Shops.* Durham, NC: Duke University Press, 2007.

Canfield, D. Lincoln. "Andalucismos en la pronunciación salvadoreña." *Hispania* 36, no. 1 (February 1953): 32–33.

———. "Observaciones sobre el español salvadoreño." *Filología* 6 (1960): 29–76.

Caravedo, Rocío. "Las ciudades como espacios mentales y lingüísticos: Reflexiones sobre la variación diatópica del español." *Orillas* 1 (2012): 1–17.

Carreira, Maria. "The Vitality of Spanish in the United States." *Heritage Language Journal* 10, no. 3 (2013): 396–413.

Carris, Lauren Mason. "La Voz Gringa: Latino Stylization of Linguistic (in)Authenticity as Social Critique." *Discourse and Society* 22, no. 4 (2011): 474–90.

Carter, Niambi Michele. *American while Black: African Americans, Immigration, and the Limits of Citizenship.* New York: Oxford University Press, 2019.

Carter, Phillip M. "Poststructuralist Theory and Sociolinguistics: Mapping the Linguistic Turn in Social Theory." *Language and Linguistics Compass* 7, no. 11 (2013): 580–96.

———. "Shared Spaces, Shared Structures: Latino Social Formation and African American English in the US South." *Journal of Sociolinguistics* 17, no. 1 (2013): 66–92.

Carter, Phillip M., and Salvatore Callesano. "The Social Meaning of Spanish in Miami: Dialect Perceptions and Implications for Socioeconomic Class, Income, and Employment." *Latino Studies* 16, no. 1 (2018): 65–90.

Carter, Phillip M., Lydda López Valdez, and Nandi Sims. "New Dialect Formation through Language Contact: Vocalic and Prosodic Developments in Miami English." *American Speech: A Quarterly of Linguistic Usage* 95, no. 2 (2020): 119–48.

Cashin, Sheryll. *The Failures of Integration: How Race and Class Are Undermining the American Dream.* New York: Public Affairs, 2004.

Cheng, Andrew. "1.5 Generation Korean Americans: Consonant and Vowel Production of Two Late Childhood Arrivals." *UC Berkeley PhonLab Annual Report* 14, no. 1 (2018): 189–220. https://escholarship.org/uc/item/5k679575.

Cheshire, Jenny, Paul Kerswill, Sue Fox, and Eivind Torgersen. "Contact, the Feature Pool and the Speech Community: The Emergence of Multicultural London English." *Journal of Sociolinguistics* 15, no. 2 (2011): 151–96.

The Chicago Manual of Style. 18th ed. Chicago: University of Chicago Press, 2024.

Chimbutane, Feliciano. "Multilingualism in Education in Post-Colonial Contexts: A Special Focus on Sub-Saharan Africa." In *The Routledge Handbook of Multilingualism*, edited by Marilyn Martin-Jones, Adrian Blackledge, and Angela Creese, 167–83. New York: Routledge, 2012.

Chun, Elaine W. "The Construction of White, Black, and Korean American Identities through African American Vernacular English." *Journal of Linguistic Anthropology* 11, no. 1 (2001): 52–64.

Chun, Elaine W., and Adrienne Lo. "Language and Racialization." In *The Routledge Handbook of Linguistic Anthropology*, edited by Nancy Bonvillain, 234–47. New York: Routledge, 2015.

Clark, Joshua, and Olivia Araiza. *Margins in Movement: Toward Belonging in the Inland Empire of Southern California.* Report. Othering and Belonging Institute, November 29, 2021. https://belonging.berkeley.edu/margins-in-movement.

Cobas, José A., Jorge Duany, and Joe Feagin. "Introduction: Racializing Latinos: Historical Background and Current Forms." In *How the United States Racializes Latinos: White Hegemony and Its Consequences*, edited by José A. Cobas, Jorge Duany, and Joe Feagin, 1–14. Boulder, CO: Paradigm, 2009.

Cohn, D'Vera, "Census History: Counting Hispanics." Pew Research Center, March 3, 2010. https://www.pewresearch.org/social-trends/2010/03/03/census-history-counting-hispanics-2/#:~:text=The%202000%20Census%2C%20which%20counted,to%20respondents%20and%20question%20placement.

Collins, Allyson. *Shielded from Justice: Police Brutality and Accountability in the United States.* Edited by Cynthia Brown. New York: Human Rights Watch, 1998.

Collins, Chris. "A Fresh Look at Habitual Be in AAVE." In *Structure and Variation in Language Contact*, edited by Ana Deumert, and Stephanie Durrleman, 203–24. Amsterdam: John Benjamins, 2006.

Coronado, Heidi M., and Audrey Darlene Paredes. "From Invisible to Visible: Documenting the Voices and Resilience of Central American Students in US Schools." *Interactions: UCLA Journal of Education and Information Studies* 15, no. 1 (2018): 21–45.

Correa, Maite. "Advocating for Critical Pedagogical Approaches to Teaching Spanish as a Heritage Language: Some Considerations." *Foreign Language Annals* 44, no. 2 (2011): 308–20.

Cortina, Regina, ed. *Indigenous Education Policy, Equity, and Intercultural Understanding in Latin America*. New York: Palgrave Macmillan, 2017.

Coupland, Nikolas. "Sociolinguistic Authenticities." *Journal of Sociolinguistics* 7, no. 3 (2003): 417–31.

———. *Style: Language Variation and Identity*. Cambridge: Cambridge University Press, 2007.

Curtis, Ariana, curator. *Bridging the Americas: Community and Belonging from Panama to Washington, DC*. Washington, DC: Smithsonian Anacostia Museum, 2016.

Cutler, Cecelia Anne. "'Keepin' it real': White Hip Hoppers' Discourses of Language, Race, and Authenticity." *Journal of Linguistic Anthropology* 13 (2003): 211–33.

———. "White Hip-Hoppers." *Language and Linguistics Compass* 9, no. 6 (2015): 229–42.

D'Arcy, Alexandra. "Like and Language Ideology: Disentangling Fact from Fiction." *American Speech* 82, no. 4 (2007): 386–419.

Davies, Bronwyn, and Rom Harré. "Positioning: The Discursive Production of Selves." *Journal for the Theory of Social Behaviour* 20, no. 1 (1990): 43–63.

"DC Home Rule." Council of the District of Columbia. Accessed November 21, 2023. https://dccouncil.gov/dc-home-rule/.

"DC-Metro Latino Research Initiative." American University. https://www.american.edu/centers/latin-american-latino-studies/latinos-in-dc.cfm.

De Fina, Anna. "Discourse and Identity." In *The Encyclopedia of Applied Linguistics*, edited by Carol A. Chapelle, 1–8. Hoboken, NJ: John Wiley, 2012.

———. *Identity in Narrative: A Study of Immigrant Discourse*. Amsterdam: John Benjamins, 2003.

———. "Orientation in Immigrant Narratives: The Role of Ethnicity in the Identification of Characters." *Discourse Studies* 2, no. 2 (2000): 131–57.

———. "Positioning Level 3: Connecting Local Identity Displays to Macro Social Processes." *Narrative Inquiry* 23, no. 1 (2013): 40–61.

De Fina, Anna, and Alexandra Georgakopoulou. *Analyzing Narrative: Discourse and Sociolinguistic Perspectives*. Cambridge: Cambridge University Press, 2008.

De Fina, Anna, and Kendall A. King. "Language Problem or Language Conflict? Narratives of Immigrant Women's Experiences in the US." *Discourse Studies* 13, no. 2 (2011): 163–88.

De Fina, Anna, and Sabina Perrino. "Transnational Identities." *Applied Linguistics* 34, no. 5 (2013): 509–15.

De Genova, Nicholas, and Ana Yolanda Ramos-Zayas. *Latino Crossings: Mexicans, Puerto Ricans, and the Politics of Race and Citizenship.* New York: Routledge, 2003.

De Houwer, Annick. "Bilingual Language Acquisition." In *The Handbook of Child Language,* edited by Paul Fletcher and Brain MacWhinney, 219–50. Oxford: Blackwell, 2017.

Del Valle, José, ed. *A Political History of Spanish: The Making of a Language.* Cambridge: Cambridge University Press, 2013.

Díaz-Campos, Manuel. *Introducción a la sociolingüística hispánica.* Newark, NJ: Wiley, 2013.

Dolberg, Pnina, and Karin Amit. "On a Fast-Track to Adulthood: Social Integration and Identity Formation Experiences of Young-Adults of 1.5 Generation Immigrants." *Journal of Ethnic and Migration Studies* 49, no. 1 (2023): 252–71.

Du Bois, John W. "The Stance Triangle." In *Stancetaking in Discourse: Subjectivity, Evaluation, Interaction,* edited by Robert Englebretson, 139–82. Amsterdam: John Benjamins, 2007.

Duany, Jorge. "Reconstructing Racial Identity: Ethnicity, Color, and Class among Dominicans in the United States and Puerto Rico." *Latin American Perspectives* 25, no. 3 (1998): 147–72.

Duff, Patricia A. "Transnationalism, Multilingualism, and Identity." *Annual Review of Applied Linguistics* 35 (March 2015): 57–80.

Dufour, D. L., and B. A. Piperata. "Rural-to-Urban Migration in Latin America: An Update and Thoughts on the Model." *American Journal of Human Biology* 16, no. 4 (2004): 395–404.

East, Dave. "My Nigga Dead (Interlude)." MP3 audio. Track 9 on Dave East, *Karma 2.* Def Jam Recordings, 2018.

Eckert, Penelope. "The Future of Variation Studies." Keynote address at NWAV40: Celebrating 40 Years of Analyzing Variation . . . But Who's Counting? Georgetown University, Washington, DC, October 28, 2011.

———. *Meaning and Linguistic Variation.* Stanford, CA: Stanford University Press, 2018.

———. "The Whole Woman: Sex and Gender Differences in Variation." *Language Variation and Change* 1, no. 3 (1989): 245–67.

"Economic Mobility Trends in the DMV." Display slides. Brookings, n.d. https://www.brookings.edu/wp-content/uploads/2022/04/GS_20220427_DMV-Economic-Trends.pdf.

Ellis, Carolyn. "At Home with 'Real Americans': Communicating across the Urban/Rural and Black/White Divides in the 2008 Presidential Election." *Cultural Studies↔Critical Methodologies* 9, no. 6 (2009): 721–33.

Eriksen, Thomas Hylland. *Globalization: The Key Concepts.* Oxford, UK: Berg, 2007.

Erker, Daniel. "The Limits of Named Language Varieties and the Role of Social Salience in Dialectal Contact: The Case of Spanish in the United States." *Language and Linguistics Compass* 11 (2017): e12232.

Executive Office of the Mayor, Government of the District of Columbia. "Mayor Bowser Signs Bill to Designate Go-Go Music as the Official Music of DC." Press release, February 19, 2020. https://mayor.dc.gov/release/mayor-bowser-signs-bill-designate-go-go-music-official-music.-dc.

Faez, Farahnaz. "Linguistic Identities and Experiences of Generation 1.5 Teacher Candidates: Race Matters." *TESL Canada Journal* 29, special issue 6 (2012): 124–41.

Farrington, Charlie, and Natalie Schilling. "Contextualizing the Corpus of Regional African American Language, DC: AAL in the Nation's Capital." *American Speech* 94, no. 1 (2019): 21–35.

Fasold, Ralph W. *Tense Marking in Black English: A Linguistic and Social Analysis*. Urban Language Series, No. 8. Arlington, VA: Center for Applied Linguistics, 1972.

Fichter, Andrew. "DC's Population Is Exploding." Greater Washington, May 26, 2016. https://ggwash.org/view/41810/dcs-population-is-exploding.

Fishman, Joshua A., ed. *Language Loyalty in the United States: The Maintenance and Perpetuation of Non-English Mother Tongues by American Ethnic and Religious Groups*. The Hague, Netherlands: Mouton, 1966.

Fishman, Joshua A. "Language Maintenance and Language Shift as a Field of Inquiry: A Definition of the Field and Suggestions for Its Further Development." *Linguistics* 2, no. 9 (1964): 32–70.

Flores, Nelson. "Silencing the Subaltern: Nation-State/Colonial Governmentality and Bilingual Education in the United States." *Critical Inquiry in Language Studies* 10, no. 4 (2013): 263–87.

Flores, Nelson, and Jonathan Rosa. "Undoing Raciolinguistics." *Journal of Sociolinguistics* 27, no. 5 (2023): 421–27.

Flores, Nelson, and Jonathan Rosa. "Undoing Appropriateness: Racio-linguistic Ideologies and Language Diversity in Education." *Harvard Educational Review* 85, no. 2 (2015): 149–71.

Flores, Nelson, Amelia Tseng, and Nicholas Subtirelu. *Bilingualism for All? Raciolinguistic Perspectives on Dual Language Education in the United States*. Bristol, UK: Multilingual Matters, 2020.

Flores-González, Nilda. "Puerto Rican High Achievers: An Example of Ethnic and Academic Identity Compatibility." *Anthropology and Education Quarterly* 30, no. 3 (1999): 343–62.

Fought, Carmen. *Chicano English in Context*. London: Palgrave Macmillan, 2003.

Freeman-Woolpert, Sarah. "Community Museum Showcases Washington, DC's Long History of Activism," Waging Nonviolence, August 2, 2018.

https://wagingnonviolence.org/2018/08/anacostia-community-museum-showcases-washington-dc-activism/.
Frey, William H. *Diversity Explosion: How New Racial Demographics Are Remaking America*. Washington, DC: Brookings Institution Press, 2018.
Fries-Britt, Sharon, and Kimberly Griffin. "The Black Box: How High-Achieving Blacks Resist Stereotypes about Black Americans." *Journal of College Student Development* 48, no. 5 (September–October 2007): 509–24.
Galvez, Martha, Josh Leopold, Cameron Okeke, and Alyse D. Oneto. *Three Decades of Mary's Center's Social Change Model: A Community Health Center's Approach to Addressing the Social Determinants of Health*. Report. Washington, DC: Urban Institute, September 2019.
García, Lorena, and Mérida Rúa. "Processing Latinidad: Mapping Latino Urban Landscapes through Chicago Ethnic Festivals." *Latino Studies* 5 (2007): 317–39.
García, Ofelia, and Li Wei. "Translanguaging." In *The Encyclopedia of Applied Linguistics*, edited by Carol A. Chapelle, 1–7. Hoboken, NJ: Wiley-Blackwell, 2014. https://doi.org/10.1002/9781405198431.wbeal1488.
Gastner, Mary Kate. "Valuing 'Others': Free African American Neighborhoods in Antebellum Alexandria." MA thesis, University of Maryland, College Park, Maryland, 2011.
Gee, James Paul. *Social Linguistics and Literacies: Ideology in Discourses, Critical Perspectives on Literacy and Education*. London: Falmer Press, 1990.
Georgakopoulou, Alexandra. *Small Stories, Interaction and Identities*. Amsterdam: John Benjamins, 2007.
Goble, Ryan A. "Linguistic Insecurity and Lack of Entitlement to Spanish among Third-Generation Mexican Americans in Narrative Accounts." *Heritage Language Journal* 13, no. 1 (2016): 29–54.
Gonzalez-Barrera, Ana. "The Ways Hispanics Describe Their Identity Vary across Immigrant Generations." Pew Research Center, September 24, 2020. https://www.pewresearch.org/fact-tank/2020/09/24/the-ways-hispanics-describe-their-identity-vary-across-immigrant-generations/.
Gorman, L. "Connecting US Latina/o Cultural Identities and Language: The Case of Mexican-Nuevomexicano Families in Northern New Mexico." In *Explorations in Ethnography, Language and Communication: Capturing Linguistic and Cultural Diversities*, edited by Stina Hållsten and Zoe Nikolaidou, 41–58. Stockholm: Södertörn University, 2018.
Green, Constance McLaughlin. *Secret City: A History of Race Relations in the Nation's Capital*. Princeton, NJ: Princeton University Press, 2015.
———. *Washington: A History of the Capital, 1800–1950*. Vol. 1. Princeton, NJ: Princeton University Press, 1976.
Green, Lisa J. *African American English: A Linguistic Introduction*. Cambridge: Cambridge University Press, 2002.

Green, Matthew N., Julie Yarwood, Laura Daughtery, and Maria Mazzenga, "Chocolate City, Vanilla Swirl, or Something Else? Race and Ethnicity in City and Region." Chapter 8 in *Washington 101: An Introduction to the Nation's Capital*, 123–43. New York: Palgrave Macmillan, 2014.

Grieser, Jessica. *The Black Side of the River: Race, Language, and Belonging in Washington, DC*. Washington, DC: Georgetown University Press, 2022.

———. Locating Style: Style-Shifting to Characterize Community at the Border of Washington, DC. University of Pennsylvania Working Papers in Linguistics 19, October 2013.

Gudmunson, Lowell, and Justin Wolfe, eds. *Blacks and Blackness in Central America: Between Race and Place*. Durham, NC: Duke University Press, 2010.

Gumperz, John J. *Language and Social Identity*. Cambridge: Cambridge University Press, 1982.

———. "Linguistic and Social Interaction in Two Communities." *American Anthropologist* 66, no. 6 (1964): 137–53.

Gutiérrez, Ramón A. "What's in a Name? The History and Politics of Hispanic and Latino Panethnicities." In *The New Latino Studies Reader: A Twenty-First-Century Perspective*, edited by Ramón A. Gutiérrez and Tomás Almaguer, 19–53. Oakland: University of California Press, 2016.

Gzesh, Susan. "Central Americans and Asylum Policy in the Reagan Era." Migration Policy Institute, April 1, 2006. https://www.migrationpolicy.org/print/4621.

Hannah, John A., Robert G. Storey, Erwin N. Griswold, Theodore M. Hesburgh, Robert S. Rankin, and Spottswood W. Robinson III. *Civil Rights U.S.A./Housing in Washington, D.C.* Washington, DC: US Government Printing Office, for the United States Commission on Civil Rights, 1962.

Harkness, Geoff. "Hip Hop Culture and America's Most Taboo Word." *Contexts* 7, no. 3 (2008): 38–42.

Harré, Rom. "Positioning Theory." In *The International Encyclopedia of Language and Social Interaction*, edited by Karen Tracy, 1–9. Hoboken, NJ: John Wiley, 2015.

Hart-González, Lucinda. "Pan-Hispanism and Sub-Community in Washington, DC." In *Spanish Language Use and Public Life in the United States*, edited by Lucía Elías-Olivares, Elizabeth A. Leone, René Cisneros, and John R. Gutiérrez, 73–88. Berlin: Mouton de Gruyter, 1985.

Heldke, Lisa M. *Exotic Appetites: Ruminations of a Food Adventurer*. New York: Routledge, 2003.

Heller, Monica. "Bilingualism as Ideology and Practice." In *Bilingualism: A Social Approach*, edited by Monica Heller, 1–22. London: Palgrave Macmillan, 2007.

Hidalgo, Margarita. "The Emergence of Standard Spanish in the American Continent: Implications for Latin American Dialectology." *Language Problems and Language Planning* 14, no. 1 (1990): 47–63.

"Hispanic Population and Origin in Select U.S. Metropolitan Areas, 2014." Pew Research Center, September 6, 2016. https://www.pewresearch.org/race-and-ethnicity/feature/hispanic-population-in-select-u-s-metropolitan-areas/.

Holland, Jesse. *Black Men Built the Capitol: Discovering African-American History in and around Washington, DC*. Lanham, MD: Rowman and Littlefield, 2007.

Holliday, Adrian. "Native-Speakerism." *ELT Journal* 60, no. 4 (2006): 385–87.

Holliday, Nicole. R. "Perception in Black and White: Effects of Intonational Variables and Filtering Conditions on Sociolinguistic Judgments with Implications for ASR." *Frontiers in Artificial Intelligence* 4 (2021). https://doi.org/10.3389%2Ffrai.2021.642783.

Hopkinson, Natalie. *Go-Go Live: The Musical Life and Death of a Chocolate City*. Durham, NC: Duke University Press, 2012.

Hornberger, Nancy H., and Shuhan C. Wang. "Who Are Our Heritage Language Learners? Identity and Biliteracy in Heritage Language Education in the United States." In *Heritage Language Education: A New Field Emerging*, edited by Donna M. Brinton, Olga Kagan, and Susan Bauckus, 3–35. Abingdon, UK: Routledge, 2008.

House-Niamke, Stephanie, and Takumi Sato. "Resistance to Systemic Oppression by Students of Color in a Diversity Course for Preservice Teachers." *Educational Studies* 55, no. 2 (2019): 160–79.

Huante, Alfredo. "A Lighter Shade of Brown? Racial Formation and Gentrification in Latino Los Angeles." *Social Problems* 68, no. 1 (2021): 63–79.

Hughes, Langston. *The Collected Poems of Langston Hughes, 1902–1967*. Edited by Arnold Rampersad and David Roessel. New York: Knopf, 1995.

Hunter, Margaret. "The Persistent Problem of Colorism: Skin Tone, Status, and Inequality." *Sociology Compass* 1, no. 1 (2007): 237–54.

Hyra, Derek S. *Race, Class, and Politics in the Cappuccino City*. Chicago: University of Chicago Press, 2017.

Ibrahim, Awad. *The Rhizome of Blackness: A Critical Ethnography of Hip-Hop Culture, Language, Identity, and the Politics of Becoming*. New York: Peter Lang, 2014.

Institute for Immigration Research. "Colombia: Colombian Population in the Washington, DC and Baltimore, MD Metropolitan Areas." George Mason University. Accessed June 1, 2023. https://iir.gmu.edu/immigrant-stories/colombia/colombia-colombian-population-in-the-washington-dc-and-baltimore-md-metropolitan-areas.

Institute for Immigration Research. "El Salvador: Salvadoran Population in the Washington, DC and Baltimore, MD Metro Areas." George Mason University. Accessed June 1, 2023. https://iir.gmu.edu/immigrant-stories/el-salvador/el-salvador-salvadoran-population-in-the-washington-dc-and-baltimore-md-metro-areas.

Instituto Cervantes. *El español: Una lengua viva.* 2016. https://www.cervantes.es/imagenes/File/prensa/EspanolLenguaViva16.pdf.
Iraheta, Ana C. "Interdental /s/ in Salvadoran Spanish: Finding Linguistic Patterns and Social Meaning." PhD diss., University of Minnesota, 2017.
Irvine, Judith T., and Susan Gal. "Language Ideology and Linguistic Differentiation." In *Linguistic Anthropology: A Reader*, edited by A. Duranti, 402–34. Hoboken, NJ: Wiley-Blackwell, 2009.
Jackson, Jonathan. "The Consequences of Gentrification for Racial Change in Washington, DC." *Housing Policy Debate* 25, no. 2 (2015): 353–73. https://doi.org/10.1080/10511482.2014.921221.
Jackson, Maurice. "Washington, DC: From the Founding of a Slaveholding Capital to a Center of Abolitionism." *Journal of African Diaspora Archaeology and Heritage* 2, no. 1 (2013): 38–64.
Jackson, Maurice, and Blair A. Ruble, eds. *DC Jazz: Stories of Jazz Music in Washington, DC.* Washington, DC: Georgetown University Press, 2018.
Jaffe, Alexandra, ed. *Stance: Sociolinguistic Perspectives.* Oxford: Oxford University Press, 2009.
Jaffe, Harry S., and Tom Sherwood. *Dream City: Race, Power, and the Decline of Washington, D.C.* New York: Simon and Schuster, 1994.
Jamal, Tazim, and Steve Hill. "Developing a Framework for Indicators of Authenticity: The Place and Space of Cultural and Heritage Tourism." *Asia Pacific Journal of Tourism Research* 9, no. 4 (2004): 353–72.
Järlehed, Johan, Helle Lykke Nielsen, and Tove Rosendal. "Language, Food and Gentrification: Signs of Socioeconomic Mobility in Two Gothenburg Neighbourhoods." *Multilingual Margins: A Journal of Multilingualism from the Periphery* 5, no. 1 (2018): 40–65.
Joassart-Marcelli, Pascale. *The $16 Taco: Contested Geographies of Food, Ethnicity, and Gentrification.* Seattle: University of Washington Press, 2021.
Johnstone, Barbara. "Ideology and Discourse in the Enregisterment of Regional Variation." In *Space in Language and Linguistics: Geographical, Interactional, and Cognitive Perspectives*, edited by Peter Auer, Martin Hilpert, Anja Stukenbrock, and Benedikt Szmrecsanyi, 107–27. Berlin: De Gruyter, 2013.
———. "A New Role for Narrative in Variationist Sociolinguistics." *Narrative Inquiry* 16, no. 1 (2006): 46–55.
———. "Place, Globalization, and Linguistic Variation." In *Sociolinguistic Variation: Critical Reflections*, edited by Carmen Fought, 65–83. Oxford: Oxford University Press, 2004.
Jones, Nicholas, Rachel Marks, Roberto Ramirez, and Merarys Ríos-Vargas. "2020 Census Illuminates Racial and Ethnic Composition of the Country." Census.gov, August 12, 2021. https://www.census.gov/library/stories/2021/08/improved-race-ethnicity-measures-reveal-united-states-population-much-more-multiracial.html.

Jones-Correa, Michael, and David L. Leal. "Becoming 'Hispanic': Secondary Panethnic Identification among Latin American–Origin Populations in the United States." *Hispanic Journal of Behavioral Sciences* 18, no. 2 (1996): 214–54.

Jonsson, Rickard, Henning Årman, and Tommaso M. Milani. "Youth Language." In *The Routledge Handbook of Linguistic Ethnography*, edited by Karin Tusting, 259–72. New York: Routledge, 2019.

Joseph, Galen. "Taking Race Seriously: Whiteness in Argentina's National and Transnational Imaginary." *Identities Global Studies in Culture and Power* 7, no. 3 (2000): 333–71.

Kay, Cristóbal. "Reflections on Rural Poverty in Latin America." *European Journal of Development Research* 17, no. 2 (2005): 317–46.

Keane, Webb. "Voice." *Journal of Linguistic Anthropology* 9, no. 1–2 (1999): 271–73.

Kendall, Tyler, and Charlie Farrington. The Corpus of Regional African American Language, ver. 2020.05. Eugene, OR: Online Resources for African American Language Project. http://oraal.uoregon.edu/coraal.

Kerswill, Paul. "Identity, Ethnicity and Place: The Construction of Youth Language in London." In *Space in Language and Linguistics: Geographical, Interactional, and Cognitive Perspectives*, edited by Peter Auer, Martin Hilpert, Anja Stukenbrock, and Benedikt Szmrecsanyi, 128–64. Berlin: De Gruyter, 2013.

———. "Migration and Language." In *Sociolinguistics/Soziolinguistik: An International Handbook of the Science of Language and Society*. Vol. 3, *Teil-band*, edited by Ulrich Ammon, Norbert Dittmar, and Klaus Mattheier, 2271–84. Berlin: De Gruyter, 2006.

Kiesling, Scott F. "Dude." *American Speech* 79, no. 3 (2004): 281–305.

———. "Style as Stance." In *Stance: Sociolinguistic Perspectives*, edited by Alexandra M. Jaffe, 171–94. Oxford: Oxford University Press, 2009.

Kijakazi, Kilolo, Rachel Marie Brooks Atkins, Mark Paul, Anne Price, Darrick Hamilton, and William A. Darity Jr. *The Color of Wealth in the Nation's Capital*. Report. Urban Institute, November 1, 2016. https://www.urban.org/research/publication/color-wealth-nations-capital.

King, Sharese. "From African American Vernacular English to African American Language: Rethinking the Study of Race and Language in African Americans' Speech." *Annual Review of Linguistics* 6, no. 1 (2020): 285–300. https://doi.org/10.1146/annurev-linguistics-011619-030556.

King, Wyman, Richard C. Emanuel, Xavier Brown, Niroby Dingle, Vertis Lucas, Anissa Perkins, Ayzia Turner, Destinee Whittington, and Qwa'dryna Witherspoon. "Who Has the 'Right' to Use the N-Word? A Survey of Attitudes about the Acceptability of Using the N-Word and Its Derivatives." *International Journal of Society, Culture and Language* 6, no. 2 (2018): 47–58.

Kirkland, Elizabeth. "What's Race Got to Do with It? Looking for the Racial

Dimensions of Gentrification." *Western Journal of Black Studies* 32, no. 2 (2008).

Klee, Carol A., and Rocío Caravedo. "Andean Spanish and the Spanish of Lima: Linguistic Variation and Change in a Contact Situation." In *Globalization and Language in the Spanish-Speaking World*, edited by Clare Mar-Molinero and Miranda Stewart, 94–113. London: Palgrave Macmillan, 2006.

Krogstad, Jens Manuel, and Ana Gonzalez-Barrera. "A Majority of English-Speaking Hispanics in the US Are Bilingual." Pew Research Center, March 24, 2015. http://pewrsr.ch/1Hvx3jh.

Krogstad, Jens Manuel, and Mark Hugo Lopez. "Use of Spanish Declines among Latinos in Major US Metros." Pew Research Center, October 31, 2017. www.pewresearch.org/fact-tank/2017/10/31/use-of-spanish-declines-among-latinos-in-major-u-s-metros/.

Kupisch, Tanja, and Jason Rothman. "Terminology Matters! Why Difference Is Not Incompleteness and How Early Child Bilinguals Are Heritage Speakers." *International Journal of Bilingualism* 22, no. 5 (2018): 564–82.

Labov, William. "How I Got into Linguistics, and What I Got Out of It." *Historiographia Linguistica* 28, no. 3 (2001): 455–66.

———. *Language in the Inner City: Studies in the Black English Vernacular*. Philadelphia: University of Pennsylvania Press, 1972.

———. *Sociolinguistic Patterns*. Philadelphia: University of Pennsylvania Press, 1972.

———. *A Study of the Non-Standard English of Negro and Puerto Rican Speakers in New York City*. Vol. 1, *Phonological and Grammatical Analysis*. Philadelphia: US Regional Survey, 1968.

Labov, William, and Wendell A. Harris. "De Facto Segregation of Black and White Vernaculars." *Diversity and Diachrony* 53 (1986): 33–44.

Labov, William, and Joshua Waletzky. "Narrative Analysis." In *Essays on the Verbal and Visual Arts: Proceedings of the 1966 Annual Spring Meeting of the American Ethnological Society*, edited by June Helm, 12–44. Seattle: University of Washington Press, 1967.

Lacayo, Celia. "Latinos Need to Stay in Their Place: Differential Segregation in a Multi-Ethnic Suburb." *Societies* 6, no. 25 (2016): 25.

Landolt, Patricia, Lillian Autler, and Sonia Baires. "From Hermano Lejano to Hermano Mayor: The Dialectics of Salvadoran Transnationalism." *Ethnic and Racial Studies* 22, no. 2 (1999): 290–315.

Lane, Jeffrey. "Rethinking the Brand–Community Relationship: Wearing a Biggie in Harlem." *Journal of Consumer Culture* 21, no. 2 (2021): 219–35.

Lavadenz, Magaly. "Como hablar en silencio (Like Speaking in Silence): Issues for Language, Culture, and Identity of Central Americans in Los Angeles." In *Building on Strength: Language and Literacy in Latino Families and Communities*, edited by Ana Celia Zentella, 93–108. New York: Teachers College Press, 2005.

Lavariega Monforti, Jessica, and Gabriel R. Sanchez. "The Politics of Perception: An Investigation of the Presence and Sources of Perceptions of Internal Discrimination among Latinos." *Social Science Quarterly* 91, no. 1 (2010): 245–65.

Lee, Jerry Won, and Sender Dovchin, eds. *Translinguistics: Negotiating Innovation and Ordinariness.* Abingdon, UK: Routledge, 2020.

Lee, Sinae. "High and Mid Back Vowel Fronting in Washington, DC." *American Speech* 91, no. 4 (2016): 425–71.

Leeman, Jennifer. "Critical Language Awareness and Spanish as a Heritage Language: Challenging the Linguistic Subordination of US Latinxs." In *The Routledge Handbook of Spanish as a Heritage Language*, edited by Kim Potowski, 345–58. Abingdon, UK: Routledge, 2018.

———. "Investigating Language Ideologies in Spanish as a Heritage Language." In *Spanish as a Heritage Language in the United States: The State of the Field*, edited by S. M. Beaudrie and M. Fairclough, 43–60. Washington, DC: Georgetown University Press, 2012.

Leeman, Jennifer, and Gabriella Modan. "Commodified Language in Chinatown: A Contextualized Approach to Linguistic Landscape." *Journal of Sociolinguistics* 13, no. 3 (2009): 332–62.

Lees, Loretta. "Gentrification, Race, and Ethnicity: Towards a Global Research Agenda?" *City and Community* 15, no. 3 (2016): 208–14.

Leonardo, Zeus, and Margaret Hunter. "Imagining the Urban: The Politics of Race, Class, and Schooling." In *International Handbook of Urban Education*, edited by William T. Pink and George W. Noblit, 779–801. Dordrecht: Springer, 2007.

Levey, Jane Freundel, Laura Croghan Kamoie, Richard T. Busch, J. Brendan Meyer, and Anne W. Rollins. "Roads to Diversity: Adams Morgan Heritage Trail." Cultural Tourism DC (2005). Accessed April 21, 2021. https://online.flippingbook.com/view/122427947/4/.

Lewis, Gwyn, Bryn Jones, and Colin Baker. "Translanguaging: Origins and Development from School to Street and Beyond." *Educational Research and Evaluation* 18, no. 7 (2012): 641–54.

Lewis, Tom. *Washington: A History of Our National City.* New York: Basic Books, 2015.

Li, Wei, ed. *The Bilingualism Reader.* Abingdon, UK: Routledge, 2020.

———. "Translanguaging as a Practical Theory of Language." *Applied Linguistics* 39, no. 1 (2018): 9–30.

Lippi-Green, Rosina. *English with an Accent: Language, Ideology and Discrimination in the United States.* 2nd ed. Abingdon, UK: Routledge, 2012.

Lipsitz, George. "Cruising around the Historical Bloc: Postmodernism and Popular Music in East Los Angeles." *Cultural Critique* 5 (1986): 157–77.

Lipski, John M. *Latin American Spanish.* London: Longman, 1994.

———. "On the Weakening of /s/ in Latin American Spanish." *Zeitschrift für Dialektologie und Linguistik* 51 (1984): 31–43.

———. "/s/ in Central American Spanish." *Hispania* 68 no. 1 (1985): 143–49.
———. *Varieties of Spanish in the United States*. Washington, DC: Georgetown University Press, 2008.
Lo, Adrienne, and Elaine Chun. "Language, Race, and Reflexivity: A View from Linguistic Anthropology." In *The Oxford Handbook of Language and Race*, edited by H. Samy Alim, Angela Reyes, and Paul V. Kroskrity, 25–46. New York: Oxford University Press, 2018.
"Load My Gun." Featuring The Lox. MP3 audio. Track 13 on Dave East and Styles P, *Beloved*. Def Jam Recordings, 2018.
Lopes, Tian, and Barb Thomas. *Dancing on Live Embers: Challenging Racism in Organizations*. Toronto: Between the Lines, 2006.
Lopez, Mark Hugo, Ana Gonzalez-Barrera, and Danielle Cuddington. *Diverse Origins: The Nation's 14 Largest Hispanic-Origin Groups*. Pew Research Center, June 19, 2013. https://www.pewresearch.org/hispanic/2013/06/19/diverse-origins-the-nations-14-largest-hispanic-origin-groups/.
Lopez, Mark Hugo, Ana Gonzalez-Barrera, and Gustavo López. *Hispanic Identity Fades across Generations as Immigrant Connections Fall Away*. Washington, DC: Pew Research Center, 2017. https://www.pewresearch.org/hispanic/2017/12/20/hispanic-identity-fades-across-generations-as-immigrant-connections-fall-away/.
Lorenzi, Jane, and Jeanne Batalova. "South American Immigrants in the United States." Migration Policy Institute, February 16, 2022. https://www.migrationpolicy.org/article/south-american-immigrants-united-states.
Loughran, Maureen Elizabeth. "Community Powered Resistance: Radio, Music Scenes and Musical Activism in Washington, DC." PhD diss., Brown University, 2008.
Low, Bronwen E. "Hip-Hop, Language, and Difference: The N-Word as a Pedagogical Limit-Case." *Journal of Language, Identity, and Education* 6, no. 2 (2007): 147–60.
Lowe, Seana S. "Creating Community: Art for Community Development." *Journal of Contemporary Ethnography* 29, no. 3 (2000): 357–86.
Luna, Ronald W. "Transforming Espacios Culturales: How the Salvadoran Community Is Establishing Evangelical Protestant Churches as Transnational Institutions in the Washington, DC Metropolitan Area." PhD diss., University of Maryland, 2008.
Lung-Amam, Willow. "An Equitable Future for the Washington, DC Region? A 'Regionalism Light' Approach to Building Inclusive Neighborhoods." In *A Shared Future: Fostering Communities of Inclusion in an Era of Inequality*, edited by C. E. Herbert, J. Spader, and J. H. Molinsky, 190–201. Cambridge, MA: Joint Center for Housing Studies of Harvard University, 2018.
Lynch, Andrew, ed. *The Routledge Handbook of Spanish in the Global City*. Abingdon, UK: Routledge, 2020.
Lynch, Andrew, and Kim Potowski. "La valoración del habla bilingüe en los

Estados Unidos: Fundamentos sociolingüísticos y pedagógicos en 'Hablando bien se entiende la gente.'" *Hispania* 97, no. 1 (March 2014): 32–46.

Lytra, Vally, and Jens Norman Jørgensen, eds. *Multilingualism and Identities across Contexts: Cross-Disciplinary Perspectives on Turkish-Speaking Youth in Europe*. Copenhagen: University of Copenhagen, 2008.

MacDonald, Victoria-María, and Juan F. Carrillo. "The United Status of Latinos." In *Handbook of Latinos and Education: Theory, Research, and Practice*, edited by Enrique G. Murillo Jr., Sofia A. Villenas, Ruth Trinidad Galvan, Juan Sanchez Munoz, Corinne Martinez, and Margarita Machado-Casas, 8–26. New York: Routledge, 2010.

Macedo, Donaldo. "The Colonialism of the English Only Movement." *Educational Researcher* 29, no. 3 (2000): 15–24.

MacSwan, Jeff. "A Multilingual Perspective on Translanguaging." *American Educational Research Journal* 54, no. 1 (2017): 167–201.

Maher, Justin T. "The Capital of Diversity: Neoliberal Development and the Discourse of Difference in Washington, DC." *Antipode* 47, no. 4 (2015): 980–98.

Makoni, Sinfree B. "A Critique of Language, Languaging, and Supervernacular." *Muitas vozes* 1, no. 2 (2012): 189–99.

Mallet, Marie L., and Joanna M. Pinto-Coelho. "Investigating Intra-Ethnic Divisions among Latino Immigrants in Miami, Florida." *Latino Studies* 16, no. 1 (2018): 91–112.

Manning, Robert D. "Multicultural Washington, DC: The Changing Social and Economic Landscape of a Post-Industrial Metropolis." *Ethnic and Racial Studies* 21, no. 2 (1998): 328–55.

Marie, Tya. *Grimey 2: Married to the King of Miami*. LaVergne, TN: Sullivan Group, 2016.

Márquez-Reiter, Rosina, and Louisa Martín Rojo, eds. *A Sociolinguistics of Diaspora: Latino Practices, Identities, and Ideologies*. Abingdon, UK: Routledge, 2014.

Márquez-Reiter, Rosina, and Adriana Patiño-Santos. "The Politics of Conviviality: On-the-Ground Experiences from Latin Americans in Elephant and Castle, London." *Journal of Sociolinguistics* 25, no. 5 (November 2021): 662–81.

Martin, Ben L. "From Negro to Black to African American: The Power of Names and Naming." *Political Science Quarterly* 106, no. 1 (1991): 83–107.

Martin, Susan. "Climate Change, Migration, and Governance." *Global Governance: A Review of Multilateralism and International Organizations* 16, no. 3 (2010): 397–414.

Martínez, Daniel E., and Kelsey E. Gonzalez. "Panethnicity as a Reactive Identity: Primary Panethnic Identification among Latino-Hispanics in the United States." *Ethnic and Racial Studies* 44, no. 4 (2021): 595–617.

Martínez, Glenn A., and Robert W. Train. *Tension and Contention in Language Education for Latinxs in the United States: Experience and Ethics in Teaching and Learning*. New York: Routledge, 2019.

"Mayors of the District of Columbia since Home Rule." DC.gov. Office of the Secretary. Accessed November 21, 2023. https://os.dc.gov/page/mayors-district-columbia-home-rule.

McDearman, Brad, Greg Clark, and Joseph Parilla, "The 10 Traits of Globally Fluent Metro Areas." Brookings Institution, October 29, 2013. www.brookings.edu/research/the-10-traits-of-globally-fluent-metro-areas/, click on the link for Washington, DC, under the "Metro Area Profiles" map, 1–2.

McGuire, Connie. "Central American Youth Gangs in the Washington DC Area." Washington Office on Latin America. January 2007. https://www.wola.org/sites/default/files/downloadable/Citizen%20Security/past/Maras_DCarea_FINAL_CM_feb_7.pdf.

Mendoza-Denton, Norma. *Homegirls: Language and Cultural Practice among Latina Youth Gangs*. Malden, MA: Blackwell, 2008.

———. "Sociolinguistics and Linguistic Anthropology of US Latinos." *Annual Review of Anthropology* 28 (1999): 375–95.

Menjívar, Cecilia. *Fragmented Ties: Salvadoran Immigrant Networks in America*. Berkeley: University of California Press, 2000.

———. "Liminal Legality: Salvadoran and Guatemalan Immigrants' Lives in the United States." *American Journal of Sociology* 111, no. 4 (2006): 999–1037.

Milligan, Melinda J. "Displacement and Identity Discontinuity: The Role of Nostalgia in Establishing New Identity Categories." *Symbolic Interaction* 26, no. 3 (Summer 2003): 381–403.

Modan, Gabriella Gahlia. "Mango Fufu Kimchi Yucca: The Depoliticization of 'Diversity' in Washington, DC Discourse." *City and Society* 20, no. 2 (2008): 188–221.

———. "The Semiotics of Urbanness: Lifestyle Centers and the Commodified City." In *The Routledge Handbook of Anthropology and the City*, edited by Setha Low, 326–41. New York: Routledge, 2018.

———. *Turf Wars: Discourse, Diversity, and the Politics of Place*. Hoboken, NJ: John Wiley, 2008.

Molina, Raúl Sánchez. *Cruzar fronteras en tiempos de globalización: Estudios migratorios en antropología*. Madrid: Alianza Editorial, 2018.

Montanari, S., K. Subrahmanyam, M. Zepeda, and C. Rodríguez. "The English Phonological Skills of Latino Spanish-English Dual-Language Preschoolers Living in Los Angeles: Implications for Practice." In *Perspectives in the Study of Spanish Language Variation*, edited by Alazne Landa, Andrés Enrique-Arias, Francisco Ocampo, and Manuel J. Gutiérrez, 465–96. Santiago de Compostela, Spain: Universidade de Santiago de Compostela, Servizo de Publicacións e Intercambio Científico, 2014.

Moore, Jacqueline M. *Leading the Race: The Transformation of the Black Elite in the Nation's Capital, 1880–1920*. Charlottesville: University of Virginia Press, 1999.

Mora, G. Cristina. *Making Hispanics: How Activists, Bureaucrats, and Media Constructed a New American*. Chicago: University of Chicago Press, 2014.

Morales, Ed. *Latinx: The New Force in American Politics and Culture*. London: Verso, 2018.

———. "Opinion: What Sarah Huckabee Sanders Gets Wrong with Her 'Latinx' Ban." CNN, January 13, 2023. https://www.cnn.com/2023/01/13/opinions/sarah-huckabee-sanders-latinx-ban-morales/index.html.

Morgan, Marcyliena. "Speech Community." In *A Companion to Linguistic Anthropology*, edited by Alessandro Duranti, 3–22. Malden, MA: Blackwell, 2004.

Morrison, Bruce A., and Paul Donnelly. "Attracting New Americans into Baltimore's Neighborhoods Immigration Is the Key to Reversing Baltimore's Population Decline." Abell Foundation, December 1, 2002.

Morrison, Judith A. "Behind the Numbers: Race and Ethnicity in Latin America." *Americas Quarterly* 9, no. 3 (August 5, 2015): 80.

Moslimani, Mohamad, and Luis Noe-Bustamante. *Facts on Latinos in the US*. Pew Research Center, August 16, 2023. https://www.pewresearch.org/hispanic/fact-sheet/latinos-in-the-us-fact-sheet/.

Muñoz, José Esteban. "Feeling Brown: Ethnicity and Affect in Ricardo Bracho's *The Sweetest Hangover (and Other STDs)*." *Theatre Journal* 52, no. 1 (2000): 67–79.

Murphy, Mary-Elizabeth B. *Jim Crow Capital: Women and Black Freedom Struggles in Washington, DC, 1920–1945*. Durham: University of North Carolina Press, 2018.

Mushin, Ilana. *Evidentiality and Epistemological Stance: Narrative Retelling*. Amsterdam: John Benjamins, 2001.

Nagel, Joane. "Constructing Ethnicity: Creating and Recreating Ethnic Identity and Culture." *Social Problems* 41, no. 1 (1994): 152–76.

Naveed, Minahil. "Income Inequality in DC Highest in the Country." DC Fiscal Policy Institute, December 15, 2017. https://www.dcfpi.org/all/income-inequality-dc-highest-country/.

NBC4 Washington. "Pupusas in Washington DC: How the Salvadoran Dish Became Unique to the District." YouTube video, November 19, 2019. https://www.youtube.com/watch?v=uACvyCTUffI.

Ndhlovu, Finex. "A Decolonial Critique of Diaspora Identity Theories and the Notion of Superdiversity." *Diaspora Studies* 9, no. 1 (2016): 28–40.

Negrón, Rosalyn. "Ethnic Identification and New York City's Intra-Latina/o Hierarchy." *Latino Studies* 16 (2018): 185–212.

———. "New York City's Latino Ethnolinguistic Repertoire and the Negotiation of Latinidad in Conversation." *Journal of Sociolinguistics* 18 (2014): 87–118.

———. "Spanish as a Heritage Language and the Negotiation of Race and Intra-Latina/o Hierarchies in the US." In *The Routledge Handbook of Spanish as a Heritage Language*, edited by Kim Potowski, 107–23. Abingdon, UK: Routledge, 2018.

Nevalainen, Terttu. "Social Variation in Intensifier Use: Constraint Only Adverbialization in the Past?" *English Language and Linguistics* 12, no. 2 (2008): 289–315.

Newman, Michael. "Focusing, Implicational Scaling, and the Dialect Status of New York Latino English." *Journal of Sociolinguistics* 14, no. 2 (2010): 207–39.

———. *New York City English*. Boston: Mouton de Gruyter, 2014.

Noe-Bustamante, Luis, Lauren Mora, and Mark Hugo Lopez. "About One-in-Four US Hispanics Have Heard of Latinx, but Just 3% Use It." Pew Research Center, August 11, 2020. https://www.pewresearch.org/hispanic/2020/08/11/about-one-in-four-u-s-hispanics-have-heard-of-latinx-but-just-3-use-it/.

Oboler, Suzanne. *Ethnic Labels, Latino Lives: Identity and the Politics of (Re)Presentation in the United States*. Minneapolis: University of Minnesota Press, 1995.

Ochs, Elinor. "Constructing Social Identity: A Language Socialization Perspective." *Research on Language and Social Interaction* 26, no. 3 (1993): 287–306.

Ochs, Elinor, and Lisa Capps. *Living Narrative: Creating Lives in Everyday Storytelling*. Cambridge, MA: Harvard University Press, 2001.

Oh, Janet S., and Terry Kit-fong Au. "Learning Spanish as a Heritage Language: The Role of Sociocultural Background Variables." *Language, Culture and Curriculum* 18, no. 3 (2005): 229–41.

Okamoto, Dina, and G. Cristina Mora. "Panethnicity." *Annual Review of Sociology* 40 (2014): 219–39.

Orloff, Patricia, et al. "Racial and Ethnic Tensions in American Communities: Poverty, Inequality, and Discrimination." Vol. 1 of *The Mount Pleasant Report*. Washington, DC: Commission on Civil Rights, January 1993. https://files.eric.ed.gov/fulltext/ED359294.pdf.

Osuna, Steven. "Intra-Latina/Latino Encounters: Salvadoran and Mexican Struggles and Salvadoran–Mexican Subjectivities in Los Angeles." *Ethnicities* 15, no. 2 (2015): 234–54.

Otheguy, Ricardo, Ofelia García, and Wallis Reid. "A Translanguaging View of the Linguistic System of Bilinguals." *Applied Linguistics Review* 10, no. 4 (2019): 625–51.

Pain, Rachel. "Gender, Race, Age and Fear in the City." *Urban Studies* 38, nos. 5–6 (2001): 899–913.

Paris, Django. "'It Was a Black City': African American Language in California's Changing Urban Schools and Communities." In *Raciolinguistics: How Language Shapes Our Ideas about Race*, edited by H. Samy Alim, John R. Rickford, and Arnetha F. Ball, 241–54. New York: Oxford University Press, 2016.

———. "'They're in My Culture, They Speak the Same Way': African American Language in Multiethnic High Schools." *Harvard Educational Review* 79, no. 3 (2009): 428–48.

Parliament. *Chocolate City.* Recorded 1975, Casablanca Records, LP.
Parodi, Claudia. "Contacto de dialectos en Los Ángeles: Español chicano y español salvadoreño." *Séptimo Encuentro Internacional de lingüística en el Noroeste* 2 (2004): 277–93.
Pavlenko, Aneta. "Superdiversity and Why It Isn't: Reflections on Terminological Innovation and Academic Branding." In *Sloganizations in Language Education Discourse: Conceptual Theory in the Age of Academic Marketization*, edited by Barbara Schmenk, Stephan Breidbach, and Lutz Küster, 142–68. Bristol, UK: Multilingual Matters, 2018.
Pearlman, Lauren. *Democracy's Capital: Black Political Power in Washington, DC, 1960s–1970s.* Durham: University of North Carolina Press Books, 2019.
Peñalosa, Fernando. *Chicano Sociolinguistics: A Brief Introduction.* Rowley, MA: Newbury House, 1980.
Pennycook, Alastair. *Critical Applied Linguistics: A Critical Reintroduction.* New York: Routledge, 2021.
———. *Global Englishes and Transcultural Flows.* New York: Routledge, 2006.
Pérez Huber, Lindsay. "Using Latina/o Critical Race Theory (LatCrit) and Racist Nativism to Explore Intersectionality in the Educational Experiences of Undocumented Chicana College Students." In *Foundations of Critical Race Theory in Education*, edited by Edward Taylor, David Gillborn, and Gloria Ladson-Billings, 77–96. Abingdon, UK: Routledge, 2023.
Pessar, Patricia R. "The Elusive Enclave: Ethnicity, Class, and Nationality among Latino Entrepreneurs in Greater Washington, DC." *Human Organization* 54, no. 4 (1995): 383–92.
Pineo, Ronn F., and James A. Baer. *Cities of Hope: People, Protests, and Progress in Urbanizing Latin America, 1870–1930.* New York: Routledge, 2018.
Podesva, Robert J. "Phonation Type as a Stylistic Variable: The Use of Falsetto in Constructing a Persona 1." *Journal of Sociolinguistics* 11, no. 4 (2007): 478–504.
———. "Stance as a Window into the Language-Race Connection: Evidence from African American and White Speakers in Washington, DC." In *Raciolinguistics: How Language Shapes Our Ideas about Race*, edited by H. Samy Alim, John R. Rickford, and Arnetha F. Ball, 203–20. New York: Oxford University Press, 2016.
———. "Three Sources of Stylistic Meaning." *Texas Linguistic Forum* 51, *Proceedings of the 15th Annual Symposium about Language and Society–Austin* (2008): 1–10.
Poplack, Shana. "Dialect Acquisition among Puerto Rican Bilinguals." *Language in Society* 7, no. 1 (1978): 89–103.
Population Change in the Washington DC Metropolitan Area. Report. George Mason University Center for Regional Analysis, April 2011. https://cra.gmu.edu/pdfs/researach_reports/recent_reports/Population_Change_in_the_Washington_Metropolitan_Area.pdf.

Portes, Alejandro, and Min Zhou. "Should Immigrants Assimilate?" *Public Interest* 116 (Summer 1994): 317–28.

Potowski, Kim. *IntraLatino Language and Identity: MexiRican Spanish*. Amsterdam: John Benjamins, 2016.

———, ed. *The Routledge Handbook of Spanish as a Heritage Language*. Abingdon, UK: Routledge, 2018.

Pozo, Valeria. "Percepción sociolingüística de los peruanos residentes en Chile acerca de su variedad del español en interacción con el español chileno." *Boletín de filología* 49, no. 2 (2014): 237–56.

Prado Robledo, Samantha. "Colorism: The Relationship between Latino/a Self-Perceived Skin Color and Assimilation." MA thesis, California State University San Marcos, 2012.

Preston, Dennis R. "The Uses of Folk Linguistics." *International Journal of Applied Linguistics* 3, no. 2 (1993): 181–259.

Price, Marie, and Lisa Benton-Short. "Immigrants and World Cities: From the Hyper-diverse to the Bypassed." *GeoJournal* 68, nos. 2–3 (2007): 103–17.

Price-Spratlen, Townsand. "Urban Destination Selection among African Americans during the 1950s Great Migration." *Social Science History* 32, no. 3 (Fall 2008): 37–469.

Prince, Sbiyha. *African Americans and Gentrification in Washington, DC: Race, Class and Social Justice in the Nation's Capital*. London: Routledge, 2016.

Pritchett, Wendell E. "A National Issue: Segregation in the District of Columbia and the Civil Rights Movement at Mid-Century." *Georgetown Law Journal* 93 (2004): 1321.

Quijano, Aníbal. "Coloniality of Power and Eurocentrism in Latin America." *International Sociology* 15, no. 2 (2000): 215–32.

Rahman, Jacquelyn. "The N Word: Its History and Use in the African American Community." *Journal of English Linguistics* 40, no. 2 (2012): 137–71.

Ramirez, Rosa María. "Were You Here? Estuviste aqui? Celebrating the History and Legacy of Centro de Arte." MA thesis, Corcoran College of Art and Design, Washington, DC, 2014.

Ramos-Zayas, Ana Y. "Racializing the 'Invisible' Race: Latino Constructions of 'White Culture' and Whiteness in Chicago." *Urban Anthropology and Studies of Cultural Systems and World Economic Development* 30, no. 4 (Winter 2001): 341–80.

Rampton, Ben. *Crossing: Language and Ethnicity among Adolescents*. London: Routledge, 2018.

———. "Language Crossing and the Problematisation of Ethnicity and Socialisation." *Pragmatics* 5, no. 4 (1995): 485–513.

Raymond, Chase Wesley. "Generational Divisions: Dialect Divergence in a Los Angeles–Salvadoran Household." *Hispanic Research Journal* 13, no. 4 (2012): 297–316.

———. "Reallocation of Pronouns through Contact: In the Moment Identity Construction amongst Southern California Salvadorans." *Journal of Sociolinguistics* 16, no. 5 (2012): 669–90.

Redfern, P. A. "What Makes Gentrification 'Gentrification'?" *Urban Studies* 40, no. 12 (2003): 2351–66.

Relaño Pastor, Ana María, and Anna De Fina. "Contesting Social Place: Narratives of Language Conflict." *Dislocations/Relocations: Narratives of Displacement* (2005): 36–60.

Repak, Terry A. *Waiting on Washington: Central American Workers in the Nation's Capital*. Philadelphia: Temple University Press, 2010.

Reyes, Angela. *Language, Identity, and Stereotype among Southeast Asian American Youth: The Other Asian*. New York: Routledge, 2017.

Richardson, Jason, Bruce Mitchell, and Jad Edlebi. *Gentrification and Disinvestment 2020*. Washington, DC: National Community Reinvestment Coalition, 2020.

Richardson, Jason, Bruce Mitchell, and Juan Franco. *Shifting Neighborhoods: Gentrification and Cultural Displacement in American Cities*. Washington, DC: National Community Reinvestment Coalition, 2019.

Rickford, John R. *African American Vernacular English: Features, Evolution, Educational Implications*. Malden, MA: Wiley-Blackwell, 1999.

Rivera-Mills, Susana V. "Use of Voseo and Latino Identity: An Intergenerational Study of Hondurans and Salvadorans in the Western Region of the US." In *Selected Proceedings of the 13th Hispanic Linguistics Symposium*, edited by Luis A. Ortiz-López, 94–106. Somerville, MA: Cascadilla Proceedings Project, 2011.

Robertson, Roland. "Globalisation or Glocalisation?" *Journal of International Communication* 1, no. 1 (1994): 33–52.

———. *Globalization: Social Theory and Global Culture*. London: Sage, 1992.

Rodríguez, Ana Patricia. "Becoming 'Wachintonians': Salvadorans in the Washington, DC, Metropolitan Area." *Washington History* 28, no. 2 (2016): 3–12.

———. "'Departamento 15': Cultural Narratives of Salvadoran Transnational Migration." *Latino Studies* 3, no. 1 (2005): 19–41.

———. "Diasporic Reparations: Repairing the Social Imaginaries of Central America in the Twenty-First Century." *Studies in 20th and 21st Century Literature* 37, no. 2, art. 3 (2013). https://doi.org/10.4148/2334-4415.1803.

———. "¿Dónde estás vos/z? Performing Salvadoreñidades in Washington, DC." In *Imagined Transnationalism: US Latino/a Literature, Culture, and Identity*, edited by Kevin Concannon, Francisco A. Lomeli, and Marc Priewe, 201–20. New York: Palgrave Macmillan, 2009.

———. "Refugees of the South: Central Americans in the US Latino Imaginary." *American Literature* 73, no. 2 (2001): 387–412.

Rodriguez, Gregory. *The Emerging Latino Middle Class*. Report. Pepperdine University Institute for Public Policy and AT&T, October 1996.

Rogers, Brandon M. A., and Scott M. Alvord. "Miami-Cuban Spanish and English /l/." In *Dialects from Tropical Islands: Caribbean Spanish in the United States*, edited by Wilfredo Valentín-Márquez and Melvin González-Rivera, 54–70. London: Routledge, 2019.

Rojas Gallardo, Darío. "Actitudes lingüísticas en Santiago de Chile: 'Agrado' y variedades geográficas del español." *Anuario de lingüística hispánica* 28 (2012): 99–116.

——. "Estatus, solidaridad y representación social de las variedades de la lengua española entre hispanohablantes de Santiago de Chile." *Literatura y lingüística* 29 (2014): 251–70.

Rosa, Jonathan. *Looking like a Language, Sounding like a Race: Raciolinguistic Ideologies and the Learning of Latinidad*. Oxford: Oxford University Press, 2019.

Rosa, Jonathan, and Nelson Flores. "Unsettling Race and Language: Toward a Raciolinguistic Perspective." *Language in Society* 46, no. 5 (2017): 621–47.

Rosado, Shantee. "Puerto Ricans, Dominicans, and the Emotional Politics of Race and Blackness in the US." PhD diss., University of Pennsylvania, 2019.

Roth, Wendy D. *Race Migrations: Latinos and the Cultural Transformation of Race*. Stanford, CA: Stanford University Press, 2012.

Ruble, Blair A. *Washington's U Street: A Biography*. Washington, DC: Woodrow Wilson Center Press; Baltimore: Johns Hopkins University Press, 2010.

Rumbaut, Rubén G. "Pigments of Our Imagination: On the Racialization and Racial Identities of 'Hispanics' and 'Latinos.'" In *How the US Racializes Latinos: White Hegemony and Its Consequences*, edited by José Cobas, Jorge Duany, and Joe Feagin, 15–36. Baltimore: Paradigm, 2009.

Rumbaut, Rubén G., Douglas S. Massey, and Frank D. Bean. "Linguistic Life Expectancies: Immigrant Language Retention in Southern California." *Population and Development Review* 32, no. 3 (2006): 447–60.

Rusk, David. *Goodbye to Chocolate City*. DC Policy Center, Washington, DC. July 20, 2017. https://www.dcpolicycenter.org/publications/goodbye-to-chocolate-city/.

——. *The Great Sort: Part I*. DC Policy Center, Washington, DC, June 26, 2018. https://www.dcpolicycenter.org/publications/the-great-sort-part-i/.

Salinas, Cristobal, Jr. "The Complexity of the 'x' in Latinx: How Latinx/a/o Students Relate to, Identify with, and Understand the Term Latinx." *Journal of Hispanic Higher Education* 19, no. 2 (2020): 149–68.

Salinas, Cristobal, Jr., and Adele Lozano. "Mapping and Recontextualizing the Evolution of the Term Latinx: An Environmental Scanning in Higher Education." *Journal of Latinos and Education* 18, no. 4 (2019). https://doi.org/10.1080/15348431.2017.1390464.

Salmerón, Josué, Cecelia Castillo Ayometzi, Kelsey Chatlosh, and Johanna Cajina Castillo. "Latinos in the District of Columbia." Washington, DC: Office on Latino Affairs, 2013. https://ola.dc.gov/sites/default/files/dc/sites/ola/publication/attachments/fy11_12_agencyperformance_officeoflatinoaffairs_responses_indices2011.pdf.

Sandoval-Sánchez, Alberto. *José, can you see? Latinos on and off Broadway*. Madison: University of Wisconsin Press, 1999.

Santa Ana, Otto. "Chicano English and the Nature of the Chicano Language Setting." *Hispanic Journal of Behavioral Sciences* 15, no. 1 (1993): 3–35.

Santa Ana, Otto, and Robert Bayley. "Chicano English: Phonology." *Americas and the Caribbean* (2008): 219–38.

Sassen, Saskia. "The Global City: Introducing a Concept." *Brown Journal of World Affairs* 11, no. 2 (2005): 27–43.

Saucier, Paul Khalil. "'We eat cachupa, not clam chowder': Mapping Second Generation Cape Verdean Youth Identity in the Greater Boston Area." PhD diss., Northeastern University, Boston, 2008.

Savage, Joanne. "Homicide and Inequality in 'The Murder Capital.'" *Journal of Ethnicity in Criminal Justice* 7, no. 1 (2009): 3–29.

Scallen, Patrick Daniel. "'The Bombs That Drop in El Salvador Explode in Mount Pleasant': From Cold War Conflagration to Immigrant Struggles in Washington, DC, 1970–1995." PhD diss., Georgetown University, Washington, DC, 2019.

Schalley, Andrea C., and Susana A. Eisenchlas, eds. *Handbook of Home Language Maintenance and Development: Social and Affective Factors*. Berlin: Walter de Gruyter, 2020.

Schilling, Natalie. "Investigating Stylistic Variation." In *The Handbook of Language Variation and Change*, 2nd ed., edited by J. K. Chambers and Natalie Schilling-Estes, 327–49. Hoboken, NJ: John Wiley, 2013.

Schilling-Estes, Natalie. "Constructing Ethnicity in Interaction." *Journal of Sociolinguistics* 8, no. 2 (2004): 163–95.

Schoenfeld, Sarah. "The History and Evolution of Anacostia's Barry Farm." DC Policy Center, July 9, 2019. https://www.dcpolicycenter.org/publications/barry-farm-anacostia-history/.

"Selected Social Characteristics, 2019 American Community Survey 1-Year Estimates, Washington-Arlington-Alexandria, DC-VA-MD-WV Metro Area." Maryland.gov, n.d. https://planning.maryland.gov/MSDC/Documents/American_Community_Survey/2019/METRO_47900_ACS_2019.pdf.

Sharma, Devyani. "Social Class across Borders: Transnational Elites in British Ideological Space." *Journal of Sociolinguistics* 25, no. 5 (2021): 682–702.

Shrider, Emily A., Melissa Kollar, Frances Chen, and Jessica Semega. *Income and Poverty in the United States: 2020*. Report Number P60-273. US Census Bureau, September 14, 2021. https://www.census.gov/library/publications/2021/demo/p60-273.html#:~:text=Median%20household%20income%20was%20%2467%2C521,and%20Table%20A%2D1).

Siegel, Jeff. "Creoles and Minority Dialects in Education: An Update." *Language and Education* 21, no. 1 (2007): 66–86.
Silverstein, Michael. "Indexical Order and the Dialectics of Sociolinguistic Life." *Language and Communication* 23, nos. 3–4 (2003): 193–229.
Singer, Audrey. *Latin American Immigrants in the Washington, DC Metropolitan Area*. Washington, DC: Woodrow Wilson International Center for Scholars, 2007.
———. "Metropolitan Washington: A New Immigrant Gateway." In *Research in Race and Ethnic Relations*. Vol. 17, *Hispanic Migration and Urban Development: Studies from Washington DC*, edited by E. Pumar, 3–24. Bingley, UK: Emerald, 2013.
———. "Twenty-First Century Gateways: An Introduction." In *Twenty-First Century Gateways: Immigrant Incorporation in Suburban America*, edited by Audrey Singer, Susan W. Hardwick, and Caroline B. Brettell, 3–30. Washington, DC: Brookings Institution Press, 2008.
Singer, Audrey, Susan W. Hardwick, and Caroline B. Brettell, eds. *Twenty-First Century Gateways: Immigrant Incorporation in Suburban America*. Washington, DC: Brookings Institution Press, 2008.
Singh, Rajendra, ed. *Towards a Critical Sociolinguistics*. Amsterdam: John Benjamins, 1996.
Skeggs, Beverley. *Class, Self, Culture*. London: Routledge, 2013.
Slobe, Tyanna. "Style, Stance, and Social Meaning in Mock White Girl." *Language in Society* 47, no. 4 (2018): 541–67.
Slomanson, Peter, and Michael Newman. "Peer Group Identification and Variation in New York Latino English Laterals." *English World-Wide* 25, no. 2 (2004): 199–216.
Smith, Tom W. "Changing Racial Labels: From 'Colored' to 'Negro' to 'Black' to 'African American.'" *Public Opinion Quarterly* 56, no. 4 (1992): 496–514.
Smitherman, Geneva. "African Americans and 'English Only.'" *Language Problems and Language Planning* 16, no. 3 (1992): 235–48.
Smitherman, Geneva. *Black Talk: Words and Phrases from the Hood to the Amen Corner*. Boston: Houghton Mifflin Harcourt, 2000.
Solis, Carmen, Edwardo L. Portillos, and Rod K. Brunson. "Latino Youths' Experiences with and Perceptions of Involuntary Police Encounters." *Annals of the American Academy of Political and Social Science* 623, no. 1 (2009): 39–51.
Song, Miri. "Introduction: Who's at the Bottom? Examining Claims about Racial Hierarchy." *Ethnic and Racial Studies* 27, no. 6 (2004): 859–77.
Sorenson, Travis Doug. "Voseo to Tuteo Accommodation among Two Salvadoran Communities in the United States." PhD diss., Texas A&M University, 2010.
Sprehn-Malagón, Maria, Jorge Hernández-Fujigaki, and Linda Robinson. *Latinos in the Washington Metro Area*. Images of America series. Charleston, SC: Arcadia, 2014.

Squires, Lauren. "Indexical Bleaching." In *The International Encyclopedia of Linguistic Anthropology*, edited by James Stanlaw, 1–4. Hoboken, NJ: Wiley-Blackwell, 2020. https://doi.org/10.1002/9781118786093.iela0455.

State Immigration Data Profiles. "District of Columbia, Language & Education." Migration Policy Institute. Accessed September 1, 2023. https://www.migrationpolicy.org/data/state-profiles/state/language/DC.

Stewart, Craig O., Margaret J. Pitts, and Helena Osborne. "Mediated Intergroup Conflict: The Discursive Construction of "Illegal Immigrants" in a Regional US Newspaper." *Journal of Language and Social Psychology* 30, no. 1 (2011): 8–27.

Suárez Büdenbender, Eva-María. "Puerto Ricans' Evaluations of Dominicans and Dominican Spanish as Reflected in Inter-Personal Interviews." *Southwest Journal of Linguistics* 30, no. 2 (January 2011): 101.

Sugiharto, Setiono. "The Multilingual Turn in Applied Linguistics? A Perspective from the Periphery." *International Journal of Applied Linguistics* 25, no. 3 (2015): 414–21.

Summers, Brandi Thompson. *Black in Place: The Spatial Aesthetics of Race in a Post-Chocolate City*. Durham: University of North Carolina Press, 2019.

Swain, Merrill. "Languaging, Agency and Collaboration in Advanced Second Language Proficiency." In *Advanced Language Learning: The Contribution of Halliday and Vygotsky*, edited by Heidi Byrnes, 95–108. London: Continuum, 2006.

Sweetland, Julie. "Unexpected but Authentic Use of an Ethnically-Marked Dialect." *Journal of Sociolinguistics* 6, no. 4 (2002): 514–38.

"A Tale of Three Cities: What the Census Says about the District and How We Must Respond." Washington, DC: DC Action for Children, 2011.

Tallentire, Jenéa. "Strategies of Memory: History, Social Memory, and the Community." *Histoire sociale/Social History* 34, no. 67 (2001): 197–212.

Tannen, Deborah. "Introducing Constructed Dialogue in Greek and American Conversational and Literary Narrative." In *Direct and Indirect Speech*, edited by Florian Coulmas, 11–32. Berlin: Walter de Gruyter, 1986.

Taylor, Paul, Mark Hugo Lopez, Jessica Martínez, and Gabriel Velasco. *When Labels Don't Fit: Hispanics and Their Views of Identity*. Pew Research Center, April 4, 2012. https://www.pewresearch.org/hispanic/2012/04/04/when-labels-dont-fit-hispanics-and-their-views-of-identity/.

Telles, Edward, and Stanley Bailey. "Understanding Latin American Beliefs about Racial Inequality." *American Journal of Sociology* 118, no. 6 (2013): 1559–95.

Telles, Edward, and René Flores. "Not Just Color: Whiteness, Nation, and Status in Latin America." *Hispanic American Historical Review* 93, no. 3 (2013): 411–49.

Thomas, Erik R. *An Acoustic Analysis of Vowel Variation in New World English*. Durham, NC: Duke University Press, for the American Dialect Society, 2001.

———, ed. *Mexican American English: Substrate Influence and the Birth of an Ethnolect*. Cambridge: Cambridge University Press, 2019.

Thomas, Julia. "Gender and /aɪ/ Monophthongization in African American English." In *Proceedings of the 37th Annual Meeting of the Berkeley Linguistics Society*, edited by Chundra Cathcart, Shinae Kang, and Clare S. Sandy, 449–63. Berkeley, CA: Berkeley Linguistics Society, 2013. https://escholarship.org/uc/item/4dw2p6h6.

Tischauser, Leslie Vincent. *Jim Crow Laws*. Santa Barbara, CA: ABC-CLIO, 2012.

Torres, Lourdes M. *Puerto Rican Discourse: A Sociolinguistic Study of a New York Suburb*. Mahwah, NJ: Erlbaum, 1997.

Torruella-Quander, Carmen. "Conversation with an Old-School DC Latina." Event presented at Historical Society of Washington, DC, 2015.

Trudgill, Peter. "Sex, Covert Prestige and Linguistic Change in the Urban British English of Norwich." *Language in Society* 1, no. 2 (1972): 179–95.

Tseng, Amelia. "Advancing a Sociolinguistics of Complexity: Spanish-Speaking Identities in Washington, DC." In *The Routledge Handbook of Spanish in the Global City*, edited by Andrew Lynch, 330–54. Abingdon, UK: Routledge, 2020.

———. "Nativized Exoticism in 'el país de todas las sangres.'" *Ethnic and Racial Studies* 47, no. 6 (2023). https://doi.org/10.1080/01419870.2023.2243306.

———. "The Ordinariness of Dialect Translinguistics in an Internally Diverse Global-City Diasporic Community." In *Translinguistics: Negotiating Innovation and Ordinariness*, edited by Jerry Won Lee and Sender Dovchin, 146–60. Abingdon, UK: Routledge, 2020.

———. "Playground Learning: African American English in Latinx Raciomultilingual Repertoires." *Journal of Language, Identity, and Education*, October 27, 2023, 1–17. https://doi.org/10.1080/15348458.2023.2263568.

———. "'Qué barbaridad, son latinos y deberían saber español primero': Language Ideology, Agency, and Heritage Language Insecurity across Immigrant Generations." *Applied Linguistics* 42, no. 1 (February 2021): 13–135. https://doi.org/10.1093/applin/amaa004.

———. "Raciolinguistic Reindexicalization, Marginalization, and Identity Construction in a Changing Asian Latino Diaspora." Sociolinguistic Symposium 23. University of Hong Kong, Hong Kong, June 7–10, 2021.

———. "Vowel Variation, Style, and Identity Construction in the English of Latinos in Washington, DC." PhD diss., Georgetown University, Washington, DC, 2015.

Tseng, A., C. Chang, T. Leal, J. S. Lee, and B. Lopez. *Research in Heritage Speaker Bilingualism: Theories, Methods, and Designs*. New York: Routledge, 2025.

Tseng, Amelia, and Holly R. Cashman. "Code-Switching Pragmatics." In *The Encyclopedia of Applied Linguistics*, edited by Carol Chapelle, 1–6. Hoboken, NJ: John Wiley, 2015.

Tseng, Amelia, and Lars Hinrichs. "Introduction: Mobility, Polylingualism, and Change: Toward an Updated Sociolinguistics of Diaspora." *Journal of Sociolinguistics* 25, no. 5 (November 2021): 649–61.

Tuan, Yi-fu. *Space and Place: The Perspective of Experience*. Minneapolis: University of Minnesota Press, 1977.

Turner, Margery Austin, and Christopher R. Hayes. *Poor People and Poor Neighborhoods in The Washington Metropolitan Area*. Washington, DC: Urban Institute, March 1, 1997. https://www.urban.org/research/publication/poor-people-and-poor-neighborhoods-washington-metropolitan-area.

Twine, France Winddance. "Brown Skinned White Girls: Class, Culture and the Construction of White Identity in Suburban Communities." *Gender, Place and Culture: A Journal of Feminist Geography* 3, no. 2 (1996): 205–24.

US Bureau of Labor Statistics. "Washington-Arlington-Alexandria, DC-VA-MD-WV Metropolitan Statistical Area: Nonfarm Employment and Labor Force Data." n.d. https://www.bls.gov/regions/mid-atlantic/data/xg-tables/r03fx9512.htm.

US Census Bureau. "American Community Survey 1-Year Estimates." Census Reporter Profile page for Washington-Arlington-Alexandria, DC-VA-MD-WV Metro Area, 2022. http://censusreporter.org/profiles/31000US47900-washington-arlington-alexandria-dc-va-md-wv-metro-area/.

———. "American Community Survey 5-Year Estimates." Census Reporter Profile page for Washington, DC, 2022. http://censusreporter.org/profiles/16000US1150000-washington-dc/.

———. "Census Bureau Releases New Educational Attainment Data." Press release. February 24, 2022. https://www.census.gov/newsroom/press-releases/2022/educational-attainment.html.

———. Quick Facts District of Columbia. "Population Estimates, July 1, 2022." https://www.census.gov/quickfacts/fact/table/DC/PST045222.

US Commission of Civil Rights. *Racial and Ethnic Tensions in American Communities: Poverty, Inequality, and Discrimination*. Vol. 1, *The Mount Pleasant Report*. Washington, DC: US Commission on Civil Rights, January 1993.

Valdés, Guadalupe. "Heritage Language Students: Profiles and Possibilities." In *Handbook of Heritage, Community, and Native American Languages in the United States*, edited by Terrence G. Wiley, Joy Kreeft Peyton, Donna Christian, Sarah Catherine K. Moore, and Na Liu, 41–49. Abingdon, UK: Routledge, 2014.

Valdez, Verónica E., Juan A. Freire, and M. Garrett Delavan. "The Gentrification of Dual Language Education." *Urban Review* 48, no. 4 (2016): 601–27.

Valencia, Richard R. "'Mexican Americans don't value education!' On the Basis of the Myth, Mythmaking, and Debunking." *Journal of Latinos and Education* 1, no. 2 (2002): 81–103.

Vallejo, Jody Agius. "Latina Spaces: Middle-Class Ethnic Capital and Professional Associations in the Latino Community." *City and Community* 8, no. 2 (2009): 129–54.

Vanderbeck, Robert M. "Vermont and the Imaginative Geographies of American

Whiteness." *Annals of the Association of American Geographers* 96, no. 3 (September 2006): 641–59.

Vandevoordt, Robin, and Gert Verschraegen. "Demonstrating Deservingness and Dignity: Symbolic Boundary Work among Syrian Refugees." *Poetics* 76 (2019), article 101343.

Vertovec, Steven. "Super-Diversity and Its Implications." *Ethnic and Racial Studies* 30, no. 6 (2007): 1024–54.

———. *Transnationalism*. London: Routledge, 2009.

Vidal-Ortiz, Salvador, and Juliana Martínez. "Latinx Thoughts: Latinidad with an X." *Latino Studies* 16, no. 3 (2018): 384–95.

Walker, J. Samuel. *Most of 14th Street Is Gone: The Washington, DC Riots of 1968*. New York: Oxford University Press, 2018.

Walsh, John C., and Steven High. "Rethinking the Concept of Community." *Histoire sociale/Social History* 32, no. 64 (1999): 255–72.

Weldon, Tracey L. *Middle-Class African American English*. Cambridge: Cambridge University Press, 2021.

Wenger, Etienne. *Communities of Practice: Learning, Meaning, and Identity*. Cambridge: Cambridge University Press, 1998.

Wennersten, John R. *Anacostia: The Death and Life of an American River*. Baltimore: Chesapeake Book Co., 2008.

Westbrook, Alonzo. *Hip Hoptionary: The Dictionary of Hip Hop Terminology*. New York: Harlem Moon, 2002.

Wiley, Terrence G. "Accessing Language Rights in Education: A Brief History of the US Context." *Bilingual Education and Bilingualism* 61 (2007): 89.

Williams, Zachary R. *In Search of the Talented Tenth: Howard University Public Intellectuals and the Dilemmas of Race, 1926–1970*. Columbia: University of Missouri Press, 2010.

Witt, Doris. *Black Hunger: Soul Food and America*. Minneapolis: University of Minnesota Press, 2004.

Wodak, Ruth. "The Trajectory of Far-Right Populism: A Discourse-Analytical Perspective." In *The Far Right and the Environment: Politics, Discourse and Communication*, edited by Bernhard Forchtner, 21–37. Abingdon, UK: Routledge, 2019.

Wolford, Tonya, and Keelan Evanini. "Features of AAVE as Features of PRE: A Study of Adolescents in Philadelphia." *University of Pennsylvania Working Papers in Linguistics* 12, no. 2 (2006): 231–44.

Wolfram, Walt. *Sociolinguistic Aspects of Assimilation: Puerto Rican English in New York City*. Arlington, VA: Center for Applied Linguistics, 1974.

Wolfram, Walt, and Mary E. Kohn. "Regionality in the Development of African American English." *The Oxford Handbook of African American Language*, edited by Sonja Lanehart, 140–60. New York: Oxford University Press, 2015.

Wolfram, Walt, and Natalie Schilling-Estes. *American English: Dialects and Variation*. Hoboken, NJ: Wiley-Blackwell, 2015.
Woods, Michael R., and Susana V. Rivera-Mills. "El tú como un 'mask': Voseo and Salvadoran and Honduran Identity in the United States." *Studies in Hispanic and Lusophone Linguistics* 5, no. 1 (2012): 191–216.
Woolard, Kathryn A. *Singular and Plural: Ideologies of Linguistic Authority in 21st Century Catalonia*. Oxford: Oxford University Press, 2016.
Woolard, Kathryn A., and Bambi B. Schieffelin. "Language Ideology." *Annual Review of Anthropology* 23 (1994): 55–82.
Yellin, Eric S. *Racism in the Nation's Service: Government Workers and the Color Line in Woodrow Wilson's America*. Durham: University of North Carolina Press, 2013.
Zentella, Ana Celia. "The 'Chiquitafication' of US Latinos and Their Languages, or Why We Need an Anthropolitical Linguistics." In *SALSA III: Proceedings of the Symposium about Language and Society*, Austin, TX, April 5–7, 1995.
———. "'Dime con quién hablas, y te diré quién eres': Linguistic (in) Security and Latina/o Unity." In *A Companion to Latina/o Studies*, edited by Juan Flores and Renato Rosaldo, 25–38. Malden, MA: Wiley-Blackwell, 2007.
———. *Growing Up Bilingual: Puerto Rican Children in New York*. Malden, MA: Blackwell, 1997.
———. "The Hispanophobia of the Official English Movement in the US." *International Journal of the Sociology of Language* 127 (1997): 71–86.
———. "Lexical Leveling in Four New York City Spanish Dialects: Linguistic and Social Factors." *Hispania* 73, no. 4 (1990): 1094–1105.
———. "'Limpia, fija y da esplendor': Challenging the Symbolic Violence of the Royal Spanish Academy." *Chiricú Journal: Latina/o Literature, Art, and Culture* 1, no. 2 (2017): 21–42.
———. "TWB (Talking while Bilingual): Linguistic Profiling of Latina/os, and Other Linguistic Torquemadas." *Latino Studies* 12 (2014): 620–35.
Zhang, Wenquan, and John R. Logan. "Global Neighborhoods: Beyond the Multiethnic Metropolis." *Demography* 53, no. 6 (December 2016): 1933–53.
Zukin, Sharon. *The Naked City: The Life and Death of Urban Authentic Places*. Oxford: Oxford University Press, 2010.

Index

AAE. *See* African American English
Adams Morgan, 1, 53, 121, 165, 169, 191–92; Day, 192
African American city, Washington, DC as, 46–48. *See also* Chocolate City; Washington, DC
African American English (AAE), 14, 22, 48, 145, 163–64, 213; and African American contact, 58–60; ambiguous positioning, 199–200, 202; attitudes towards, 123–26; as second language, 114–15; characterization of, 130; contact, conflict, and community, 121–23; and contemporary Latinx repertoires, 115–21; and cultural assimilation, 122–23; features, 116–17; as "ghetto" language, 124–25; ideological continuity and change, 203–4; influence of, 113–14; morphology and syntax, 118; multilingual repertoires, 61, 194; multiple discourses, 70; normalization of, 124; normalizing "sounding Black," 155–56; and polycentricity, 127; positioning of, 199–200; and racialized displacement, 172; and "sounding local," 132–38, 155–56; sounding Washingtonian, 175–79; Washingtonians using, 166, 169. *See also* Black English
African Americans, 4, 43, 169, 194, 198, 200, 208–10; ambiguous referents, 154–56; association with urbanness and toughness, 31; attitudes toward Black English, 123–26; and Black English as second language, 114–15; contact with, 58–60; and DC as African American city, 46–48; and DC as global city, 51–53; discrimination against, 224n18; and gentrification, 48–50; and Latinidad in nation's capital, 22, 27; and Latinx linguistic repertoires, 113–14; socialization with, 123; socioeconomic diversity among, 225n19; sounding Washingtonian, 175–79; Washingtonians *versus* gentrifier and, 164–66; and Whiteness of gentrifiers, 173–74
Afro-Latinxs, 7, 22–23, 126, 156, 211
afrodescendientes, 209
Albury, Nathan, 203
Alim, H. Samy, 24
all-American pastime, celebrating, 1–3
Alonso, participant, 57–58, 113, 115, 195
ambiguous referents, 153–57
American Civil War of 1861–65, 46
Anacostans, 44–45
Ángel, participant, 81, 116, 118, 130–31
anthropolitical linguistic perspective, 213–14
Aparicio, Edwin, 63
Aparicio, Francis, 29, 34, 158
Aranda, Elizabeth, 67
Argentina, 8–9, 102, 106, 117, 130, 199, 231n18
Argentinean Spanish, 99
Asians, 15–16, 49, 52, 64, 76, 211
authenticity, constructing: conclusions, 193–97; languaging identity, 161–64; overview, 160–61; putting down roots, 179–89; racializing the city, 191–93; real Washingtonians, 189–91; reminiscence, 166–75; sounding Washingtonian, 175–79; Washingtonians *versus* gentrifiers, 164–66
Avilés, Quique, 56, 147, 195, 209–11

Bacon, Christylez, 114
Bader, Michael, 51

Bailey, Benjamin, 4
baleadas, 86
Banks, Michelle, 195
Barrio, El (neighborhood), 53–54
Benítez, José, 59, 68, 99
Benor, Sarah Bunin, 25, 38, 112
Benton-Short, Lisa, 51
big-D Discourses, 31
bigger picture, raciomultilingual perspective: language and identity, 28–30; race and ethnicity, 30–32
bilingualism, 4–5, 11–13, 24, 29, 36–38, 84, 129, 151, 203; continuum of, 60; deriding, 146–47; evaluating, 78; and heritage languages, 38–39; and identity construction, 145–46, 155; marking what is considered "authentic" language, 196; misunderstanding, 82–84, 106; multilingual repertoires, 38; racializing, 125, 129; realities of, 82; stigmatization of, 155; supporting as part of culture, 72–73, 75; translanguaging in bilingual communication, 75–77
Black English, 48, 114, 162; attitudes toward, 123–26; as a Second Language, 114–15, 125, 208; stereotypical pejoratives, 154–55. *See also* African American English
Black ESL, 125
Black Prince George's County, Maryland, 52–53
Blackness, 178, 194, 196, 200, 208–9, 210–11; normalization of, 59; stigmatization of, 67–68, 125–26, 154
Blommaert, Jan, 25–26
Bolivia, 8–9, 55, 61, 78, 116–17, 130, 148
Bourdieu, Pierre, 150
brechas, 152–53
Brown v. Board of Education, 47
Brown, Chuck, 186
Bucholtz, Mary, 24, 125, 196

Cadaval, Olivia, 7
Callesano, Salvatore, 68, 100
Cándida, participant, 76–77, 116

Caribbean Spanish, 67–68, 97, 102
Carolina, participant, 116, 148–49
Carter, Phillip, 59, 68, 100
Centeno-Meléndez, José, 44
Central America, 8–9, 22, 44, 56, 61, 66, 69, 84, 104, 130, 138–39, 147–48, 157
Central American Spanish, 4, 14, 68, 93–94, 97, 102, 104
Chile, 8–9
Chocolate City (DC), 43–44, 121, 165, 193–94, 214; DC as African American city, 46–48; as immigrant destination, 50; reminiscing about, 166–76; Washingtonians *versus* gentrifiers, 165–66
city, claims to: community and continuity, 184–86; next generation of Washingtonians, 186–88; overview, 179–82; teaching Washingtonian values, 188–89; Washingtonians *versus* Transients, 182–84
city/suburb pattern (sociolinguistic surveys), 115–21
"*ciudades hermanas*" (sister cities), 62
classed personhood, 150–51
close friends, use of Spanish with, 74
code-switching, 29, 75–77, 124–25, 204, 213
cohesion, 64–69
Colombia, 8–9, 12, 67–68, 97–99, 111, 116–17, 149, 153
Colombian Spanish, 97–100
Columbia Heights, 1–2, 20, 53, 56–58, 88, 118–19, 121, 153, 165–66, 192–93
commonsense, 30, 39, 127
community: and authenticity, 191–92; bilingual, 37; community narrative, 70; contact, conflict, and, 121–23; and continuity, 184–86; DC Latinxs, 53–58; and roots, 182–83; and urban areas, 191–92; and Washington, DC, 57–58, 84, 138–41, 167–69, 184–89; term, 36–37. *See also* gentrification; Washington, DC
Como deberíamos hablarlo, attitude, 96–100
conflict narratives, 145–47
continuity, 164, 166, 182, 184–86

Index 281

Cubans, 66, 68, 100, 153
Cuban Spanish, 68, 100

DACA. *See* Deferred Action for Childhood Arrivals
data: analyzing, 13–14; conducting research, 6–13
DC accent, 164, 176–77, 195
DC Afro Latino Caucus, 211
DC Latinidad, 1–3; and Latinxs in DC, 53–70; overview, 43–44; in Washington, DC, 44–53
DC Latinxs, 9–10, 17, 21, 71, 108, 177–78; African American contact, 58–60; allyship with, 15–16; bilingualism of, 125, 155; characteristics of, 157, 166, 210; dialect attitudes, 100; diversity characterizing, 22; diversity, divisions, and cohesion, 64–66; examining connections of, 13; and gentrification, 171; imagining collective identity, 161; interaction between systems of meaning, 126–27; multilingual repertoires, 60–61; perception of Salvadorans, 138–39; presence in DC, 53–58; race and ethnicity, 30; and Salvadorans, 61–63; scalar semiotics, 205; social figure of, 129, 205; sociolinguistic context, 7–8; sociolinguistics of place and identity, 3–5; sounding Washingtonian, 179; Spanishes, 84–87; speaking AAE, 123, 200; speaking English, 109, 119–20, 199; speaking Spanish, 72, 105; toward raciomultilingual perspective, 5–6, 24–27; views on African American language and culture, 27. *See also* Washington, DC
DC pragmatic norms, 168–69, 190. *See also* pragmatics
De Fina, Anna, 60
deculturalization, deficit discourses of, 149–53
Deferred Action for Childhood Arrivals (DACA), 66
Día de Muertos (Day of the Dead), 7, 54

dialect: attitudes, 96–100; contact, 92–96; different dialects of English, 112–13; downgrading, 95; variation, 13–14. *See also* sociolinguistic variation
diaspora, emerging new meanings in, 24–27
"*Dime con quién andas, y te diré quién eres,*" phrase, 23–24
discrimination, language and, 110–12
discursive heterogeneity, 157–58
diversity, 64–69
divisions, 64–69
DMV. *See* Washington, DC
Dominican Republic, 8–9, 98, 117
Dominican Spanish, 99
Douglass, Frederick, 47

Ecuador, 8–9, 81, 103, 133, 141
El Salvador. *See* Salvadorans; Salvadoran Spanish
Emanuel, participant, 20, 48, 82–83, 87, 116, 121–23, 139–41, 171, 184
English, speaking: different dialects, 112–13; language discrimination, 110–12; survey participants, 109. *See also* African American English (AAE); Latinx English (LE)
Erker, Daniel, 5
"Esquineros" project, 7, 58

Faez, Farahnaz, 8–10
family, Spanish spoken with, 74
Félix, participant, 138–39, 148
Fishman, Joshua, 39–40
Flores, Nelson, 5, 24
food, symbolism of, 170–72
fractal recursivity, 31

Gal, Susan, 31
García, Ofelia, 5, 25
Gee, James, 31
gender: grammatical, 40, 41, 144; participants and, 12, 42, 116t, 117t, 119, 156
gentrification, 48–50, 56–58; changing metropolises, 206–7; and characteristics of gentrifiers, 164–66;

gentrification (cont.)
  community versus, 182–84; and description of Adams Morgan Day as "White people selling tacos," 191–93; engaging with racialization of DC identity, 174–75; and racialized displacement, 58, 170–72; reminiscence of time before, 164–66, 180; Washingtonians versus, 164–66; and Whiteness of gentrifiers, 17, 154–55, 172, 173–74, 178, 192, 200
Georgetown University Language and Communication in the Washington, DC Metropolitan Area Project, 10
ghetto, term, 124–25
global cities: changing metropolises, 206–7; DC region diversity, 72; decentering hegemonic gaze, 212–13; "I, Too" (poem), 207–12; overview, 205–6; Washington, DC, as, 51–53
globalization, 24, 28, 32–33, 206
"glocal," 52; class dynamics, 147–49
go-go, 43–44, 160, 167, 186
Gracia, participant, 20–21, 135–38, 156–57, 173–74
Grieser, Jessica, 48
gringos (White Americans), 142–43, 155
Guatemala, 8–9, 12, 77, 116, 129–30, 152
Gumperz, John, 37

Hablan con el acento de su mamá, term, 92–96
"hablando bien" (speaking well), 97–99
Hart-González, Lucinda, 64–66, 100, 199
Héctor, participant, 76–77, 87, 116–18, 132–33, 141–47, 173, 179
hegemonic gaze, decentering, 212–13
heritage languages, 24, 28, 31–32, 38–40, 73, 77, 82–83, 105, 214
Hip Hop Nation Language (HHNL), 120
Hispanic, term, 40–42
Hispanics, 80, 111, 136
Home Rule Act of 1973, 124
Honduras, 8–9, 85–86, 104, 139, 157
Hughes, Langston. See "I, Too" (poem)
Hughes, Sallie, 67

hybridity, 29
hyperarticulation, 177

"I, Too" (poem), 207–12
Ibrahim, Awad, 115, 208
identity, languaging: bigger picture, 23–24, 28–32; communication as self-definition of, 23–24; defining terms, 35–42; Latinidad in Washington and, DC, 21–23; overview, 19–21, 161–64; and sociolinguistics of migration, 32–33; and theorizing Latinidad, 33–35; toward raciomultilingual perspective, 24–27
identity, sociolinguistics, 3–5
immigrant generations, 8–10
immigrants, and Washington, DC, 50–51
indexicality, 13, 17, 20, 28–31, 36, 48, 106, 137, 156, 172, 176, 195, 200–201
Inés, participant, 129–30, 152
international, term, 66
international, identity term, 65–66
International Latinx, 143, 147–49
Irvine, Judith T., 31
Islander, 49

Jim Crow laws, 47, 224n18
José, participant, 116, 133, 149–51, 155

Kennedy, John F., 45–46
King, Kendall, 59
King, Martin Luther, Jr., 2, 47–48

Labov, William, 4, 132, 136, 139, 144, 214
Lamont Park, 54
language: choice of, 12. See also specific languages
Language Access Act, 111–12
language and identity, raciomultilingual perspective, 28–30
language boundaries, raciolinguistic ideologies crossing: and narrating Self and Other, 132; overview, 129–31; and social figures, 131; and "sounding local," 132–37
languages, naming, 36. See also specific languages

languaging, term, 35–36
Latin America: Blackness stigmatization in, 126; color-related social hierarchy in, 26–27; social hegemonies, 67
Latin Americans, 149, 150, 198, 205; Latinidad in Washington, DC, 21–23; origins of, 9; symbolic capital, 151; White Latin Americans, 106–7
Latin@, term, 40–42
Latine, term, 40–42
Latinidad: imaging local Latinidad, 153–58; theorizing, 33–35; in Washington, DC, 21–23. *See also* DC Latinidad
Latino, term, 40–42
Latinoamérica, term, 40–42
Latino/a/x/e/u, term, 34
Latino Festival, 1
Latinx: AAE influence in linguistic repertoires of, 113–26; contact, conflict, and community, 121–23; contemporary repertoires, 115–21; dialect attitudes, 96–100; dialect contact, 92–96; and different dialects of English, 112–13; and discursive heterogeneity, 157–58; distinguishing between gringos and, 142–43; international, 147–49; marker of identity, 77–84; multilingual repertoires, 60–61; multiple discourses on, 69–70; "Othered" Latinx, 144–45; posh, 143–44; and Salvadoran Spanish, 100–105; Salvadoran stereotype, 68–69; Salvadorans in DC, 61–63; social meaning of Spanish among, 71–107; and superdiversity, 64–69
Latinx, term, 40–42
Latinx English (LE), 14, 112–13, 162; contemporary Latinx repertoires, 115–21; "sounding Washingtonian," 175–79
Latinx identity, Spanish as marker of: conclusions, 105–7; discourses of language inadequacy, 81; and exclusion, 78–80; and linguistic insecurity, 81–84; and pride in identity, 77–78; pushing back against exclusion, 80–81

Latinxs: African American contact, 58–60; backgrounds of, 55–56; community growth, 56; establishing roots of, 53–55
Learner English, 112–13
leeches. *See* gentrification
linguistic insecurity, 81–84
linguistic repertoires, 5, 13, 17, 24–25, 37–38, 59–61, 112–15, 123–27, 154–56, 195–96, 200–202, 214. *See also* Marcos; multilingual repertoires
local identity, constructing, 193–97; languaging identity and, 161–64; overview, 160–61; and putting down roots, 179–89; racializing city, 191–93; real Washingtonians, 189–91; reminiscence, 166–75; and sounding Washingtonian, 175–79; Washingtonians *versus* gentrifiers, 164–66
local Latinidad, imagining: ambiguous referents, 153–57; and discursive heterogeneity, 157–58. *See also* Salvadorans
Luna, Casilda, 55, 210

majority-minority city. *See* Washington, DC
Malcolm X Park, 2
Manplesa, La, 54–55. *See also* Mount Pleasant
Manplesa, La (film), 54–55
Marcos, participant, 19–20, 44, 57, 193–97; linguistic repertoire, 161–64; overview, 160–61; putting down roots, 179–89; racializing city, 191–93; real Washingtonians, 189–91; reminiscence, 166–75; sounding Washingtonian, 175–79; Washingtonians *versus* gentrifiers, 164–66
Maryland, Spanish in, 72–73
meaning, interactions of systems of, 126–28
metalinguistic commentary, 91–94, 164, 176
metropolitan area (DC), 1, 6, 16, 42; Latinidad in, 21–23; race/ethnicity in, 49; Spanish in, 71–75
Mexicans, speech norms of, 92–96

Mexico, 8–9, 62, 88, 93
"mi gente," voicing, 141–47
Miami, Florida, Latinx population in, 68
migration: changing metropolises, 206–7; decentering hegemonic gaze, 212–13; "I, Too" (poem), 207–12; overview, 205–6
migration, sociolinguistics of, 2–33
Modan, Gabriella, 58, 165–66, 169, 174, 180, 215
Modan, Galey, 7
Mora, G. Cristina, 33–34
moral positioning: overview, 179–82; and right to the city, 169, 187–88
Mount Pleasant, 1–2, 7, 20, 53–54, 56, 62, 121–22, 165–66, 174, 180, 193
multilingualism, centering, 24–27, 201–3
multilingual repertoires, 37–38, 39, 60–61
Mvze, Anna, 119–20

named languages, 36
naming "Latinx," 40–42
narrative, medium, 132, 162; and identity, 13, 132, 135–36, 139, 141–46, 164, 168, 175, 181, 199–200, 210; and voicing, 155. *See also* storytelling
Native Americans, 49
Negrón, Rosalyn, 34, 67, 100, 196
New England chowder, symbolism of, 170–72
New York, NY, Latinx population in, 67–68
New York Times, 174
Noemí, participant, 81, 133–35, 141, 156–57, 203
Noemíscalar semiotics and recentering, 204–5

Okamoto, Dina, 33–34
1.5 generation, 8–10
organized heterogeneity, 33
origins, Latin American, 9
"other," 162, 173, 212; narrating, 132; Latinx, 64, 144–46

Panama, 8–9, 116
panethnicity, defining, 33–34

Paraguay, 8–9, 80, 116
Paris, Django, 178
participants, ages of, 11
parties with friends, use of Spanish at, 74
Peninsular Spanish, 97–100
peripheral insider, researcher positionality, 14–16
persona, 129, 131, 145–46. *See also* social figures
Peru, 8–9, 16, 56, 61, 93, 97–98, 110–11
Peruvians, speech norms of, 92–96
Peruvian Spanish, 92, 97–99
Pía, participant, 93–94, 97, 99
place, sociolinguistics of, 3–5
polycentricity, 26, 127
posh Latinxs, 143–44
positioning, 13–14; among Latinxs, 158; and identity, 28; and ambiguity, 67–68, 153; deficit positioning, 141, 199, 202; moral positioning, 179–80; Washingtonians *versus* gentrifiers, 164, 166, 187
Potomac River, 45
Potowski, Kim, 212
pragmatics, 168–69, 190. *See also* DC pragmatic norms
Preston, Dennis, 203
Price, Marie, 51
Prince George's County, MD, 45; and race, 52–53, 128
Prince of Petworth, 174
Proposition 227, 72–73
Puerto Ricans, speech norms of, 92–96
Puerto Rico, 8–9, 39
Pupusa Power, term, 171
pupusas, 86

race and ethnicity, 30–32, 34–35, 39, 96, 100; and DC identity, 161, 166, 171, 173–74, 191–93; and gentrifiers, 161, 166, 163, 173–74; and localness, 143, 146–48, 154, 156, 174, 194, 215; and raciomultilingual perspective, 30–32; and social class, 102, 105, 136, 142–43, 147–48, 156; and stereotypes, 64,

67–69, 98, 154; and superdiversity, 64
racialized displacement, gentrification and, 58, 170–72
raciolinguistic perspective, 24–25
racialized multilingualism, centering, 201–3
raciomultilingual framework, advantages of, 200; centering racialized multilingualism, 201–3; ideological continuity and change, 203–4
raciomultilingual perspective: as bigger picture, 28–32; moving toward, 5–6, 24–27
raciomultilingual Self and Other, voicing: centering Salvadorans, 138–53; conclusions, 158–59; crossing language boundaries, 129–38; imagining local Latinidad, 153–58
Real Academia de la Lengua Española (Royal Academy of the Spanish Language), 40–41, 98, 100
real Washingtonians, 189–91
reggaetón, 152
reminiscence: engaging with racialization of DC identity, 174–75; gentrification and racialized displacement, 170–72; overview of, 166–69; Whiteness of gentrifiers, 173–74
research, ideologies borne out of, 67–68
researchers, positionality of, 14–16
Rigores, Francisco, 211
Robledo, Samantha Prado, 67
Rodríguez, Ana Patricia, 59
Roebuck, Roland, 211
roots, putting down: authenticity, 164, 166; community and continuity, 184–86; next generation of Washingtonians, 186–88; overview, 179–82; teaching Washingtonian values, 188–89; Washingtonians *versus* Transients, 182–84
Rosa, Jonathan, 5, 24, 34–35, 106–7
Rosario, Carlos, 55
Royal Academy of the Spanish Language. *See* Real Academia de la Lengua Española

Sabogal, Elena, 67
Salvadorans, 61–63; and ambiguous referents, 153–57; centering, 138–41; deficit discourses of deculturalization, 149–53; and discursive heterogeneity, 157–58 , 199, 210; naming "glocal" class dynamics, 147–49; positioning Salvadoran Spanish, 198–99; speech norms of, 87–92; stereotype of, 68–69; voicing "*mi gente*," 141–47; *voseo* and, 86–87
Salvadoran Spanish, 17, 22, 70, 100, 162; as ambiguous referent, 125, 154–57; centering Salvadorans, 140; colloquial term "*se come la 's*'," 87–88; commenting on, 199; and conflict narratives, 145–47; constructed dialogue, 103–4; crossing language boundaries, 129–31; dialect contact, 92–96; and discursive heterogeneity, 157–58; expressed concerns about, 90; negative stereotypes, 103; non-White, 102–3; normalization of, 101, 127; and positioning, 202; similarities between dialects, 104–5; stigmatization of, 102, 199; viewing as vulgar, 101–2; *voseo* as major feature of, 86
Samuel, participant, 95, 110–11
scalar semiotics and recentering, 204–5
se come la "s," term: Salvadoran participants, 88–89; showing elision in Spanish, 88; stigmatization of, 87–88; style-shifting, 90; unweakened /s/ production, 90–92
second language, Black English as, 114–15
second-level indexicalities, 176–77
Self, narrating, 132
Skeggs, Beverly, 150
Smithsonian Center for Folklife and Cultural Heritage, 7, 115
Smithsonian Folklife Festival, 3, 114
social class, 47, 66, 102, 125, 151, 154
social figures, 129, 131; ambiguous referents, 153–57; discursive heterogeneity, 157–58; imagining local Latinidad, 153–58; and "sounding local," 132–37; voicing "mi gente," 141–47

sociolinguistic ideology, 24–27
sociolinguistics, 3–5
sociolinguistic scales, 25-27, 126–27, 143, 159, 204
sociolinguistic socialization: AAE influence in Latinx linguistic repertoires, 113–26; local/broader systems of meaning, 126–28; overview, 108; speaking English, 109–13
sociolinguistic variation, 21, 121. *See also* dialect: variation
"sounding local," 132–37; social figure and, 131
Spanglish, 29, 75–77, 96, 147
Spanish: in DC metropolitan area, 71–75; diversity of Spanishes, 84–105; opportunities for, 73–75; social meaning of, 71; Spanish as marker of Latinx identity, 77–84; translanguaging in bilingual communication, 75–77
Spanishes, diversity of, 85; descriptions of DC Spanish, 85; dialect attitudes, 96–100; Mexican speech norms, 92–96; overview, 84–87; Salvadoran Spanish, 100–105; Salvadoran speech norms, 87–92
stance, 13–14, 28, 58, 94, 124, 132, 141, 146, 163, 172, 180-181, 189, 196, 205
storytelling, 28, 132, 162. *See also* narrative
style-shifting, 90
suburbanization, 48
super-diversity, 33, 51, 64
Sweetland, Julie, 178

Temporary Protected Status (TPS), 66
terms, defining: community, 36–37; heritage languages, 38–40; Hispanic, 40–42; languaging, 35–36; Latin@, 40–42; Latine, 40–42; Latino, 40–42; Latinx, 40–42; multilingual repertoires, 37–38; named languages, 36
Thirteenth Amendment, 47
Tiempo Latino, El, 61, 62
TPS. *See* Temporary Protected Status
transients, Washingtonians *versus*, 182–84, 146, 165, 182–84, 205

translanguaging, 13–14, 17; in bilingual communication, 75–77; and identity, 38, 75–76, 162; multilingual repertoires, 38; similarity to code-switching, 29, 220n22; and "sounding local," 132. *See also* Spanglish
Treaty of Guadalupe Hidalgo, 40
Treinta, Los (show), 56–58
turf wars, 169

Union Market (Washington, DC), 170–72, 190
United States: color-related social hierarchy in, 26–27; global cities in, 51–53; and heritage languages, 39; naming in, 40–42; social meaning of Spanish in, 71–107; superdiversity in, 64–69. *See also* Washington, DC
urbanities, changing, 32–33
Uruguay, 8–9, 69
US Census, 8, 39–40, 42
US Commission on Civil Rights, 122

Vallejo, Jody Agius, 151–52
Valley Girl, accent, 31
Venezuela, 8–9, 116
Vertovec, Steven, 51
Virginia, Spanish in, 72–73
voicing, 76, 78, 86–87, 113, 117, 144–45, 155–56, 158, 164, 169, 172, 176–77, 232n25, 235n30
voseo, 14, 86–87, 96, 102, 199

Waletzky, Joshua, 132
Washington Hispanic, 61–62
Washington Nationals, 1
Washington Post, 61, 62, 63, 160, 174
Washington, DC, 198–200, 214–16; as African American city, 46–48; African American contact with, 58–60; analyzing data from, 13–14; book structure, 16–18; community growth in, 56; conducting research in, 6–13; constructing local identity and authenticity in, 160–97; DC Latinidad, 43–70; demographics, 51–52; as

immigrant destination, 50–51; dialect contact in, 92–96; four quadrants of, 45; gentrification of, 48–50, 56–58; as global city, 51–53; languaging identity, 19–42; Latinidad, 21–23; Latinx community in, 1–3; Latinxs in, 53–70; multilingual repertoires, 60–61; multiple discourses on, 69–70; overview of, 43–46; race/ethnicity in, 49; racializing city, 166, 171, 173, 191–93; raciomultilingual dynamics in, 19–42; reminiscence of, 166–75; researcher positionality, 14–16; and roots of Latinx community, 53–55; Salvadorans in, 61–63; Salvadoran Spanish in, 100–105; Salvadoran stereotype in, 68–69; social meaning of Spanish, 71–107; sociolinguistics of place and identity, 3–5; sociolinguistic socialization in, 108–28; superdiversity in, 64–69; toward raciomultilingual perspective, 5–6; various Spanishes in, 84–105; voicing raciomultilingual Self and Other in, 129–50

Washingtonians: authenticating identity of, 189–91; community and continuity, 184–86; next generation of, 186–88; sounding, 175–79; teaching Washingtonian values, 188–89; *versus* transients, 182–84

Washingtonians, characteristics of, 164–66

Wei, Li, 5, 25

Welty, Antonio, 55

White English, characterizing, 124–25

White Latinos, 142, 146, 155, 173

Whiteness, 17, 31, 35, 67, 115, 198, 200, 204, 209; ambiguous referents, 154–55; associating Vermont with, 184; associating with privilege, 143–44; being seen as "other," 162; capitalization of, 218n27; incompatibility with, 178–79; indexing, 172–74, 177; normalization of, 159; and urbanness, 191–92, 194–95

Williams, Anthony, 48

Wolfram, Walt, 4

World Bank Latinos, term, 65–66

World War II, 50

Zavala, Cindy, 153

Zentella, Ana Celia, 4, 59, 68, 213–14

Zukin, Sharon, 189–90

About the Author

Amelia Tseng is assistant professor of linguistics and Spanish in the Department of World Languages and Spanish, and affiliate faculty in the Department of Anthropology and the Center for Latin American and Latino Studies, at American University. She has published numerous articles and book chapters and is lead author of *Research in Heritage Speaker Bilingualism: Theories, Methods, and Designs* (with Charles Chang, Tania Leal, Jin Sook Lee, and Belém López, 2025) and co-editor of *Bilingualism for All? Raciolinguistic Perspectives on Dual Language Education in the United States* (with Nelson Flores and Nicholas Subtirelu, 2020). Tseng is primary investigator on the Washington, DC Latinx Language and Identity Project (DCLLIP). She has been interviewed numerous times on National Public Radio and recently began speaking about linguistics on children's radio.

www.ingramcontent.com/pod-product-compliance
Lightning Source LLC
LaVergne TN
LVHW040902200725
816610LV00001B/17